Voyages of Abus

Voyages of Abuse

Seafarers, Human Rights and International Shipping

A.D. Couper
with C.J. Walsh, B.A. Stanberry and G.L. Boerne

Pluto Press

LONDON • STERLING, VIRGINIA

First published 1999 by Pluto Press
345 Archway Road, London N6 5AA
and 22883 Quicksilver Drive, Sterling, VA 20166–2012, USA

British Library Cataloguing in Publication Data
A catalogue record for this book is available from the British Library

ISBN 0 7453 1545 3 hbk

Library of Congress Cataloging-in-Publication Data
A catalog record for this book is available

Designed and produced for Pluto Press by
Chase Production Services, Chadlington, OX7 3LN
Typeset from disk by Gawcott Typesetting, Buckingham
Printed in the EU by T.J. International, Padstow

Contents

Tables and Figures

List of Tables

List of Figures

Acknowledgements

Part of this book was written while I was Director of the Seafarers International Research Centre (SIRC) at the University of Cardiff. I am indebted to my colleagues, Chris Walsh, Ben Stanberry and Geoff Boerne. Each contributed to the research and compilation. I was responsible for the work overall as primary author and editor. The views expressed are ours and not necessarily those of the University or SIRC.

I wish to thank the International Transport Workers' Federation (ITF) for access to their files. Likewise I am grateful to the Flying Angel and Stella Maris missions to seamen for their material and especially to several chaplains of these and other missions who sent letters and tape recordings, only a small amount of which could be used in this study.

It is not possible to acknowledge by name (at their request) the many people who took part in interviews and made comments on specific chapters, particularly on the case study. These included former managers of the Adriatic Tanker Company of Greece, ships' captains, bankers and commercial companies who were involved or had special knowledge of the events. I am grateful to them for their co-operation and frankness which served to validate documentary information.

Critical comments were made on the draft by representatives of the wider shipping industry. I trust that in response it is sufficiently clear in the book that our concern is for the human rights of seafarers serving on substandard ships. These owners are threats to the lives of seafarers and their families, they obtain unfair economic advantages over decent companies, and they create very adverse perceptions of the shipping industry which is resented by seafarers, unions, the better shipping companies and the more responsible section of the world maritime press.

I am particularly grateful for the many forthright articles of the latter which have appeared in *Lloyd's List* and *TradeWinds* over the past decade. These also helped us piece together the picture of widespread abuse of workers in a global industry which is difficult to see as a whole, even by participants, and is generally hidden from public view.

Alastair Couper
Cardiff, 1999

1

'Us Poor Seamen'

This book is about seafarers employed within the sector of merchant shipping which is regarded as substandard. By substandard we include ships defective in structure and equipment, and those with low wages and poor working and living conditions. Very often they are the same vessels. In this substandard sector of shipowning, seafarers are exploited and abused, and respectable shipping companies are exposed to unfair competition.

The abuse of seafarers comes to the attention of most people only when a ship is abandoned in a local port and appeals are made to assist the crew, an event which is not something new but in recent years has been increasing.

Many seafarers have in fact throughout history been subjected to abuse, dangerous and difficult work, and separation for long and unpredictable periods from homes and families. They have frequently raised their voices in complaint but have not often been heard. When the English seaman Edward Barlow returned from a twenty-month trip on the *Queen Cathrane* in 1663 he and his shipmates' wages were reduced to pay for items of cargo damaged during the voyage:

> ... after going with many a hungry belly and thirsty stomach, and many a stormy and dark night with cold and wet coats, and hoping to receive what they have worked for with sweat and toil after venturing their lives amongst all manner of dangers, for to enrich others at home in all manner of pleasures and delights, wanting nothing that can please their senses; and in this manner are they recompensed, when the poor seamen are no more in the fault than the man that never saw a ship in all his lifetime.[1]

Nearly two centuries later in 1853 the Revd John Ashley – who subsequently founded the Missions to Seamen – ventured out to ships lying for weeks off Cardiff. He asked the Captain of one vessel if they were ever visited: 'With a look of sovereign contempt the Captain answered "Visit us sir? No sir, as long as they can get anything by us poor seamen, I believe they will leave us to perish like dogs."'[2]

1

More than a century later in 1995 the Second Officer, Radio Officer and Bo'sun of the Adriatic Tanker *Nova Progress* appealed to the journal *TradeWinds*, that the crew had been abandoned ashore after eleven months' service, they had no wages and could not get home: 'our families welfare is dramatically changing from bad to worse. In fact we are up to date slaves of ruthless owners. We hope you will publish our letter in your newspaper and maybe somebody will save us.'[3]

Exploitation of the seafarer has always been easy, and has become more so with globalisation of the shipping industry, the use of flags of convenience, and the subterfuge of the real owners registering each ship of their fleet under a different company in various countries.

Changing Conditions

Added to the complexity of the position of the seafarer in law are the changing work and social environments of seafaring. In the past, under common hardships and isolated from the shore, seafarers formed a community on board ship with its distinctive traditions and nautical language. Teamwork and social interdependence were features of this community and the shared experiences created a bond between members of a crew. This bonding reached back to family life in the days when the crews of ships were drawn from common country areas, towns and villages, and there were systems of mutual support amongst families ashore.

Commonality of origins was still frequent on many ships in the nineteenth century, although it is unlikely that a foreign-going vessel was ever nationally or ethnically homogeneous. Now with enormous technological changes, the vast capital requirements of modern shipping and the search for methods in reducing running cost, there have been dramatic changes in crew size and national composition. The recruiting agents seek crews wherever they can find them in the world, with minimum acceptable competence at lowest levels of cost. In order to remove even the limited national labour laws and related legislation, flags of convenience (FOC) are used, but even on national-flag ships there are now many foreign seafarers. Consequently, there are extensive national, ethnic and cultural differences to be found in the crews of vessels, and vast differences in living and working conditions, all of which creates misunderstandings, stress and often accidents.

This sketch of change in the structure and composition of merchant ship crews is a generalisation masking enormous variations. The conditions under which seafarers serve in national ships vary from good to very bad. Similarly, even under flags of convenience there is sometimes a total crew from a single country, and there are responsible FOC owners who respect the seafarers and treat them well. There are other FOC shipowners who, as in the past, exploit the crew as far as possible, and show a total disregard for the well-being of seafarers and their families. Yet others under both national and FOC may start out with good intentions but lack of skill in dealing with difficult market conditions, incompetence and bravado may drive them down the road to financial disaster, and on the way they will attack the easiest targets, the wages and welfare of the crew, to save costs.

Seafarers are the least resilient in the maritime world to such economic shocks, the most vulnerable in their remoteness from law, uncertain of their relationships and status in a multicultural social structure, and all suffering from a lack of regular communication with their families. This marginalisation of seafarers as a section of the world working population renders them even more vulnerable to economic exploitation than in the past.

Seafarers have told their stories of deprivation to chaplains at the Christian Missions to Seamen, to the International Transport Workers' Federation (ITF) Inspectors, and sometimes to the press. Several of these accounts were put together by the Revd Paul Chapman in his book, *Trouble on Board* (1992);[4] some of the underlying causes and the possible remedies were touched on within his vivid accounts drawn from stories and letters. The Australian authorities in the same year published *Ships of Shame*, a report about vessels on which, amongst other disgraceful conditions, 'seafarers were abused and exploited by officers and managers alike'. The ships were unsafe and the owners hidden and dubious. It is obvious, the report stated, 'that some ship owners, managers and charterers are profiting at the expense of the working and living conditions of the crew'.[5]

Structure of the Book

Chapter 2 describes the functions of international shipping. Emphasis is placed on developments since 1973 when major changes began to affect economics, labour and the flags and structure of the world fleet. The owners and institutions of shipping are outlined as an introduction to the globalised industry.

Chapter 3 moves on to the recruitment and training of seafarers drawn from many countries, the multi-national characteristics of the crews of merchant ships, and the implications of these. The general conditions of seafarers in the modern era, and the work and hazards of sea-going are dealt with, and finally the problems and relationships with families are highlighted.

Chapter 4 presents a more substantive picture of the instability of modern merchant shipping by addressing the causes of a series of company failures and the incidence of fraud. It also considers some of the consequences of these events on seafarers, and provides the examples of the evidence for abuse world-wide on a ship-by-ship basis.

Chapters 5, 6 and 7 are components of a case study of one company – the Adriatic Tanker Company of Greece. This examines in detail the evolution of the company, its financing and management, and its subsequent failure. It puts the abuse and abandonment of seafarers in a specific context, and focuses on experiences of the crews of two ships (see below under 'The Case Study').

Chapter 8 discusses the 'friends and allies' of the seafarers in general, and in relation to the case of Adriatic Tankers. In this chapter the International Transport Workers' Federation and the various Christian missions feature as major players.

Chapter 9 covers in detail the extent to which seafarers are protected by law, and it provides a compendium of legislation on their legal rights, many of which are of no avail when it comes to abuse and abandonment.

Finally, in Chapter 10 we conclude that while there are short-term measures which must be taken to protect world seafarers, radical long-term changes are also required in the regulation of an industry which is now the most globalised of all economic activities. In this respect there is an emphasis on new forms of 'governance', and the transfer of more authority from the flag states of registry to the international community.

Those Involved

The major players in the sequence of events are diverse and global. They include the flag states, port states, the owners, managers, charterers, classification societies, P&I (Protection and Indemnity) clubs, insurers, crew recruiters, lawyers, courts, banks, lender asset recovery agencies, crisis management companies, trade unions and the International Transport Workers' Federation (the ITF), Flying Angel and Stella Maris seafarers' missions, local charities, the press and some thousands of seafarers of many nationalities. Others who impinge on the scene include the International Labour Organisation, the International Maritime Organisation and numerous governments.

It will become apparent that the case study and a few other references relate to Greek-owned shipping to a greater extent than others. This is understandable since Greek citizens are the world's biggest shipowners. They own some of the best shipping companies and ships, but also in their midst operate some of the most reckless entrepreneurs who display little concern for sailors. It is the voice of seafarers on ships owned by many countries and sailing under numerous flags that we try to make heard in this book.

The Database

There are only scattered bodies of statistics with which to measure the extent of serious abuse and abandonment of seafarers internationally. The best single source available to the researchers was the material held in the files of the ITF. These comprise cases notified to the ITF by seafarers, trade unions and ITF inspectors. Incidents were initially verified by the ITF, including making contact with the shipping companies involved, and, if necessary, were followed up as cases. The cases usually extended over many months of enquiries and legal processes.

The sample period covered was 1994–97, and included 992 cases. A case in this context ranges from the problems of part of a crew to a whole crew (see Chapter 4). In addition to these, the files relating to around a hundred Adriatic Tanker vessels were examined as the basis of a detailed case study.

The ITF records were virtually confined to parties that conveyed complaints to the Special Seafarers' Department (SSD). In this respect it is a self-selected sample. It is difficult to substantiate if these 992 cases of abandonment and abuse over a period of four years represents an almost total picture, or are merely the tip of the iceberg.

In addition to the ITF records, an extensive literature survey was made extending over the same period. This covered published reports, newspapers and journals. Of particular importance for the case study of Adriatic Tankers were the articles in the journal *TradeWinds* and the daily *Lloyd's List*. A series of interviews with seafarers, concerning life on board and seafarer families, was conducted in several places by the researchers, and also recorded by chaplains of the Flying Angel and Stella Maris seafarers' missions.

The Case Study

One specific reason for adopting a case-study approach in Chapters 5, 6 and 7 was to be able to peel away the layers of deception from the substandard ship to expose the underlying rogue company. Many previous references to the bad conditions on merchant ships refer to 'rogue ships' and leave it at that. There are in fact no rogue ships, only rogue companies, the owners of which are responsible for the substandard condition of the vessels. The case study gets to the heart of one such company.

The second reason for this approach was to show in detail the historical context of the rise and fall of a company in a period of deregulation. The Adriatic Tanker Company of Greece emerged during the major structural changes initiated in the 1970s. This was a period of some economic chaos and the general expansion of transnational companies seeking low costs in employment, freedom from taxation and unregulated labour on a world-wide basis.[6] These corporations have no commercial allegiance to a particular country, but they are beneficially owned in the most developed parts of the world. The shipping industry was already well down this path of globalisation by 1970 using flags of convenience, and there had also been deregulation within some national flags enabling crew recruitment from beyond the flag state. The conditions of the late 1970s consequently gave opportunities for the emergence of fairly buccaneering entrepreneurs who eventually set the competitive standards for more traditional shipping enterprises.

The details of the case cover the emergence of the Adriatic company, its ability to raise finance and its management behaviour. The study also focuses on two ships to provide more insights into the trials and tribulations of individual seafarers and their families, and the efforts by the international trade union movement, the Christian missions and the maritime press to help them.

In this case study we are not specifically targeting the Adriatic company. Adriatic was picked because it was a major shipping organisation, and still survives under superficial camouflage in the globalised market. There are many other companies which could have been chosen for the case, but their available records are less detailed. Some of these are outlined in Chapter 4, and they include beneficial owners residing in many countries. For reasons already given, Greek-owned companies appear paramount. But the nationalities of other owners or organisations which are referred to critically in the book include Chinese, Nigerian, Russian, Romanian, South Korean, Singaporean, Turkish and Ukrainian. There are also beneficial owners with bad records whom we have not cited (to avoid repetition of types of abuses) which include companies in Cyprus, Guinea (West Africa), Israel, Indonesia, the US (Miami), Norway and the UK (London).[7]

This list, and the subsequent accounts, may serve to show that the case study of Adriatic was not a one-off but is typical, albeit on a big scale, of the substandard companies engaged in exploiting world seafarers.

2

International Shipping

Since the early days of organised commerce, shipping has been an international business. To facilitate the carriage of goods between countries the shipping industry has functioned through codes of commerce, bills of exchange and bills of lading, and through charters, contracts, mortgages, liens, underwriting insurance, cargo insurance, arbitrators, brokers and agents, and laws and ethics.[1]

Many of these instruments and established shipping procedures stem from British nineteenth-century commerce: at that time, about half of international seaborne trade was carried by British vessels. As other states began to displace the predominance of Britain in merchant shipping, the need for international laws and unified procedures was still acknowledged and adopted, and institutions such as the Baltic Exchange in London continued in the tasks of matching ships and cargoes world-wide.

Throughout the modern era until the early 1970s, maritime states which had predominated in the nineteenth century still controlled most of international shipping. They had well-established companies with distinctive vessels, management styles and trade routes. New ships were generally ordered when replacements were required, or against growth in world trade. The vessels were paid for from the retained profits of the company, or by minimum bank loans made on the basis of creditworthiness and measurable trading prospects.

Large oil companies and other end users of raw materials still had their own fleets in 1970 sailing mainly under national flags, and they chartered in additional tonnage from independent shipowners. Most bulk charters were arranged at the Baltic Exchange and liner shipping conferences were still strong and could determine freight rates and schedules, as they were dominated by the traditional maritime countries. Ships in turn would be surveyed, classified and insured by only a few reputable organisations based in these countries and having agencies world-wide.[2]

The pre-1970s period was thus one of relative stability and prosperity for shipowners, although seafarers worked long hours and many were still absent from home for trips of over one year.

Nevertheless, compared with the pre-Second World War period, life at sea had greatly improved for most, and was safeguarded by postwar national and international legislation.

In recent years, and particularly since 1973, shipping has become even more international, but much less stable. In its financing, ownership, shipbuilding, crewing, and trans-national involvement, the shipping industry has emerged as the most globalised of all economic activities. There is now virtually unimpeded international mobility of capital and labour in the industry, few barriers to entry and a free choice to shippers of competing ships in the bulk markets and in most of the liner trades.[3]

Ships are also able to sail unimpeded throughout the world under freedom of the sea. On the high seas the only law a ship must observe is that of the country whose flag is flown (the flag state). When a ship crosses the twelve-nautical-mile territorial sea boundary of another state it retains navigational rights provided its passage is innocent, that is, not prejudicial to the adjacent coastal state. Only when the ship enters a foreign port is it subject to the laws of other countries under port-state jurisdiction. It is this mix of flag-state sovereignty, and the need for compliance with international conventions, which, as will be appreciated later, contains elements of contradiction and conflict in a new globalised era.[4]

The Globalising Processes in Shipping

The marked shifts to a new structure in shipping after 1973 were not simply a continuation of trends – they came to represent a qualitative change. National shipping moved from international to global, in the sense that Hirst and Thomson characterise the image of globalisation as 'one in which distinct national economies and, therefore, domestic strategies of national economic management are necessarily irrelevant'.[5] The new economic structure in shipping was made even more global with the opening of the previously protected socialist economies of eastern Europe.

The primary triggers for the acceleration of change included the October 1973 Yom Kippur War, the sudden rise in oil prices, cutbacks in production, successive closures and reopenings of the Suez Canal, the Iranian Revolution of 1979, and the related world economic recession. Shipping thereby moved from an environment of stability to one of near chaos. Shipbuilding orders soared for large vessels when long Cape of Good Hope passages had to be made in place of canal transits – these orders continued under shipbuilding subsidies in Japan and South Korea even when the Suez Canal was available. This, and cutbacks in trade revealed enormous surpluses in shipping.

The New Economic Environment

The rapid changes which took place in shipping amounted to a technological revolution and also involved fundamental shifts in financing and operating. Technological advances included moving from the 28,000 DWT (deadweight tonnage) supertankers of the late 1950s to the 250,000 DWT VLCC (very large crude carriers) of the 1970s as the common means of transporting crude oil, and on upwards to the half-million-ton tanker. Similarly, economies of scale were sought in the dry bulk trades, with the replacement of 10,000 DWT tramps by vessels of 40,000 and upwards to 200,000 DWT in the space of two decades. In the general cargo sector, the changes were even more profound: each container vessel replaced about seven conventional break bulk liners.

The technological revolution involved greater capital requirements. The traditional method of accumulating capital for ship replacement by retained profits was inadequate. The companies now turned more to bank loans. The effects of this were quite profound. Previously, the owner would have nearly 100 per cent equity in the ship, and attaining this put a limit on the number of vessels purchased. Now it was possible to borrow 80–90 per cent of ship costs and more than one vessel could therefore be purchased at any time.

Not only were banks and other financial institutions more than willing to lend vast sums for shipping but new shipbuilding entrepreneurs offered easy credit terms for orders. Many governments likewise gave tax concessions to national and foreign owners for fleet expansion under their flags. This ease of raising and repaying loans brought new entrepreneurs into shipping; many borrowed against promised (and bogus) future charters and became multimillionaires (or bankrupts) in the process. In the container liner section in particular, capital requirements were such that consortia had to be created.

Shipping in the new economic environment became highly geared to debt. Finance and the market process generated an uncontrolled shipping surplus which became more visible after 1973. Unlike the previous system, owners now had to meet inescapable interest and capital repayments above all else. The cash-flow problems involved and the consequences are illustrated in the case study (in Chapter 6).

Freight rates ultimately fell under subsequent competitive and other pressures, and the big end-users of shipping, such as the oil majors and steel corporations began to dispose of their own fleets and to charter ships of competing independent owners at low freight rates. Shipping profitability thereby declined. This was accompanied by cost-cutting exercises.

Cutting Crew Costs

The fastest and easiest target for reductions in cost, as many saw it, was the price of sea-going labour. Crew costs (depending on the flag) could comprise recruitment and training, wages and salaries, insurance, pensions, travel, victualling and leave payments. These could represent 40 per cent of ship operating costs (that is, crewing, stores, repairs, insurance, lube oil and administration). Whereas other costs such as capital repayments were fixed and variables (fuel and port dues) were normally common to all the shipowners, the cutting of crew costs could come within their province, and this could give some the competitive edge if reduced to the minimum, whatever that proved to be.[6] Alternatives were the securing of government subsidies to combat cheap labour ships, and the reservation of cargo for national flags with stipulations that shippers use the national flag.

Most enterprises turned predominantly to competing in crew cost reductions. This was achieved in two ways. First, there were the technological changes already noted: enormous increases in productivity per person employed in shipping had been achieved as a result of economies of scale and reduced time in ports. In addition crew sizes on these new vessels were reduced from 40–50 per ship to 20–30 with the introduction of multi-skilling, labour-saving equipment and unstaffed engine rooms.

The second cost-cutting device was the use of flags of convenience (FOC), whereby registration was arranged in a foreign state. The shift to FOC meant renting a foreign flag at a relatively low price. This gave freedom to recruit from any part of the world at reduced wages and conditions. It also allowed companies to escape from national taxation, and from some ship safety and on-board health and social requirements. Comparing wages alone, by 1996 a chief officer from north-western Europe would earn about $7500 per month, from India $3100 and from the Philippines $2000. There were wider national differences for ratings drawn from different countries. When all conditions of crew and ship were taken into account, the operating costs of a high-standard ship and crew could be three times greater than those of substandard vessels with deplorable crew conditions.

It was now possible to compete hard on crew costs and to manipulate most costs on a global basis. A single vessel could be financed, mortgaged, built, registered, owned, managed and insured all in different countries. It could be chartered to yet another country, leased back to the country of beneficial ownership and engaged in trading world-wide. The world fleet through these processes changed in structure, flag, ownership, ship types and shipboard society.

The Structure of World Shipping

The vessels which conduct world trade can be divided into five main groups by tonnage: oil tankers (36 per cent), bulk carriers (36 per cent), general cargo (14 per cent), container ships (6 per cent) and others (8 per cent). Within these groups there are hundreds of specialised types (including combined bulk and oil OBO (ore-bulk-oil) ships, chemical, gas, wine and fruit juice tankers, and woodchip and car carriers) and also about 250 or so large cruise ships which, unlike cargo vessels, are not responding to a derived demand for goods in different parts of the world, but are meeting a direct desire of people for sea voyages and recreation. This is the fastest growing sector of modern shipping.

In aggregate there about 85,000 merchant ships, of these 46,000 carry 5000 million tons of cargo each year between 1000 or so main ports. Table 2.1 shows the twenty most important maritime countries, and the ships they have registered under national and foreign flags.

The foreign flags shown in Table 2.1 are primarily flags of convenience. The beneficial owners of these ships are still mainly in the traditional maritime countries of western Europe plus the US and Japan. At the end of the Cold War the fleets and seamen of the former Soviet Union and the countries of eastern Europe entered into global activity, and there was a rise of shipping in China, Hong Kong, South Korea, Singapore, Taiwan and Brazil. The flags of convenience which had been common to Liberia, Panama and Honduras had now extended to the Bahamas, Bermuda, Cyprus, Malta, Vanuatu, Tuvalu, the Marshall Islands, the Maldives, St Vincent and some other small states. Table 2.2 shows the tonnage distribution of major FOC (open-registry) fleets in December 1996.

Table 2.1　The twenty most important maritime countries, 1996

Country of domicile of parent company	Number of Vessels			Deadweight tonnage			Foreign flag as % of total	Total as % of world total
	National flag	Foreign flag	Total	National flag	Foreign flag	Total		
Greece	912	2 003	2 915	46 444 947	71 954 723	118 399 670	60.77	17.41
Japan	922	1 829	2 751	22 116 501	65 171 700	87 288 201	74.66	12.84
United States	482	732	1 214	13 134 699	35 994 699	49 129 398	73.27	7.22
Norway	836	568	1 404	28 127 282	20 781 990	48 909 272	42.49	7.19
China	1 594	378	1 972	23 162 264	13 095 430	36 257 694	36.12	5.33
Hong Kong	104	503	607	5 401 167	28 079 400	33 480 567	83.,87	4.92
Republic of Korea	501	303	804	10 253 709	12 869 037	23 122 746	55.66	3.40
United Kingdom	388	510	898	5 269 713	15 875 697	21 145 410	75.08	3.11
Germany	478	984	1 462	6 140 698	11 918 853	18 059 551	66.00	2.66
Russian Federation	2 595	239	2 834	12 231 787	5 113 585	17 345 372	29.48	2.55
Taiwan Province of China	179	254	433	7 577 719	7 534 148	15 111 867	49.86	2.22
Sweden	203	163	366	2 099 323	12 490 165	14 589 488	85.61	2.15
Singapore	402	252	654	8 876 995	5 544 741	14 421 736	38.45	2.12
Denmark	439	219	658	7 215 240	5 337 867	12 553 107	42.52	1.85
India	381	57	438	11 172 932	1 252 316	12 425 248	10.08	1.83
Italy	452	151	603	7 654 238	4 359 353	12 013 591	36.29	1.77
Saudi Arabia	69	58	127	1 078 603	9 749 334	10 827 937	90.04	1.59
Brazil	205	20	225	7 178 283	2 538 505	9 716 788	26.12	1.43
Turkey	420	23	443	8 997 546	107 859	9 105 405	1.18	1.34
France	178	105	283	4 313 260	3 446 166	7 759 426	44.41	1.14

Source: UN Review of Maritime Transport, 1997.[7]

Table 2.2   Tonnage distribution of major open-registry fleets, December 1996

Country	Total	
	Ships	Thousand DWT
Panama	3 478	108 904
Liberia	1 515	92 714
Cyprus	1 348	33 050
Bahamas	959	35 579
Malta	930	27 535
Bermuda	80	5 082
Vanuatu	126	1 757
Total	8 436	304 621

Source: UN Review of Maritime Transport, 1997.[8]

Since the early 1980s an alternative (quasi-FOC) has appeared as 'second registries'. These are more closely related to the governments of the traditional maritime countries of western Europe. They offer most of the advantages of FOC for owners, with the exception of some required conditions on employment, for example the master or senior officers may have to be nationals of a primary state or the EU. Second registries include DIS (Denmark), GIS (Germany), Isle of Man (UK), Kerguelin (France), Madeira (Portugal) and NIS (Norway). The second registries are referred to also as 'off shore' or 'international'. They represent an attempt to retain a semblance of national flags, remove the owners from some FOC stigma, and give greater credence to a genuine link between the ships and flags they are flying.

The Shipowners

Ownership of the world fleet of merchant ships is still retained largely by the developed market economy (DME) countries. Of the 758 million DWT in 1996 some 543 million belong to the DME states (directly and through FOC), but developing Asia owned by that time 109 million DWT. The ownership of the world merchant fleet has also been changing within these country groupings. In the 1950s the oil majors owned most oil tankers; by the 1990s over 65 per cent of tankers were independently owned, some 18 per cent were state owned or by smaller oil companies, about 6 per cent owned by oil producers, and only around 11 per cent by the oil majors.[9] The largest independent tanker owners are Greek companies. The new names and big players in the tanker markets have been Niarchos, and Onassis, in Greece, Ludwig in the US and C.Y. Tung and Y.K. Pao in Hong Kong.

In the dry-bulk trades, there are even more independent owners. Some are massive enterprises such as the company of the Norwegian, Erling Naess. Many major dry-bulk enterprises emerged from small shipping companies and entered the big ship league through raising loans from banks or on the world financial markets. Most of them reverted to FOC to cut costs. Several owners in tankers and dry bulk registered each of their ships as a separate company under FOC, which makes it difficult to identify in many cases who the beneficial owners are, and it avoids cross liabilities between these ships.

The liner companies have practically all moved to container shipping and the massive capital required for this has involved the forming of consortia. The combination, for example, of the old established British liner companies such as Blue Star, Blue Funnel, British and Commonwealth, Ellermans, Furness Withy, Port Line, P&O and Shaw Savill, are incorporated in Overseas Containers Ltd (OCL) and Associated Container Transport (ACT) as well as elsewhere. Others including the German Hapag-Lloyd, the Dutch Ned Lloyd, and the American President Line all contain multiple interest. The largest container company in the world however is a relatively new entrant; the Evergreen Marine Corporation of Taiwan.

In the refrigerated (reefer) trades, the specialised fruit, meat and dairy carriers have concentrated their vessels into a massive pool with ship ownership over at least six companies. The chemical trades also have highly specialised vessels owned by a few major companies such as Stolt-Neilsen of Norway, and are multi-national in management, crewing and operations. There are in addition some small-scale independent chemical shipowners engaged in short-haul distributions.[10]

The fastest growing sector of the shipping industry is cruising. This is almost all under FOC (Bahamas, Liberia and Panama). Of the 4.7 million GRT cruise fleet (1996) 2.5 was owned by US shipowners, 0.6 million Greek-owned, and 0.5 British-owned.[11]

The Institutions of Shipping

Public and private organisations are involved in several aspects of regulating shipping at international, regional and national levels. The principal international bodies are the United Nations agencies – the International Maritime Organisation (IMO) and the International Labour Organisation (ILO). The UN Conference on

Trade and Development (UNCTAD) was also very active in shipping during the 1960s and 1970s but is now less so. These bodies facilitate the making of international conventions through intergovernmental meetings and with the participation of several private organisations, some of which have UN consultative status.

The process of making an international convention can be protracted, involving working parties and expert technical and legal committees, formal and informal consultations, and a final high-level diplomatic conference. In this process, consensus is sought between nation states, and also from sectoral interests within and between states. Consequently, the final outcome is full of compromises and framed along minimal requirements. Sometimes even this is not attainable as binding legislation in international law, and only a recommendation is sought, which will provide guidelines for states and sectoral interests.

The UN organisations which bring conventions into being are not themselves directly involved in enforcement. This is a matter for the flag states, and only those flag states which have ratified the conventions. The UN bodies often have the means of monitoring flag-state compliance, and can bring defects to the attention of these states. In addition vessels which are in violation of international safety legislation can be detained in ports under the port-state jurisdiction of countries which have the mechanisms for carrying this out.

Several major private organisations with international scope have the power to influence both the formulation and enforcement of UN regulations. They can, for example, make representation to their governments, may participate in working parties and committees, and provide interpretations and guidance to their members on conventions. These bodies include the shipowners' organisations – the International Chamber of Shipping (ICS), the International Shipping Federation (ISF), the Baltic and International Maritime Council (BIMCO), the Association of Independent Tanker Owners (Intertanko) and the Association of Independent Dry Bulk and Carrier Owners (Intercargo). Shippers (cargo owners) and port organisations are also active in pressing their particular interests, which may not coincide with those of shipowners. The International Maritime Industries Forum (IMIF) in turn tries to provide a discussion base with inputs from bankers and other lenders to shipping. Important also is the *Comité Maritime International* (CMI) made up of Maritime Law Associations from many countries, and the Nautical Institute.

On the maritime labour side, the International Transport Workers' Federation (ITF), which is in effect an international trade union, exerts influence on conventions as they are negotiated through the UN machinery, and especially at ILO meetings. The ITF also monitors and takes action against ships violating international law and ITF employment norms.

The standards of construction of ships are supervised internationally on behalf of governments (flag states) and shipowners by classification societies. The larger and older societies are grouped under the International Association of Classification Societies (IACS). Classification societies have safety rules for construction and carrying out surveys to determine if a ship is still 'in class'. The largest, and oldest, classification society is Lloyd's Register, established in 1760. There are about ten major societies (including Bureau Veritas, American Bureau, Det Norsk Veritas) and some forty or so minor societies. As there is not always consistency in survey criteria, a shipowner can shop around societies ('class-hopping') in order to obtain a class certificate.

Other commercial organisations which exert influences and have rules binding on their members are the many Protection and Indemnity (P&I) clubs. These are mutual insurance organisations. Each member makes a premium contribution, and claims which are brought by any other member due to ship accidents, cargo damage or deaths and injuries of seafarers, are borne by the membership as a whole. The club members are naturally interested in the conditions of club ships and crews and the risks which other members expose them to. An owner who poses very high risks, or who has not paid his premium, can be thrown out of the club.

In addition to international bodies, there are regional organisations, including the European Union (EU). Within the EU lies the Economic Commissions (EC). These embody Directorate DG7 (Waterborne Transport) which, amongst other things, encourages enforcement measures in relation to international conventions, and facilitates EU directives which are binding on each member state. The EU rules on the conditions of ships apply not only to EU-flag vessels but to foreign-flag ships entering EU ports under a unified EU regime of port-state control.

Finally, there are a number of non-governmental organisations (NGOs) which act as pressure groups in, for example, marine environmental protection and human rights. The various Christian missions to seafarers monitor conditions on ships, and at various levels, including through their unified International Christian Maritime Association (ICMA), they exert pressures on policy makers and shipping companies, and provide assistance to seafarers.

The activities of these and other bodies are detailed in relation to substandard shipping in various sections of the book, and legal functions are discussed in Chapter 9.

Conclusion

International shipping has undergone enormous financial, technological and structural changes over the last three decades. It has suffered from a self-inflicted surplus of ships and destructive market competition which has extended to many of the institutions of shipping. Shippers now expect low freight rates, and some shipowners find the means of providing these by cheap crewing mainly under FOC, reduced crew sizes, cuts in maintenance and avoidance of national taxes.

In this globalised environment, well-run companies with good management and seafarers can still survive. The less efficient, greedy and unscrupulous (most of which are under FOC and others' national flags) engage in fraud, go bankrupt through incompetence and/or drive the conditions of crew and ship safety to low levels and challenge the better shipowners in the market.

The legislative and regulatory processes which govern shipping are complex and depend on law-making at international levels and implementation by nation states. As most of shipping finance, labour, operations, politics and problems are global in scope the requirement for nation-state enforcement is often irrelevant. Indeed the sovereign immunity of the flag can be a means of protecting the substandard company.

The main problem for the seafarer is a downscaling of employment conditions on the grounds that crew costs must be reduced in order to compete in the international market. Shipping already provides very low costs of transport: in 1997 a ton of cargo could be carried one mile for a little more than one cent. The real costs, as will be seen later, can be higher in human and environmental terms.

3

Seafarers and Employment

Introduction

Crews of merchant ships must be self-sufficient and able to improvise. They are responsible for the safety of the vessel, care of the cargo, maintenance and repairs; they need to be prepared for fire, weather damage, evacuation and other emergencies without assistance from the shore. Similarly, there can be illnesses and injuries which require attention without direct medical assistance.

The work and rest regimes of the 24-hour shipboard community are necessarily stringent. There may be a total of only twelve to twenty seafarers, divided between officers and ratings, and covering deck, engine room and catering functions. Ratings now tend to be general purpose and able to work across traditional departments. There is still a hierarchical structure on most foreign-going ships, but with small crews even senior deck officers are in boiler suits at various times and are multi-skilled. Some are qualified as polyvariant, combining navigational and engineering professional certificates. Added to what were the normal duties of the officer of the watch is now the work of the radio officer, who is no longer employed on most cargo vessels.

Workloads depend on the trade and type of vessel, but all are lengthy compared with shore occupations. There is little scope for substitution if a watchkeeper is ill: usually someone has to carry extra duties. On long voyages with small crews, life can be lonely and boring, and on coastal and short sea trades, exhausting. In both the seafarer is away from home for periods of a few months to over one year.

In spite of its drawbacks, sea-going has always attracted adventurous young men, as well as some women. There have been social misfits and those escaping from unsatisfactory home lives, but for the vast majority of seafarers it is a way of earning a living, although often a temporary one, and it has been fulfilling and rewarding for generations of people drawn from ports, coastal areas and islands around the world.

The work of seafarers in transporting raw materials, fuels, food-stuffs and manufactured goods throughout the world is vital. It is generally unseen and unheard except during a pollution incident, and usually unappreciated, except at times of war. Merchant ships move in their thousands over the oceans and have knit the countries of the world into tight interdependencies.

This chapter looks briefly at the work, the life and the hazards of modern seafaring. It takes small cross-sections of activities rather than in-depth analysis and is intended as a background to the accounts of unfair treatment meted out to many sailors who carry out these tasks, often under difficult and sometimes hazardous conditions, and always remote from homelands and families.

Recruitment

As a result of globalisation and structural change, the majority of ordinary seafarers (as distinct from officers) come from Asia. Most seafarers work mainly on the ships of independent shipowners who charter out their vessels to major oil companies and other industrial interests. Others are employed on container liners, ferries and cruise vessels. There are about one and a quarter million seafarers within the main sector of the world merchant fleet. The significance of Third World countries in the supply of crews is illustrated by Table 3.1 which shows the top ten supply countries.

Table 3.1   The top ten labour-supplying countries, 1995

	Countries	Seafarers
1.	The Philippines	244 782
2.	Indonesia	83 500
3.	Turkey	80 000
4.	China	76 482
5.	India	53 000
6.	Russia	47 688
7.	Japan	42 537
8.	Greece	40 000
9.	Ukraine	38 000
10.	Italy	32 300

Source: BIMCO/ISF 1995.[1]

In these countries seafarers are recruited by several methods. The bigger shipping companies may have direct recruitment by personnel departments; this is particularly the practice for acquiring senior officers. Management companies may recruit for several shipping firms who are their principals, and frequently private agencies will carry out recruitment on a speculative basis by advertisements. Sometimes a state mercantile marine office will recruit for national and foreign shipping, and occasionally seafarers' unions may also be involved in recruitment.

Table 3.1 shows the Philippines is by far the largest source of seafarers. There are about 300 manning agencies in the country, and they are approved by the Philippines Overseas Employment Administration (POEA) to supply seafarers to accredited shipping companies. The POEA is a government agency which comes under the jurisdiction of the Ministry of Labour and Employment.

Most of those recruited are males. Out of a world total of 1.25 million merchant seafarers only 1–2 per cent are female. Table 3.2 gives an indication of gender imbalances from a survey of EU recruitment. Sweden and Denmark stand out as exceptional.

Table 3.2   Distribution of women seafarers in parts of the EU

Country	Total no. of seafarers	Women seafarers	Women as per cent of total
Belgium	1,350	60	4.4
Denmark	9,809	1,478	15.1
Finland	5,218	294	5.6
Germany	17,178	920	5.3
Italy	25,000	300	1.2
Sweden	15,117	3,518	23.3
UK	31,392	1,463	4.7
Total	105,064	8,033	7.6 %

Source: Minghua, Zhao (1998).[2]

Most women are employed in catering and hotelling on board cruise ships and ferries. Senior posts amongst deck and engine-room staff are unusual. Of the 1603 German captains there are only four women, and one of the most progressive companies in the UK, BP Shipping, had only one woman chief officer in 1997.

There is a world surplus of ratings and a shortage of officers. In the traditional maritime countries (TMCs), with the decline in national flag shipping and cutbacks in training, there have been widespread closures of schools of navigation for cadets and officers. It became apparent in the 1990s that there was a critical shortage of officers for the future, and that it was common for many ship-ping companies to continue to employ European officers and to draw crews from developing countries. Competition is intense among labour-supplying countries, especially in relation to finding jobs for ratings. Countries offer, or claim, comparative advantages in levels of training, language, reliability and competence. Liberal (from the employer's point of view) terms of contracts are provided and often low levels of remuneration and social benefits accepted.

The majority of seafarers from the developing countries are on average much younger than the smaller numbers now drawn from the TMCs. Another feature of most seafarer employment of today is the lack of long-term job security. This applies even for some offi-cers and captains, but with a shortage of these ranks there is more security. There are few company contracts for ratings, work is for a single voyage and career prospects uncertain. This deters many good potential recruits from entering what could still be diverse and rewarding careers afloat and eventually ashore.

Training of Seafarers

With the globalisation of recruitment has come an increasing concern about the standard of seafarers crewing the world's ships, and the training that they undergo. A shipowner with a vessel manned by officers and crew from several countries has no way of knowing the quality of the seafarers working for him, particularly if he has relied on a manning or management agency for recruitment.

Training methods and standards still vary considerably and the quality of seafarers qualified by training establishments and gov-ernments differs from country to country, and even between training establishments within countries. The majority of seafarers now come from Asia, primarily the Philippines, Indonesia, India and China. The government of each country has laid down their own minimum requirements for training and each differs in some respects from the others. This is true also for many other parts of the world.

In 1978 the International Convention on Standards of Training, Certification and Watchkeeping for Seafarers (STCW) was adopted in an attempt to guarantee standards and the guidelines to achieve these. One of the reasons for stricter examination requirements was that a growing number of forged certificates of competency were being discovered particularly from the Philippines. It was found that officers were buying certificates from corrupt government officials without the need to undertake any formal training. This resulted in the dangerous situation whereby the officer of the watch on a foreign-going vessel would have little training for the job.

The 1978 STCW was only partially successful due to the problems of flag-state implementation of sufficiently rigorous training, examinations and monitoring, and also the rapid changes in technology and ship sizes which rendered some aspects obsolete.

There was increasing pressure to lay down new international minimum standards of training, and by 1992 a revised STCW was produced in the form of an Associate Code to the 1978 Convention. To ensure that parties implemented this (STCW 95), the IMO is in the process of creating a 'White List' of countries that comply with the training requirements. If a country is not included in the list, its certificates of competency will not be recognised by other member states, and ships employing officers from unrecognised states may be detained by port-state control.

Because so many European Union-flagged vessels sail with crews from several countries outside the EU, Brussels commissioned a study of training in the East in order to have a first-hand database on the training facilities in, to begin with, China, India, Indonesia and the Philippines. This included visiting colleges in these countries to see at first hand the facilities provided.[3] In addition to local and regional colleges there are a number of training centres set up by individual shipping companies from the UK, Germany and Norway to train seafarers from their own vessels, usually under FOC. This concept tries to ensure that companies receive adequately trained seafarers and avoids fraudulent certification.

Under STCW 95, the training of seafarers may improve considerably. The standardisation of instruction will reinforce globalisation of the industry by ensuring that almost any seafarer will be qualified to work on any ship.

Nationality and Cultural Diversity

As a result of the globalisation of the shipping industry, ships' crews are already nationally, culturally and linguistically diverse. About 80 per cent of world merchant ships have more than one nationality on board, many have seven or eight, and large cruise ships have more than thirty. As an example, Table 3.3 shows the places of origin of seafarers sailing under the flag of Cyprus.

Table 3.3   Places of origin of the majority of seafarers under the flag of Cyprus, 1995

	Officers	Ratings	Total
EU Nationals	1609	—	1609
Other European	1080	—	1080
Indian	478	620	1098
Burmese	133	434	567
Indonesian	31	207	238
Filipino	1793	6139	7932
Russian	2072	2536	4608
Polish	—	693	693
Other Asian	24	—	24
Ukrainian	165	204	369
Kiribati	—	220	220
Other	61	1721	1782
TOTAL	7446	12774	20220

Source: Cyprus Shipping Council 1995.[4]

There has of course always been some national diversity of seafarers on merchant ships. In the nineteenth century, British vessels had sailors and firemen drawn from the Indian subcontinent, Somalia and Yemen. But generally crews were fairly homogeneous until the 1970s. Shipping companies with trade links to specific parts of the world often signed on crews in these areas. Similarly they had crews sent from company homeports to join ships elsewhere in their country. Whole crews would have as a result been drawn from the Clyde, north-east England, Liverpool, south Wales, London, Hamburg, Marseilles, Yokohama, Hong Kong, Bombay, and so on. In India, a serang (petty officer) would select recruits in his home area for his ship. Such local procedures were widespread. For example, Gelina Harlaftis writes about Greek seafarers: '... a considerable number of vessels were manned by crews originating not merely from the same Island but often from the same village. The AB or deck boy might well have been the Captain's son, nephew or cousin.'[5]

Consequently up until recent times there would have been on many vessels a common language, culture and even kinship. There were hierarchical, class, and even caste divisions on board, but these were well-understood within a crew. Nowadays the racial, national and cultural mixes are very complex, and can lead to misunderstandings, stress and even violence.

The Divided Ship

For the seafarer, the ship is both a home and a workplace. On many ships these days the social community aspects of life have deteriorated due to a reduction in crew size and multi-national employment. There are foreign-going cargo vessels with only ten to twelve crew, most others have about twenty. Since it is a 24-hour working society, a watch-keeper will spend eight hours on duty (either 12 to 4; 4 to 8; or 8 to 12, both a.m. and p.m.) and will have other duties and broken sleep. During recreation periods there are few people about. Even with those awake, communication is not always easy.

There is still a hierarchical structure on most vessels. A gulf exists between officers and ratings and the master and chief engineer may remain removed even from the officers. The age range is often wide in a small crew, which likewise can create frictions over behaviour. Differences in language, race, education and cultural diversity further compound communication difficulties, and the smooth functioning of a shipboard community.

Many ships are thus very different socially from those operating in the 1970s. And although on-board relationships were seldom close and long-lasting in those days they were generally free from serious frictions. Hill, in his study *The Seafaring Career* (1972). observed, 'The seafarer tends to develop a highly skilled way and ability to make a quick, easy, jovial temporary relationship with those with whom he sails.'[6] This is much more difficult in a small multi-national society, where status, mores, religious taboos, humour, food and recreational preferences are diverse, and especially when most have to try and communicate in a common language (primarily English) which is not their own. This in itself creates tensions due to different meanings attributed to the same words by different cultures. It tends also to undermine team work and can lead to accidents. For example, in the *Scandinavian Star* fire of 1988, 'The fire was observed by the motorman who was Honduran, who then reported the fire to the watch engineer who was Filipino. The two men did not share a common language and consequently had to communicate by hand signals.' Similarly, in the *Scandinavian Star* fire of 1990, 'The crew had been hired on the understanding they spoke English but clearly they did not and this was a significant factor in the death toll of 158 people.'[7] As in the cases of the *Scandinavian Star*, communication problems with mixed crews may surface critically during emergencies – when people panic, it is said, they panic in their own languages.

On long voyages, in a socially divided ship, loneliness and boredom can set in. Off-watch sailors may confine themselves to the single-berth cabins common on the modern vessel. They will watch videos, smoke, perhaps drink, and have long periods of escapist sleep.

Some managers argue that provided seafarers are well trained for their technical tasks, only a basic functional common language and maritime vocabulary is needed. Others point out that off-duty social interaction depends on the ability to communicate well, and that this has implications for the smooth and safe working of the ship:

> The language that is spoken as far as the ship's work is con-
> cerned, that's quite easily understandable. But the social aspect
> of things on board is destroyed. There is no social interaction,
> and that is possibly one of the reasons that people do not wish
> to come to sea, because they safely assume that they are going
> to be four months on that ship. In that four months, the ship is,
> say, 80 days at sea, you are looking at 80 days of minimum con-
> versation almost being in jail. (SIRC management interviews
> 1997)[8]

A captain of a high-tech gas carrier with a well-trained multi-national crew shows the positive side to this type of crewing, provided communication skills are good: 'I have noticed a certain evolution of certain nationalities gaining a mutual respect for each other and their different cultures, culminating in increasingly happier ships. The combination of their different ideas is interesting and they compliment each other' (SIRC interviews, 1997).[9]

Good and Bad Ships and Shipowners

On the best-crewed ships with senior officers well aware of language and cultural differences, and an understanding shore management, on-board problems are at least minimised. In some companies, in addition to well-thought-out recreational facilities, there are policies of work enrichment whereby decisions regarding the ship community, such as leave periods and budgetary and accommodation matters, are devolved to the ship, and on-board committees convened. On many Australian vessels, officers and ratings use the same dining and recreational facilities. On some of the worst ships, seafarers are treated almost as slaves and do not always know who they are working for. There are vast on-board differences between ships and even on the same vessel, sailors from different countries doing the same jobs may be on different contracts and wage scales.

Wages

A basic attraction of seagoing is obviously good wages and the opportunity to save money. Young seafarers from developing countries have 'savings targets', including marriage, buying land, a house or a boat; they will leave the industry when these are attained – or in disillusionment if the target is not reached after several years. This is also partly a feature of developed-country seafarers, although it may appear later in their careers, when the attractions of travel, and the freedom of being at sea and away from home have worn thin.

On bad ships belonging to rogue shipowners, wages are often (as is documented in the next chapter) attacked. Seafarers are unpaid for months during a voyage and after leaving the ship. What is even worse for the seafarers is when the monthly allocation of earnings they have arranged for their families (the allotment) is also not honoured by the company, and the families are left destitute.

The good shipowner operating a FOC vessel with mixed crewing has this to say:

> If you pay people on time and treat people well then the chances are they are going to come back to your ships. This is something which is very important to us and is one of the reasons that our mix of Indians and Filipinos has been successful, because the people know when they go on board we are going to play our part. If you have a situation where people, to use wages as an example, are not paid on time, then that is obviously going to create tensions on the ship which are going to manifest themselves in different ways and I think by making sure we get our side of the bargain right I think we minimise any potential problems, social or otherwise, on the ships. (SIRC interviews, 1997)

Seafarers sailing under Greek captains have also reported that on ships with very poorly paid ratings, some captains have allowed inflated overtime sheets to be passed to the company management in order to help their crews (SIRC interviews 1997).[10]

Victualling/Nutrition

Food can be another difficulty, especially with multi-cultural crews. Vietnamese and Koreans mixing with Russians and Europeans have experienced health problems due to on-board diets. There are ships with excellent crew menus, although crew members sometimes experience problems with overeating and obesity. A cook reports his experiences on good ships:

> Breakfast ... Cornflakes, cereals, fruit juice, bacon, egg, black pudding, baked beans – tea, coffee, toast whichever they want. For lunch they have soup, entree, a main course, a dessert, cheese and biscuits with coffee or tea and then for night time you have again soup, entree, main course, cold meat salad, a desert, fruit. Again you put out the suppers and you have cold meat salads, and today the menus compared to 20 years ago – they were very bad. Today they're fantastic and that's only a rough menu. A menu from any ship – from a coaster to a deep sea.[11]

On a poorly catered vessel, Father Sinclaire Oubre of the Apostleship of the Sea records:

> The crew complained much about the food on board. When we went to the messroom, lunch was being served. There was a beef curry for lunch and one orange was available for each crew member. In asking questions, it was more that food was tightly rationed and the variety was far below contracted standards. This would match the situation that was explained to us regarding the fresh water. The fresh water was rationed by the captain until midnight of the day of our visit. The kitchen had a significant number of roaches and other insects crawling on the counters and along the walls.[12]

At the extreme lower end the *St Petersburg Press* reported in 1995 on a vessel in that port: 'The crew had been forced to scrounge for whatever food they can lay their hands on – they recently cooked and ate a stray dog.' The radio officer of the ship explained, 'We ate a dog recently that we caught in the port area, not because Vietnamese like eating dogs – we were just too hungry.'[13]

It is obviously very difficult to generalise about life on modern merchant ships. There are very good vessels and socially responsible companies which treat seafarers well, others are merely tolerable but provide a living, but possibly about a quarter of merchant ships are unacceptably bad in some respects.

Hazards of Seafaring

It is not possible to go to sea without some discomfort and risk. There are dangers in most occupations, but sea-going presents higher levels of risk and has lower levels of safety and survival than most other occupations due to separation from emergency and medical services. The community on board a merchant ship needs therefore to be particularly well-trained, safety conscious and self-sufficient. But even the best seafarers can be overwhelmed by the physical circumstances of the sea given an unseaworthy vessel, bad working conditions and a poor social environment.

Ships are regularly lost but there are marked differences between losses by flag. Several FOCs rate highly as hazardous, but some national flags also have a bad record (see Appendix 2). Each year there are ships lost from stress of weather, fire and other causes. Total losses vary, for example from 321 ships (1.9 million GRT) in 1991 to 179 (0.9 million GRT) in 1996.[14]

On coastal and short sea voyages, one of many problems which contribute to accidents is fatigue. This can become chronic when seafarers get only fragmented and disturbed sleep due to fast and intensive turn-around in port, followed by watch-keeping. Watch-keepers in the hours between 0000 and 0600 are particularly fatigue-prone as the circadian rhythm then goes down to its lowest levels, when people should be asleep.[15]

The ship itself can present a dangerous working environment with hard steel architecture, steep ladders, deep holds and tanks and moving equipment. In heavy weather there is violent rolling and pitching, wet slippery conditions; there is always noise and vibration. The cargoes carried may involve danger to the crew, from exposure to chemicals, gases and fumes. In this respect the seafarer cannot escape the effects of leakages, as the ship is his home.

As the ship moves around the world, the seafarer can encounter infectious diseases, including malaria, hepatitis, tuberculosis and HIV. Stress from on-board and home worries contributes to suicides at sea. In an analysis made by SIRC of deaths of British seafarers on board ships from 1982 to 1995, there were 68 certain and probable suicides. Of these the biggest contributory causes were 'family problems and divorce'. Other categories were financial, work-related, depression and 'serious mental illness', as well as 'not known'.[16] Table 3.4 also shows some of the typical entries for foreign seafarers taken from official inquiries on deaths of seafarers on multi-cultural ships. It highlights the family problems that can beset isolated seafarers who become frustrated and depressed.

Table 3.4   Examples of suicides on board

Age	Suicide	Comments
27	Hanged	Family problems in Manila and had not received a letter for a long time.
31	Jumped overboard	Had shown signs of depression. Had family problems.
36	Jumped overboard	Mental problems because of family problem, unable to sleep. Under-supervision by fellow crew.
37	Hanged	Made request for repatriation, had been granted by master who said he would give him flight details in due course – had been drinking heavily.

Source: Roberts (SIRC, 1998).[17]

With the limited number of people working on a ship there is not the compensatory absenteeism that occurs in work ashore. Seafarers press on with duties under stress, fatigue and illness so as not to let themselves and their shipmates down. The lack of adequately trained medical personnel on board adds to the hazards. A few ships do have doctors, and in most there are sick bays and contact with physicians ashore through radio medical services. Life on board is made less risky and more tolerable by good training, accommodation designed for comfort and safety, recreational facilities and proper food. There are many ships which meet these standards but others present real dangers to the lives of seafarers in every respect.

Table 3.5 indicates the causes and number of lives lost at sea, on vessels above 100 GRT as an average over a four-year period. However, the basis of this calculation is returns mainly from OECD countries. No deaths on FOC vessels were reported and only Poland presented adequate information from the former socialist countries.

Table 3.5   Average per annum mortality of seafarers

Causes	Seafarer Deaths
Maritime disasters	1 102
Occupational accidents	419
Illness	521
Missing at sea	74
Homicides/suicides	91
Total	2 207

Source: Nielsen and Roberts (SIRC, 1998).[18]

Finally we note another external hazard which has reappeared more virulently in recent years: the violence experienced by seafarers during pirate attacks. Table 3.6 shows the regions where this danger is most prevalent, and Table 3.7 shows the types of occurrences during the first six months of 1995.

Table 3.6   Piracy incidents, 1995

Area	No. of Incidents
Indonesia	34
China	29
Brazil	17
Somalia	14
Hong Kong	12
Others – Iran, W. Africa, Arabian Peninsula	66

Source: IMB (1996) and Andrew Grey, *Lloyd's List* (1996).

Table 3.7   Main types of pirate attacks reported, January–June 1995

Boarding	37
Attempted Boarding	15
Hijack	12
Fired on	9
Detained	8
In Port Attacks	5

Source: Andrew Grey, *Lloyd's List* (1996).[19]

Seafarers have met ugly deaths or sustained severe injuries during pirate assaults on their ships. Several hundreds have been taken hostage and others have been cast away when the ship was hijacked. The MV *Anna Sierra*, for example, was boarded in the Gulf of Thailand in September 1995 by thirty pirates armed with machine guns; the crew was set adrift on a small boat and raft, the ship's name was then repainted to *Arctic Sea* and its cargo of sugar sold in China.[20]

The Family

The seafarer is no different from most people, with the exception that he or she leaves home for long periods to earn a living. But the family of the seafarer does depart from what would still be considered normative life ashore, and this is one of the most difficult aspects of seafaring. The work cycle means frequent family farewells and reunions. The interim periods of separation vary from a few weeks to over twelve months, depending on the trades and types of ships. Family worries are common enough as stress factors in normal shore-based occupations, as are working conditions, job security and finance. For the seafarer these can be enormously compounded by concerns with ship safety and conditions, and the inability to share worries with the family and even with other members of the crew.

On some occasions wives accompany captains and officers, but this is usually only convenient in the early or late stages of marriage. The normal situation in the family of seafarers is for wives to stay at home and act as single parents. They make critical domestic decisions and deal with family problems. How well they manage depends partly on the community in which they live and their levels of social integration. In small coastal and island societies from which many seafarers are, or were, drawn, there are extended families, maritime traditions and mutual support. In large, more heterogeneous port towns, networks of support may be more diffuse or absent. Trade union organisations, missions to seamen, the International Committee for Seafarers Welfare (ICSW), and bodies such as the Seamen's Wives Association of the Philippines assist, but they cannot fulfil the role of a substitute parent with the children.

When the seafarer returns home the periods of leave are generally happy occasions when the family is together as a whole, but they can also be fraught with misunderstandings. Taylor et al. examined the psychosocial effects of even regular short two-week cycles of absence and return on wives, and concluded, '... around one third of the wives in our samples reported some form of stress associated with their husband's intermittent absences, either anxiousness when he was away or recurring arguments when he was at home'.[21] The effect of longer absences, in particular, when children have changed considerably, is more complex; there is a small range of literature on some aspects of these problems.[22]

The families of most career seafarers probably do cope well enough with the stress of long absences. They are more secure financially than the average lone parent with children, and often they consider absences at sea as a temporary part of life until specific economic targets have been achieved. On the other hand, these and other economic commitments are moving targets which tend to prolong careers at sea.

When a seafarer returns to a ship after leave, he misses his family. He may have anxieties during the voyage which he cannot share with shipmates. A recording of part of the conversation between a Filipino seafarer and Karen Lai, a lay chaplain with the Apostleship of the Sea, is an example:

> *Seafarer*: If he is dead then they will be alone. I am sorry for them. I think too much about this. I cannot work. I cannot think about my job.
> *Karen*: Did you tell anyone on board what happened?
> *Seafarer*: No, I don't speak my problems to them. They have their own problems. We only talk about normal things. No one wants to hear the other one's problems.[23]

In this instance, as in many others, the mission was able to facilitate home contact and also provide the spiritual comfort this particular seaman needed.

The seafarer has to find ways of continuing family relationships – this is made easier if regular telephone contact can be achieved, financial security sustained and predictable leave periods observed. When they cannot communicate with the family, are deprived of wages, and are denied the right to return home, the seafarer and his family are reduced to helplessness and desperation.

Conclusions

This general background on the employment of seafarers has, among other things indicated that the seafarer and the seafaring way of life has undergone radical changes over the past three decades.

Recruitment is now on a world-wide basis and carried out by numerous types of agencies. Large numbers of seafarers are recruited by third party management companies and then sent to ships. Under flags of convenience it is therefore often difficult for a seafarer and his family to know precisely who is their employer. The employment procedures are virtually unregulated, jobs are insecure, and crews are generally multi-national and predominantly male. There is monitoring of ship and crew conditions by port-state control officials and ITF inspectors, but these are, in effect, only spot checks.

International competition and the open market for labour have exercised downward pressures on conditions. There have been reductions in ships and training support in the traditional maritime countries and consequently there are world shortages in well-trained and qualified officers, and a surplus of ratings available from the developing countries. Processes of rebalancing recruitment and training are taking place, and new legislation has been enacted, but problems of application and enforcement remain.

The changing geopolitics in globalisation, the associated free play of the markets, and the related declines in the systems of accountability have left the way open for dubious and incompetent people to become major owners in shipping. They have found refuge in FOCs, and under a few national flags. The effects of this on world seafarers are main issues in subsequent chapters.

4

Failures, Frauds and Abuses

The instability of much of world shipping since the early 1970s has been accompanied by company failures, fraudulent behaviour and increased abuse of seafarers. The accounts of shipping enterprise failures which follow include Greek, Japanese, Russian, Singaporean and Swedish companies. In some ways these failures are also a reflection of the changes in shipping finance that have taken place since the 1960s. As the size and cost of vessels have increased, their economies of scale in terms of efficiency and controlling operating costs have had to be paid for by higher capital commitments. Consequently, and in contrast to the successful old-established shipowners who borrowed as little as possible, the financing cost element within modern shipping has assumed increasing importance.[1]

However, when we consider the failure of a specific company, it is seldom that a single cause can be identified (leaving aside deliberate crime which is also involved). The factors are multiple and complex. There are seven aspects worth highlighting – when several of these converge, they are capable of leading shipping companies towards bankruptcy, with losses to investors and disasters for seafarers:

- a management which is over-speculative and generally inadequate
- the initial ease of provisions of large amounts of capital which banks and fund managers want to invest
- financiers with inadequate knowledge of shipping
- a ready supply of shipbuilding capacity and second-hand ships
- doubtful surveys giving over-valued assets
- unpredicted changes in the market conditions, and
- the inability to meet interest payments from cash flows.

These points cover a range of detailed factors, but at the highest level of generalisation they are true of most recent failures of shipping companies.

In reports of the failures referred to in this chapter little information is given on the seafarers. Their fate seemed of minimal interest to those winding up a company, and records, where they exist, are fragmented and difficult to access. Comparatively, as measured in human and social costs, the seafarers are the main victims and their plight is reflected early in the events. Some of the companies cited, or the mortgagees, eventually responded quite responsibly to the plight of the seafarers. Others simply ignored them.

The purposes of the first part of this chapter are therefore to refer to a few major collapses and thereby indicate that the failure of Adriatic Tankers on which we focus later is not so unusual. The second part considers the abandonment and abuse of seafarers generally – again to show that the behaviour of Adriatic management is not an aberration, or an isolated occurrence confined to one company, flag, or country of beneficial ownership.

Causes of Company Collapse

Tidal Marine

In 1972, the collapse of Tidal Marine was the direct result of the owner financing his company's growth on the back of its purported, and often fictitious, chartering commitments.[2] These charters were used as a form of security in the acquisition of bank finance and in recourse to the equity markets, which allowed the company to grow from just three vessels in 1969 to 45 by 1972. The vessels involved were a combination of second-hand oil tanker and dry cargo vessels. The collapse in 1972, resulted from a severe cash-flow crisis within the firm. This was attributed to the lack of revenue from charters, because the charter commitments, upon which the growth had been based, turned out to be largely fictitious. In addition, fraud also took place in the over-valuation of vessels for which purchase loans were then sought.

Upon the collapse, banks found that they had financed vessels of Tidal Marine in excess of 100 per cent, as opposed to the believed 75 per cent due to the over-valuation of the vessels. Whilst several of those involved, including some bankers, were subsequently charged with fraudulently obtaining over $60 million of loans, the case brought into question how a company with no track record was able to obtain financing so easily.[3]

Colocotronis

Another collapse, that of Colocotronis in 1975, demonstrated the liability to shipping companies caused by large shipping investments – which subsequently turn out to be ill-timed. In the case of Colocotronis, liquidity problems developed as the result of ordering two ULCCs (ultra-large crude carriers) in 1975. The company already represented the fifth largest Greek-owned fleet, operating 50 vessels (totalling 3 million tons), but had investment finance of $320 million tied to the company. These investment loans to Colocotronis had been widely syndicated with 15 per cent held by German banks, 40 per cent US and other European banks and the remaining 15 per cent with smaller syndicates. Action taken by the major creditors led to the transfer of equity of over 1 million tons to West German interests, the enforced sale of 23 vessels and the farming-out to management of most of the rest of the fleet.

Some of the leading bankers, such as Deutsche Schiffharts, and some smaller lenders, were able to absorb or dramatically reduce their outstanding exposure on the Colocotronis fleet. Only European-American, which was left with exposure on 12 vessels out of a portfolio of 17, resorted to taking over management of the tonnage, depriving the owner of any further say in the continued operation of the fleet. European-American were also unusual at the time for setting up syndicates with little or no knowledge or experience of the shipping industry – though as the case of Adriatic experience shows, this still occurs today.[4]

Saleninvest

In some other instances, a single factor may be identified as the trigger. The collapse of the Saleninvest empire in 1984, was largely the result of external conditions influencing its trading markets. Changes to dollar exchange rates combined with the collapse of the reefer, dry cargo markets and rigs, caused losses in all sectors of its operations. Despite the attempts of the Swedish government, and other parties, including domestic and foreign banks to restructure the company with SKr1.2 billion, the company collapsed with losses in excess of SKr360 million.[5]

Sanko

The dramatic Sanko collapse during 1985 illustrates the dangers of easily obtainable finance without adequate market knowledge. This involved almost one-sixth of the Japanese fleet (or 3 per cent of the world's total). Outstanding liabilities totalled Y1000 billion, with nearly half to financial institutions, including Y233 billion attributable to three domestic Japanese banks. The final stage in the collapse of Sanko was the result of speculative ordering of 125 handy-sized bulk carriers in a move to set the company on recovery, at a time when the freight markets had sunk to all-time lows on the expectations of recovery.[6] A similar exercise in 1973, ordering 50 ships again during a recession, had fortunately been followed by economic upturn. The final failure prompted the observance that 'In an industry noted for its volatility and instability, reliance on aggressive expansion strategies will not always be successful.'[7]

Again the three principal banks involved in the main financing of the loan to build Sanko's new ships, were observed either to have had an inadequate knowledge of the industry or not to have heeded the warning signs. Despite at least one major restructuring and various attempts at others, Sanko was finally forced into bankruptcy. The company was ultimately restructured under court supervision.[8]

Regency Cruises

In the case of Regency Cruises (1995–97), the final failure was attributed to the knock-on effects of the late delivery of a new vessel, combined with a slump in the industry and a failed public stock offering. The event was quite sudden and the company ceased operations overnight, filing for Chapter XI bankruptcy protection in New York with debts approaching $200 million. The impact of this overnight collapse on the crews was particularly significant.

Like Adriatic, Regency had already been involved in some conflict over pay and conditions of seafarers with the International Transport Workers' Federation before its collapse. In this more recent case, some information on the effects of the collapse on the crews is available, and it shows that this varied considerably with each vessel. In the case of the *Regent Star*, Kawasaki, the vessel's reported beneficial owner, paid off the 400 seafarers, using Epirotiki Cruise Line as agent to repatriate the 49 nationalities on board.

In the case of the *Regent Spirit*, 100 crew were left with outstanding claims,[9] as were the crews of the *Regent Sea* and *Regent Sun* all stranded in Nassau. They had little money, the air conditioning had broken down and the food had run out.[10] Unlike many of the passengers with travel insurance, the assurance of wages owed to the seafarers was left to the mercy of those taking over the vessels.

The Baltic Shipping Company

An even larger collapse triggered by changing external conditions is that of the Baltic Shipping Company. The Baltic Shipping Company represented the largest of the communist-controlled merchant fleets of the former Soviet Union, operating extensive liner services world-wide, owning 180 vessels and with over 15,000 employees. However, following the break-up of the Soviet Union and the collapse of the trading system during the transition to a free market economy, the fortunes of the company rapidly declined. Privatised in 1991, it found itself burdened with an ageing fleet, high overheads, shrinking trade and heavy debts. Despite making profits of Rbl215.82 billion in 1994, there were losses of Rbl3.21 billion in 1995[11] – it is said that some managers disappeared with money and in 1996 the company was formally declared bankrupt.

The arrest of vessels around the world exacerbated the already serious financial problems for both the Baltic Company and the seafarers. Many seafarers became stranded on the company's vessels, relying on local charities to support them while waiting for their wages or the sale of the vessels. By the beginning of 1997, two-thirds of the vessels in the fleet had been sold off to pay debts, for Rbl8 billion, in addition to the sale of property and other assets held by the company.[12]

Unimar Maritime Services

A more recent example of a shipping company failure due partly to inadequate management, apart from Adriatic Tankers, has been the case of Unimar Maritime Services. The collapse has been attributed by the company to a deterioration in its relations with Russian joint venture partners. However, one of these, Northern Shipping, accused Unimar of mortgaging/disposing of vessels on bareboat charter from the firm without authority, and even using the sale of one vessel to cover its own debts. Most of the capital for the venture was reported to have come from the Russian company, with Unimar in control of the day-to-day operations. Allegations were made about inappropriate use of the available funds, mostly concerning the amount of money that was spent on the company's lavish new office building in Athens. This collapse has many similarities to that of Adriatic, with registered ownership of the vessels resting with single-ship companies based in Panama and Malta.

By December 1996, virtually all the Unimar vessels had been arrested on behalf of various creditors. Those placed under a separate management company in an attempt to save them also failed, with the sale/arrest of at least two of these vessels. Overall the fleet appeared to be in a poor condition with the fear that even vessel sales would leave creditors and crews with little chance of recovering debts of several million dollars. At this point the company had effectively collapsed financially and operationally, with P&I liability cover also withdrawn, making resumption of trading increasingly unlikely.[13]

Little is known in detail of the impact on the crews of these vessels; however, the ITF had specific dealings with the crew of the *Unipower*, a general cargo vessel built in 1965. The crew, already owed five months' back pay, beached the vessel for scrapping against the advice of the ITF in London, thus compromising their ability to receive outstanding wages. Once a vessel is scrapped, it effectively 'disappears', and with it a crew's entitlement to outstanding moneys. Whilst some money was received and the crew repatriated, $100,000 remains outstanding.

Dragonix

In 1997 the Dragonix group of companies based in Singapore began to experience severe financial problems and one of its major shareholders fled Singapore with debts estimated to be in the millions.[14] He was not contactable after the arrest of the ships. Due to this abandonment, the crew of the *Dragon Supreme* were left with no water, food, electricity or wages and in desperation had to resort to obtaining the arrest of the vessel. The crew approached the Danish Sailors' Church in Singapore claiming that they had received no money to send home for their families for nine months. The arrest allowed the Sheriff's office to arrange for provisions to be sent to them by a local agent. Another vessel had been at anchor in China for over five months with the crew owed two months' wages. The company was believed to have purchased four vessels in 1997 alone,[15] indicating an expansion too rapid to be controlled, and managers with very high personal expenditures from company earnings.

These cases serve to illustrate that the international shipping industry has found, sometimes to its cost, that where reliance has been placed on relatively easily obtained and somewhat recklessly offered outside investment capital, the industry has become increasingly vulnerable to changing trading and economic conditions because of the urgency of financiers to protect the large sums involved. There is no doubt also that there are incompetent and unscrupulous owners and managers. It is the seafarers and their families that suffer from this system through no fault of their own.

Consequences to Seafarers from Company Collapse and Neglect

The hardships on seafarers arise from sometimes unfortunate, more often incompetent, management and also from a total disregard for seafarers as human beings. They have been seen mainly as factors of production to be manipulated and dispensed of at will. Before focusing on the Adriatic case a brief account of this deliberately disgraceful (and to good owners, unacceptable) aspect of international shipping will serve to put the Adriatic study in the context of widespread abuse.

It may seem extraordinary to anyone with a basic business sense that the means by which an enterprise makes its money should be poorly maintained. However, there are shipowners who fail to understand that the most important elements aboard their ships are the crews. A ship will not reach its destination and its cargo will not be delivered in good condition without a competent crew. All the more extraordinary then that the crew are often the first to feel the effects of cost-cutting or of fraudulent practices perpetrated by the shipowner.

Seafarers have been seen as an easy target throughout history. They have been cheated and abused both afloat and ashore. A seafarer going ashore at the end of a long trip, his pockets stuffed with a year's pay, was a natural target for thieves, crimps, pimps and conmen. At sea he lived a hard life under the command of men who had often had a similar upbringing but displayed extraordinarily little sympathy for those that followed them. A seafarer's life has not changed under some flags and owners.

The Diversity of Complaints

An indication of the diversity of issues involved in abuses may be appreciated from a survey over a four-year period of 992 cases from the files of the ITF's Special Seafarers' Department (SSD) Actions Unit.[16] This survey does not include the hundred Adriatic Tanker vessels which are discussed in detail in Chapters 5, 6 and 7.

Table 4.1   List of principal complaints, 1993–96

Issue	Number
Disputes over wages	418
Abandonment and repatriation	84
Collective agreements	55
Unseaworthy and substandard ships	53
Victimisation and blacklists	43
Unfair dismissal	33
Substandard accommodation	25
Medical treatment	23
Delayed allotments	22
Personal injury	16
Loss of life	9
Agency fees	5

The cases shown are not individual seafarers but are a part of or a whole crew, some are from passenger vessels and therefore the figures represent a large number of seafarers. The majority of cases emanate from flag of convenience vessels. These cases are only those that were brought to the notice of the ITF – hundreds more must go unreported every year.

Table 4.2   Principal flags from which complaints emanate

FOC	Number	Second Reg.	Number	National	Number
Panama	181	NIS	9	Romania	50
Cyprus	173	GIS	8	Russia	35
Malta	138	DIS	5	Greece	30
Liberia	69			Lithuania	15
Bahamas	64			Ukraine	11
St Vincent	64			Germany	9

The following examples are extracts from the ITF reports and from the press, missions to seamen and interviews. They follow as closely as possible the descriptions of the complainants.

Abandonment

The worst abuse a seafarer can suffer is abandonment, which usually occurs far from home and when he has little or no money. In addition there is usually a sizeable backlog of wages owed to him. A crew abandoned by a shipowner in a country where they probably cannot speak the language and where an appeal to the legal system may prove pointless, can find themselves facing disaster and their families facing penury.

Usually when a ship is abandoned there are many unpaid bills and the communications service is one of the first services to be withdrawn from the vessel. Thus it is often difficult for the seafarer to contact his family and they may not be certain of his whereabouts. Contact is important because the family's allotments will have ceased to be paid and they may be suffering.

The files show the types of abandonment incidents reported by seafarers – most of these, as with other complaints, will have been acted upon after authentication. For example, the crew of the *St Nicholas* who were abandoned in a Nigerian port in 1995, became dependent on a local charity for food as they had no supplies or funds aboard the vessel. In another case in 1994 an abandoned crew who had arrested their vessel in West Africa were obliged to stay with their ship the *Leona 3* (from Liberia) for a lengthy spell while the local courts heard their case. The problem was further exacerbated by the fact that the shipowner was bankrupt and the crew were unsure where their claim stood with regard to other creditors. The months spent waiting for the court to make a decision were wasted.

There are a number of cases where a shipowner has abandoned a crew after they have demanded their owed wages, if the amount of wages owed is greater than the value of the ship (a distinct possibility with a small vessel or one without a cargo on board). Then the owner is likely to disappear rather than pay the crew. One crew were abandoned after demanding the wages which they had contracted for, as opposed to the wages which they had received when they arrived on board. Often these back wages cannot be reclaimed. A Russian master was criminally charged by the owners when he decided to sell off part of the ship's cargo in order to pay for provisions and some wages. The abandoned crew had not been paid for several months.

In 1994, a Turkish crew were pushed out of an agent's office and on to the street in Bombay after the *Hasan Bey* (Turkey) had sailed and they had gone to the office to be paid. The agent had claimed that they would be paid when they arrived home but they refused to believe him. They were in Bombay without money but were assisted by NUSI, the ITF affiliate seafarers' union in India. Even worse off was a lone Portuguese seafarer who was thrown off the *Santa Cristina* (Honduras) in 1988 and left on the quay when it sailed.

Seafarers have been abandoned after they have been shipwrecked. Owners have blamed the crew for the wreck and refuse to repatriate them, or have simply ignored survivors once they have been brought ashore. A Ghanaian crew were shipwrecked and abandoned in Madagascar in 1994 and were unable to return home for a considerable time because the *Semo's* (Liberia) owner could not be traced. A crew can also be abandoned when a ship is sold, leaving the new owner to deal with the problem of wages owed.

On the *Goddess Orori* (Nigeria), the vessel was detained by the authorities in Malta because she was said to be in an unseaworthy state. The ship's owner then blamed the crew for the vessel's detention and refused to pay them what they were owed in wages. The ship's agents were also not paid and so would not provide the vessel with stores. The seafarers only survived with the aid of donations from charities, the Maltese public and help from the ITF.

In the case of the *Intersea* (Honduras) the crew were owed several months' wages, and lodged a claim while the ship was in a Bulgarian port. The owner disappeared as soon as the claim was made, and for two years the seafarers had to try and resolve the case. Some of them eventually settled in Bulgaria with little chance of returning to their national homes.

In 1997, the owner of the *Alimos 1* (Panama), sent a telex to the ship threatening to abandon the crew if they did not allow the discharge of the cargo and sail the vessel back to Piraeus. The crew had not been paid for ten months and were owed an estimated US$132,000. The owner offered to pay only US$10,000.

Abandoned seafarers have, however, turned out to be fairly resourceful and in some cases have married local women and started businesses in the port of abandonment. Two Filipino ratings opened a successful jewellery shop after they were abandoned in Colombo. However, the prosperity of these endeavours may often depend on the sympathy of the local immigration authorities. Many of Adriatic Tankers' seafarers fell foul of the police in Rotterdam while abandoned ashore awaiting their wages. The police were sympathetic, but the seafarers were well over their allotted transit time and they were required to see that they were repatriated whether they had been paid or not. Another case in Rotterdam involved two Egyptian watchmen placed on a vessel by the owner: they were unpaid for four years and only managed to leave the ship when paid off by a new owner.

Repatriation Refusals

Repatriation is a problem that arises from abandonment; however, it does stand as an issue in itself. A seafarer has a right to expect repatriation at the end of their contract and at certain other times, but may have considerable difficulty in achieving this.

Some of the contracts drawn up by both manning agents and shipowners are in the employer's favour, for example, where a seafarer's wages cease if he becomes ill or if the company decides to end his employment, wherever the vessel may be. This sort of agreement usually incorporates a clause requiring the seafarer to pay his own repatriation costs as well as the costs of his relief.

It is not always possible to repatriate a crew precisely at the end of their contract due to the very nature of a vessel's operations. For this reason, a contract of employment will often have a clause varying the length of a trip, plus or minus two months or so. However, it is not at all uncommon for a crew to ask for assistance when they are well over their stipulated contract time. Owners will use the ship's trading pattern as an excuse to retain a crew for as long as possible. Difficulties in transferring money and communication problems are often cited as excuses for telling the crew to remain on board for 'just one more port'. At times that port will be one that is closer to the seafarers' homes and so will be cheaper for repatriation. This is occasionally preferred by some crews, but is a poor excuse for working them well over their contracts' lengths.

A Russian crew which had completed their contract, went on strike to pressurise the owners to pay and repatriate them. However, the master anchored the vessel off the coast in a position where they were unable to get ashore and attempted to starve them into submission. Breaking contract is also dealt with in unfair ways. When the Ukrainian crew of the *Illyria* went on strike in 1995 waiting for wages they had been owed for some time, the ship's owner managed to persuade the port police that the crew were troublemakers and demanded that they be taken to the local jail. He would not repatriate them until they had signed a false document stating that they had received their full pay.

Cheating on Wages and Intimidation

Repatriation arrangements are also seen as an opportunity to cheat seafarers out of their earnings. Many of them live in remote areas of their countries and once they are on their way home, they are vulnerable to deception. A seafarer who had been paid off with his voyage wages was taken to the airport by the agent who then tried to persuade the man to sign for his severance pay which would be paid to him at the other end. Fortunately the man was not so naive: it later turned out that the owner had no intention of paying and had used this ruse before. A staff agency in the Philippines was found to be withholding seafarer's allotments from their families with the excuse that the money was to be used to repatriate those seafarers.

Wages clearly feature highest in the list of seafarers' complaints and are linked with intimidation. It is often difficult for someone at sea to find out whether or not they are being paid regularly and up to date. Communication with banks and those at home is the problem: it may take some time to receive the news that no allotments were being received.

Research has shown that an average time for a seafarer to wait before making a complaint to someone outside the company or the ship is four months, either because he suffers from a lack of information or this is about the time when his patience runs out. The act of complaining is no guarantee that he will be paid in the near future or indeed at all. Often seafarers will be afraid to ask about the wages that they are owed, either through intimidation or through fear of losing their employment with the company. Many cases show that pressure is put on those who have a legitimate right to complain not to do so.

There is ample evidence that where wages have been successfully reclaimed, attempts have been made once the ship is at sea to retrieve the money by force or intimidation. The intimidation may be in the form of threats against the seafarers' families in their homes through a staff agent or other owner's representatives or they may be against the seafarers themselves. Owners and manning agents who are known to employ these intimidatory methods are sometimes obliged by the unions or authorities to sign a waiver, stating that they will not try to retrieve the wages paid or blacklist the seafarers. This does not always work. A Sudanese crew wrote a letter withdrawing their claim for the wages that they were owed, but there was evidence that the seafarers had been taken off the ship to a detention centre and made to sign the letter and there was thought to be intimidation of their families. A Turkish captain sent an armed gang aboard his ship the *Porfirios* (Greece) in 1994 in an attempt to drive off the crew, who refused to leave until they had been paid the agreed rates.

If a wage claim has been successful and the crew of a vessel paid in full and up to date, the owner has been known to attempt to claw back the extra amount, by making deductions from subsequent earnings. These deductions take the form of false claims for services or goods that have not been supplied. The Polish third officer of the *Iolcos Pioneer* (Panama) had a claim made against him in 1994 for 127 phone calls that he had supposedly made to a country in which he did not even live!

A ship's crew may sign an agreement when they are recruited in their own country and then flown to another part of the world to join their vessel. However, when they arrive, they are told that the original agreement (often on ITF terms) is invalid and they have to sign a new agreement at a lower wage. If they refuse, they are informed that there is no job and that they are responsible for their own repatriation costs. They have little choice but to agree.

A method of paying crews below minimum rates which is fairly common is double bookkeeping. This is where two sets of account books are kept aboard the ship. One set is for inspection by the authorities and the ITF and shows the wages stipulated in the agreement; the other set, which is for the owner only, shows the lower wages that the owner actually pays. The crew are obliged to sign both sets of books.

Wages differ by nationality and complaints are received regularly from seafarers who are receiving less pay than others on board their ships by virtue of their race and the local agreements that they have signed. In March 1995, a Russian engineer aboard a Turkish flagged ship the *Asena 1* (Turkey), complained that the Turkish crew members were being paid regularly while he was months behind with his wages.

There are many excuses and devices used for the non-payment of wages and for delaying allotments to families. Some owners blame their banks and the difficulty of moving currency from one country to another while others claim that they have forwarded the crew's wages to the manning agents and it is the agents who are at fault. Exchange rates used by owners or written into agreements can often be suspect and it is very rare indeed for them to favour the seafarer.

A notorious case of a wages dispute occurred aboard the South-Korean owned *Glory Cape* (Panama) in 1994. She was arrested off the Australian coast for the non-payment of crew wages. There had been a long-standing dispute between the vessel's Indonesian crew members and the Korean master. The dispute came to a head at the port of Dampier, Western Australia with the crew refusing to sail with the vessel. They were, however, persuaded to stay aboard by an undertaking that the vessel would move out to an anchorage and wait there until the dispute was solved with the assistance of the ITF.

In breach of that undertaking, the master attempted to sail under the cover of night. On discovering this, some of the crew members tried to escape from the ship using one of the lifeboats but found that their attempted departure had been anticipated by the master and officers who had lashed down the boats with steel cables. Those attempting to escape from the vessel were then attacked by other crewmen armed with crowbars and led by the first officer. Blows were exchanged and the crew members whose escape from the ship by lifeboat had been thwarted, either jumped or fell overboard. One of them later died. (See also Chapter 9.)

The shipowner is not alone in trying to prevent a crew from receiving their owed wages. A manning agent attempted to sue a crew for delaying the ship because they had gone on strike in an attempt to recover months of unpaid wages. A Chinese seaman complained that his signature was forged on a pay-sheet to indicate that he had accepted a lower wage than he was contracted for. Signature forgery seems to be fairly common, along with the attempted bribery of officials to turn a blind eye. There are many reports of ships of the Black Sea Shipping Company (BLASCO): in 1996, they had 200 vessels under the Ukrainian flag, by 1998 most had been shifted to FOC. The Ukrainian crewing agents, it was reported to the ITF, threatened the crews and their families with violence if there were any wage claims.

The fear of intimidation is well-justified as is shown in case after case. A Peruvian shipowner sued the crew for striking to obtain months of owed wages. He claimed against them for lost revenue incurred while the ship was lying idle. Another crew were threatened by their own rather doubtful union when they went on strike in order to claim wages owed to them, and the owner of a Colombian ship threatened his crew with violence and legal action if they did not agree to sail his vessel back across the Atlantic to South America. They had signed on to fly to Europe to collect a vessel he had bought. On arrival they found the ship to be a barge not fit for ocean voyaging, only certified for a limit of twelve miles off shore. However, in the face of the threats, they were forced to sail on this dangerous voyage.

It is clear also that some ship's officers have little knowledge of crew management and are unfit to hold positions of responsibility on board. A chief officer on the *Chios Dream* (Panama), in 1994, used violence against a crew from El Salvador and Nicaragua, also withholding their overtime payments, while another sacked a group of Burmese seafarers whose only misdemeanour was to enquire about their overtime rates. One Filipino crew arranged through the ITF to have a lawyer meet them at the airport to prevent the owner or manning agent from robbing them of the wages they carried.

Crudely forged letters withdrawing pay claims have been received by unions – these are so obviously fakes they could not possibly be taken seriously. A man was locked up on board his ship to stop him leaving despite the fact that his contract was over and he was awaiting payment of his owed wages. He was held for three weeks before he managed to escape and swim ashore while the vessel was at anchor off the coast.

The Selfinvest Maritime Company of Romania is not only accused of abuse, cheating on wages and abandonment of its seafarers, but it actually took a court case against a crew as intimidation. The case was based on damages which the owner claimed were caused by the crew while waiting for wages to be paid.

Sexual Harassment

Sexual harassment is known at sea, despite the small numbers of women sailing on cargo vessels. A female cook was forced to sleep with the ship's captain to keep her job and by the threat of destroying her family life at home. The master also tried to get her to sign back on to the same vessel using the same pressure. But we know that sexual harassment is not confined to females. Amongst several reports in the 1990s, three seamen from the *Marilia A* (Malta) sought help from the Hong Kong Mariners' Club, claiming sexual assault on board.

Political Pressure

Crews are subject also to political pressures, for example, Chinese sailors have long been under threat from their own government not to make any trouble on board. This has been part of that country's policy to induce shipowners to use Chinese crews. The policy has, however, led to many of them being badly treated or underpaid by owners who are aware that they are unable to retaliate. The seafarers know that a complaint, however justified, will be reported to their manning agents and they will face action when they return home.

Refusal of Medical Treatment

Medical care is a basic right for seafarers and it is the duty of a shipowner to provide that care world-wide. The concern from the owner's point of view is that a crew member will be certified unfit and a replacement will have to be found and flown out to the ship. With today's short turn-around time, any delay to the vessel is costly. This attitude is well-illustrated by the number of cases shown in the ITF files.

If a crew member has been injured severely enough to be a possible candidate for compensation, an agent may take the man directly to the airport rather than to the doctor. In this way the seafarer will be offered a lower rate of compensation in his own country than he may have received had he claimed abroad. In 1995 a Russian seafarer was injured aboard the *Sverdlovsk* (Russia) in an American port and the US courts awarded him an amount of compensation that was well above that which his company would have paid him. In another case, indicating how far cost saving can go, the dead body of a seafarer was kept aboard a ship for eight months before the authorities were informed.

To prevent a seafarer seeing a doctor there is often collusion between the owner, master and agent. The master prevents the seafarer seeking medical attention either through loyalty to or fear of the owner. The agent will want to impress the owner with how cheaply he can turn the ship around knowing that any costs saved will be welcomed. One Polish fitter returned to his ship the *Reefer Princess* (Liberia) in 1994 after a visit to the doctor with advice from the doctor to rest for 15 days. The master did not want a non-working seafarer and paid him off, repatriating him at the fitter's own expense. In another case aboard the *Baltic Universal* (Sri Lanka) in 1993, a second officer was refused medical attention by the master who then went on to forge a letter to the company from the second officer requesting repatriation at his own expense.

There are, however, some seafarers who are unable to leave their ships despite being medically unfit to carry out their duties. One crew member who was lucky enough to visit a doctor was refused repatriation by the master even though he had a double hernia and could not work. He was obliged to struggle on through the voyage until the ship reached a port closer to his home. A doctor's recommendation that a heart patient be repatriated from the *Al Karim* (Malta) was ignored by the master who felt that the expense was not justified. In 1996, another seafarer landed with pneumonia was taken to hospital where the doctor recommended that he be repatriated. However, the agent told the master of the vessel the *Flag Mersindi* (Greece), that the man was fit enough to sail with his ship. Intervention by the authorities elicited a promise from the company that he would be flown home but later efforts to reach him led them to believe that he was still aboard the ship. In other cases, an owner tried to repatriate an officer with two broken legs to avoid medical costs at the port where the ship lay, and a seafarer with brain damage was returned to his ship after only a short spell in hospital.

Some seafarers are obliged to sign contracts that state that he will cease to be paid if he falls ill and will be repatriated at his own expense. It is also increasingly common for a contract to state that venereal disease is treated on the seafarer's own account. Under one agreement, a Chinese seafarer aboard the *Steel Flower* (Panama), had 40 per cent of his wages deducted in 1995 when he fell ill. One shipowner claimed injury compensation from his insurance company for an injury that occurred to one of his sea-farers. However, he failed to pass on the award to the seaman despite claiming that he had done so. Another case concerned a man who received no compensation for his severe injuries because the vessel's owner had not paid the P&I premiums and the ship's cover had been cancelled.

Sometimes an ill seafarer will have to take matters into his own hands. In 1995 the second officer of the *Admiral 1* (St Vincent Islands), went to the extent of instructing a lawyer to approach the company demanding that he be allowed to see a doctor. He com-plained afterwards that he had been mistreated on board because of this. Another crewman, on the *Coffee Express* (Honduras), was so worried at being denied access to a doctor that he paid for kidney treatment rather than continue suffering.

On board the *Ashley* (Liberia), the Filipino chief engineer suffered severe burns to his face and legs in a hydraulic fluid fire off the Azores. Despite requests from other officers, the master refused to seek medical care and advice for the chief. The burned man was left to treat himself with alcohol and water and it was not until twelve days later, when the vessel had crossed the Atlantic that the port authorities in Mobile, Alabama in the US insisted that he be taken ashore for treatment. He was repatriated to be met by his wife who had no knowledge of his injuries. As he later said, 'If the master can treat the chief engineer so badly, what would he have been like if the injured man had been a rating in a lower position on board?'

Victimisation

Victimisation of seafarers takes many forms. It may be perpetrated by the owner, the master and the officers or it may come from fellow seafarers. This can include threats of violence against a seafarer or his family. Many sailors are afraid to speak out against shipboard con-ditions due to fear of reprisals. Phone calls are made from ashore or letters are smuggled off ships to missions and unions to avoid scrutiny. Owners have sacked whole crews on discovering that they have joined a union or been in contact with the ITF.

There is often a racial element to victimisation and with today's mixed-race crews there is plenty of opportunity for it to occur. A number of the cases mentioned below refer to mixed nationalities, but these are not necessarily in constant disharmony – each is an individual case on board an individual ship.

On board the *Atlas* (Liberia), a Sri Lankan found he was on a ship with a Greek crew. He discovered he had signed on under his own national agreement, and was being paid considerably less than the Greeks. This compares with a case in 1995 where the mixed crew of Greeks and Pakistanis aboard the *Sea Raider* (Panama), were under the same agreement, yet the Pakistani seafarers were paid less than their Greek counterparts. One crewman complained of unfair treatment when he found he was the only Filipino aboard a vessel with three other nationalities who united against him. Some companies make a point of employing crews of different nationalities at different rates on the same ship. This is an attempt to defeat any crew concerted action and solidarity.

For some owners, contact between their crews and the unions or the ITF is grounds for dismissal. Even possession of union literature can be dangerous. Five Turkish seamen were sacked when the owner discovered their contact with the ITF. The radio officer of one vessel was removed for trying to expose double bookkeeping. On another ship, crew members who refused to hand back a union-secured pay rise, were dismissed without severance pay. Others who succumbed to the owner's threats were able to 'buy back' their jobs.

There are manning agents that produce 'blacklists' of seafarers who have defended their rights. These are in the form of a sheet of portrait photographs showing seafarers with their names, ranks and licence numbers displayed. There is a warning printed on the sheet stating that the seafarers shown have on some occasion contacted the ITF to help claim wages owed. These 'blacklists' alert other manning agencies or prospective employers that the seafarers shown are considered 'troublemakers'.

Another of these 'blacklists' notes that 5000 copies have been printed and that it is circulated to all manning agents and employers 'for their files'. It is clearly an attempt to deny the seafarers their right to employment. Some play on national sensibilities by stating that the men shown 'bring a bad name' to seafarers of that nation, thus attempting to alienate them from their fellow nationals.

Poor Food

Food is an important part of shipboard life and, with a considerable mix of nationalities, cultures and religions, there is great variation in diet requirements. Seafarers have become ill and stressed due to unfamiliar food being continuously served to them. Often there is only one cook who will produce the accustomed food of only one culture. A crew of Ukrainian seafarers were threatened with violence when they complained of the poor quality of food. On a Romanian ship the *Avrig*, in 1995, Bangladeshi crew members claimed that they were fed once every two days, whereas the rest of the crew who were Romanian received their food daily.

Ship's food is an easy target for a disgruntled crew but a Ukrainian seaman was threatened with dismissal for complaining about the food aboard his vessel, the *Toyvo Antikaynen* (Ukraine) in 1995. The master had a particular interest in the complaint because he was suspected by the crew of selling off the ship's stores. On the other hand a cook was sacked for being over-generous with the victuals aboard the *Kiwi* (Malta). The owner dismissed him for 'giving the crew too much to eat'.

Unfair Dismissal

A master was dismissed merely for informing the owner of a pay demand by the crew. The owner considered that it was the master's duty to dissuade the crew from asking for a fair wage or for payment on time. A chief engineer was dismissed when he refused to pump the ship's oily bilge-water over the side in violation of the local pollution regulations. Yet another chief engineer was sacked in 1995 by the master because he claimed that his ship, the *Concord Aska* (Panama), which had been in a collision, was not seaworthy. The master wished to avoid cargo interests making a subsequent case against the vessel.

The concern over threats to jobs is increased by the fact that the seafarer is likely to be far from home. This may result in having to meet his own repatriation expenses and pay the travel costs of a relief. Such arrangements allow a shipowner to wield an effective influence over crews.

Unfair and Dishonoured Contracts

Ordinary seafarers are often quite unsophisticated and are therefore not necessarily familiar with legal terminology used in their contracts. Although many contracts are quite straightforward some contain clauses that are blatantly unfair or misleading. A seafarer is often not permitted to have a copy of the contract he signed upon joining his vessel and has to rely on either the master's or the owner's interpretation of its contents and clauses. Someone may have little chance to read through what they are committing themselves to in the rush of signing on to a ship. The contract may in any case not be written in a language he understands, or it may be translated incorrectly to him in order to make it seem more attractive. However, should a dispute arise, the written contract will be upheld by the owner.

Should a case concerning breach of contract reach a court, it may require translation to the language of the court involving more time and expense. Having got that far the case may then be thrown out on the grounds that the court has no jurisdiction to hear it. This was a particular problem with one of Adriatic Tankers' crews abandoned in Europe. The court decided that as the vessel flew a Panama flag, the case should be brought in Panama, which, to an abandoned crew who had not been paid for months, was impossible (see Chapter 7).

Most contracts contain a clause on compensation payable in the event of death or injury and this is an area where contract abuse is most prevalent. Contracts often state an amount payable to a seafarer who has suffered an accident on the ship. The amount due will vary with the extent of the injury. However, some owners look upon the compensation payable as a burden to be minimised wherever and however possible.

One method of reducing liability is to take advantage of a seafarer from a poorer country by offering what seems an 'attractive' initial pay-off for the injury. This will in fact be only a percentage of what is actually due according to the contract. On receipt of this 'attractive' sum the seafarer will be required to sign a waiver over any other claim that may be due so that by the time he discovers what his rights really are it is too late to claim the full amount. One case concerned a seafarer who had lost a leg in an accident aboard ship. He was flown back to his home and after various manufactured delays, was offered a sum that was only one-tenth of the rate the contract stipulated, and payable, as usual, on signing a waiver to any further claim. Quite respectable P&I clubs have been involved in these practices.

The following contract clauses, drawn from a large collection of seafarer employment contracts under both national flags and FOC, would be considered unfair by most people:

- Cost of any medical care ashore after repatriation shall be borne by the seafarer.
- If the vessel is lost, sold, laid up or being repaired, the shipowner has the right to terminate this contract without notice. (The same contract requires the seafarer to give 15 days' notice to terminate the contract from his side.)
- The form of medical treatment given by a doctor is at the sole discretion of the master.
- That I [the seafarer] shall not seek any assistance from the International Transport Workers' Federation or any of its affiliates while I am on board the vessel or in any port.
- No compensation shall be payable in respect of any injury, incapacity, disability or death resulting from a wilful act on his own life by the seaman.
- If the vessel should be prejudiced by the ITF, I should inform my agent or the ship's captain and if I receive any amount it will be held on trust to be returned to my principal or agent upon my repatriation. In no case shall I be cleared by my agent without returning the said amount.
- We the undersigned authorise ... to proceed with any legal action against us in case we refuse to pay all our outstanding obligations.
- In case of discharge of the seafarer for disciplinary reasons, the owners or the master shall have the right to deduct the cost of maintenance and repatriation from the seaman's balance of wages.
- The following causes draw termination of this contract: ..., striking, ...
- I venture on this voyage at my own risk.
- Anybody who would be caught habitually being seasick will not receive salary.
- The master is entrusted with the owner's cash and if such cash is lost while in the master's care, it shall be repaid with 12 per cent interest.
- You will be required to work such hours as will be required by the master. If overtime work is required, you will perform any such overtime work without any addition or extra payment.
- You are responsible for your transportation costs according to the following geographical areas:
  1. If your residence is in Europe, to the European port where you board the vessel or to Miami if the ship is operating in the Caribbean.

2. If your residence is in South America you are responsible for your air transportation to Miami.
3. If your residence is in Asia, you are responsible for reaching the vessel in Europe or Miami.

- The total cost for our services is US$588. Payment will be made in two parts:
  1. US$198 will be paid immediately as a retainer fee, thereby allowing us to activate your file and begin our work towards finding a suitable position for you.
  2. US$390 will be paid once you receive a firm job offer ... Your signature of this agreement will constitute your consent to have the final payment deducted from your first salary payment or paid in advance.

- I understand that I am obliged to pay monthly dues at a rate of 10 per cent of my monthly foreign currency salary as settlement of organisational and technical matters concerning me. These deductions shall be made by the shipowner and included in the present contract. I understand that I am also obliged to pay into ... Ltd account the sum of 60,000 roubles when first registering for work as a processing fee in connection with hiring.

- Prior to embarkation a deposit of $500 is required to be lodged with our offices as a guarantee for repatriation expenses.

- Mr ... is to pay US$65 each month as the administration fee.

- During the term of his external assignment, Party B (the seafarer) shall hand over 30 per cent of his foreign currency to Party A (the owner/agent) as behavioural guarantee money to secure the performance of contractual duties.

- I hereby declare, willingly agree and understand that in case I will be found drunk during my service on board the vessel, I will pay a penalty of US$1000 as an officer and US$500 as a rating and will immediately be disembarked.

- Any financial disagreements whatsoever between the crew member and master will be solved prior to the crew member signing off. Any financial disagreements which are not approved in writing by the master will not be taken into account after the crew member has signed off.

- Should the captain of our vessel be forced to affect any backpay to us as extorted by ITF through intimidation or blackmail, the undersigned seamen commit ourselves by signing this affidavit, that we shall return this backpay money promptly and in full to the master upon departure from the said port. We likewise promise and agree to sign every month with a DOUBLE PAYROLL if required by our master to safeguard our future sea careers.

Employment Agency Illegal Practices

Although the inferior shipowner is usually blamed for most of the crew's problems, some recruitment agencies are no better. Numerous shipowners use these agencies to staff their vessels. Many agents are genuine, but there are those who are, as of old, rogues.

If an agency is contracted to manage a crew then they will be responsible for paying the seafarers and also forwarding allotments to their families. The seafarer will then have a contract with the agency and not the shipowner. If the manning agent is dishonest the shipowner will not necessarily be aware of this; however there are cases where the two have been worked together to cheat crews.

The ILO Convention No. 9 on Placement of Seafarers 1920 (see Chapters 7 and 8) stipulate that any agent supplying a crew to a shipowner must charge a recruitment fee to the owner and not to the seafarers. This convention is often ignored as seafarers seeking employment often have to pay a considerable percentage of their anticipated wage in advance.

Recruitment fees are often charged to both the seafarer and the shipowner. These payments represent one of the major protests from seafarers but is usually only expressed to mission chaplains or quietly to ITF inspectors because of the fear of retribution. The manning agents have the power of blacklisting and threatening seafarers' families at home in order to keep the men from revealing illegal practices.

This means that seafarers often join a vessel already in debt to the agency and are in fear of their jobs until the 'joining fee' is paid off. There have been cases where the crew members have been unable to complete a voyage through no fault of their own and therefore still owe the manning agent money when they arrive home. Until that fee is repaid, the seafarers are unable to gain employment on another vessel. The ITF have blacklisted agencies who carry out illegal recruitment practices but there are many of them still operating.

The sums demanded of seafarers are as high as US$3000; as these practices are carried on in the poorer nations, this sum can represent a considerable proportion of the wages earned by a seafarer during a trip. Those who complain about the practice to the authorities are seldom successful in obtaining justice. A Sri Lankan seafarer found that the marine authority sided with the agency and sacked him. The agency then took the man to court claiming defamation and he was prevented from going back to sea for five years.[17]

Adriatic Tanker Company's collapse highlighted many of these practices. Because the company abandoned its ships and crews around the world, the crews had to be helped by the ITF, its affiliates and charities. When legal action was taken against the company it was found that a great number of seafarers, notably Russians, owed sums of money to recruitment agencies. Some of these agencies confronted seafarers who had been repatriated, in order to extort the sums owed despite the fact that few of the abandoned seafarers had received anything like their full wage. Burmese sailors were under a similar burden when they reached home with their own government demanding taxes on wages that had never been paid to the seafarers.

A contracting agency can cheat the seafarer in many ways. The shipowner may pay the agency in good faith for a crew, but have no control over how much the agency pays the crew. In one case a crew was satisfied by receiving company notices of the payment of allotments to their homes until some of the families started complaining that they had received nothing. It turned out that the agency was holding on to the money for as long as possible in order to gain maximum interest at the bank.

There are also bogus agencies. In 1997, a company with an address in London posed as a recruitment agency and advertised for seafarers to join a cruise vessel. The agency required a US$500 deposit from prospective crew members to secure positions on board. On investigation it was found that the cruise vessel did not exist and neither did the recruiting agency.[18]

Because the practice of fee charging is illegal, the employing agents have devised a number of ways in which the recruitment fee can be hidden. They deduct the fee monthly from the seafarers' family allotment or get the joining seaman to sign for an advance that he has not in fact received. Some require seafarers to sign a clause denying that any payment has been made for recruitment, for example: '... the employee hereby solemnly declares that he has NOT paid to the Owners or their Agents or Master or any other relative party concerned, any commission or tickets or fees or any other charges in respect to his recruitment on the above vessel'.

Unseaworthy Ships

A ship can be regarded as unseaworthy for many reasons. Some owners have little consideration for the state of their vessels provided they continue to make profits. Crews are obliged to take ships to sea that have little or no life-saving equipment; working navigational instruments or proper crew composition or amenities.

Increasingly, port-state control is trying to prevent unseaworthy ships from sailing before essential repair work or missing equipment is made good and crew is up to standard. However, the authorities in a busy port cover only a percentage of the vessels visiting that port and it is inevitable that defects will be overlooked. This, coupled with the ineffective nature of port state control in some countries, allows the substandard shipowner to continue to run dangerous ships.

In 1995 the UK's Marine Safety Agency detained one of Adriatic Tanker Company's vessels on the Thames. The *Countess* (Panama) a chemical tanker, was held on 42 separate counts, ranging from corroded deck plates to inoperative toilets, in fact so bad was the ship's plumbing that portable toilets were provided for the crew. The *Countess* was so dirty that the remaining crew were eventually moved ashore while repairs were carried out. The ship had suffered serious neglect for years with little or no materials being provided for the necessary maintenance; leaking pipes and broken fire hydrants added to the deck corrosion. Safety equipment was damaged or non-existent: had an emergency occurred while the vessel was at sea the crew would have had little chance of survival. For a chemical tanker to have reached such a state of disrepair was a disgrace. Her cargo was both valuable and dangerous and better care would have been expected of such a vessel.

This ship was in such a poor state of repair that she was towed off her discharge berth, being judged too dangerous to move under her own power. In addition the multi-national crew had not been paid for four months and bad feelings were running high. They had been intimidated by the owner and manning agents to the extent that half of them were afraid to accept the offer of union help. On arrival in the UK, the master had taken up a collection amongst the crew to buy food for the next part of the voyage. One crew member, a Chinese national, took advantage of the situation to ask the British authorities for asylum.[19]

The *Kathleen D* (Honduras), was a 30-year-old vessel trading in the Caribbean. She had been designed as a short-sea trader in European waters but was now carrying containers in an open hatch without cell guides. She had already been detained by the US Coast Guard three times in 1995 for various defects and was held again at Mobile, Alabama in December of that year.

The Coast Guard found serious wastage in the bow steel, and life-saving equipment was lashed down making it impossible to use quickly in an emergency. The crew were unable to launch the emergency boat and the Coast Guard judged the vessel to be unseaworthy until repairs had been carried out. They quoted that a list of 125 deficiencies could have been made out for the vessel but they wanted the major repairs carried out first. The owner accompanied the Coast Guard on their inspection trying to persuade them that the detention was unnecessary and that the ship should be allowed to sail.

The repairs were, however, carried out to the Coast Guard's satisfaction although they warned the master that if the ship was not better maintained, the crew's lives could be at risk. One of the captain's problems was that a relative of the owner was sailing as supercargo and was interfering with the running of the ship. This led also to speculation that the vessel's stability may not have been as secure as the captain would have wished.

The *Kathleen D* sailed a few days after inspection and foundered and sank 150 miles south of Mobile. The sole survivor described how the crew had abandoned the vessel. They had tried to lower the lifeboat which had jammed on one of the falls before dropping into the sea. The crew jumped after it but only he reached the boat:

> After the sinking the owner refused to pay any compensation to the families of the seafarers or even to acknowledge their requests. He had pressurised the crew to take a dangerous ship to sea carrying a cargo for which she was not designed and he wanted no part of the consequences.[20]

Survey by MORI for the ITF (1996)[21]

Almost all the above accounts are examples communicated by seafarers to the ITF, and as far as possible they have been expressed in the same straightforward terms as contained in the 992 cases in the files. The researchers were also given access to a survey conducted for the ITF by the MORI organisation. This was a statistically valid sample of 6504 questionnaires returned to MORI from vessels registered in 93 states. It included seafarers from 14 of the principal labour-supplying countries.

From the point of view of this book, the MORI statistical exercise has proved useful as yet another form of validation, and it also revealed some features not apparent from the ITF files and the interviews with seafarers and managers.

In summary the MORI findings include the following points. The age of seafarers is predominantly between 31 and 40, the youngest nationalities are Filipino and Chinese. Some 45 per cent are employed through manning agencies and 34 per cent by shipowners and managers. Practically all are in casual employment. The sample sheet showed that 11 per cent of seafarers had to pay for their jobs but this varied greatly by nationality with 43 per cent of Indonesian seafarers being the highest in having to do so.

Under their financial situations, 23 per cent of seafarers support five or more persons on their wage, and 22 per cent in this category earn less than $500 per month. The lowest-paid nationals are from Russia and eastern Europe as well as Indonesians, Filipinos, Chinese and Africans. Fifty per cent of seafarers on FOC ships and 49 per cent on national-flag vessels earn less than the ITF benchmark of $1100 per month (as of 1996).

Of those owed wages 'against their will', 66 per cent were on Russian-flag ships and also many under Romanian and Maltese flags. In terms of crew satisfaction with conditions, Romanian-flag vessels were the worst, while Filipino seafarers reported improved working conditions over the past five years.

When it came to unfair treatment because of race or nationality, 29 per cent of all seafarers on FOC and 21 per cent under national flags reported having experienced this. The worst culprits were 'vessels registered under German, Panamanian, Greek and Japanese flags'. Of all nationalities, Filipino and Indonesian seafarers suffered most physical abuse in the year preceding the survey and 18 per cent of all seafarers endured mental abuse. Interestingly, 'junior officers reported the highest incidence of abuse at 26 per cent'. Some 4 per cent of all seafarers reported that their families had been threatened in the previous year.

In terms of trade union rights, 14 per cent of all seafarers reported receiving warnings against contacting trade unions. This occurred most frequently in the MORI coverage on Maltese (23 per cent) and Romanian (59 per cent) flag ships.

On perceptions of on-board safety there were great variations between ships of different flags. Eighty per cent of seafarers on Norwegian vessels rated their safety as good compared to 35 per cent on Russian ships and 17 per cent on Romanian.

5

Adriatic Tankers I: A Short History of the Company

The abuse of seafarers is by no means prevalent throughout the shipping industry, but neither is it confined to obscure and fly-by-night owners. Abuse occurs as a matter of strategy under specific conditions in companies owning major fleets. Under what conditions this strategy is adopted, why, and how it is pursued is best examined through a detailed case study. This study focuses on the Adriatic Tanker Shipping Company of Greece. The case, as will already be evident, is not the first of its kind, nor will it be the last – unless the processes of change, or something like them, discussed in the final chapter of this book take place.

This short chapter provides an overall perspective on the rise of the Adriatic company and its subsequent foundering. The management and financial arrangements of the company and the consequences of its practices on seafarers are analysed in the subsequent chapters.

Greek Shipowners and Shipping

The Adriatic Tankers company was founded in Greece – the owner was a former captain. Many Greek shipowners have been sea captains. In their early days as owners of one-ship enterprises, they sailed in command until sufficient capital, trading reliability and creditworthiness were built up. They then came ashore and developed their companies, always with an eye to the sale and purchase of ships as an important component of the business. These small companies often continued to be run by one man who controlled the related management, and there was intermarriage between the families of company owners. Overseas offices were also staffed by relatives and the Greek shipping communities which grew up in far-flung places often retained close business and family links with Greece.

Most of these early Greek captain-owners came from the Aegean and Ionian Islands – these island communities contributed cash as shareholders and supplied seafarers in a system of mutual dependence. Such crewing practices still existed in the early 1990s when much of the Greek-flagged fleet was crewed by nationals. However, on Greek owned vessels which are flagged out there are few Greek ratings, and pressures are being exerted in Greece for more legislation to reduce the requirements for employing Greek nationals on Greek-flag vessels. Consequently Greek shipping is in a process of considerable change.

The growth and success of the Greek shipping industry historically has been largely attributed to several features of Greek maritime culture, including the entrepreneurial approach of the shipowners; the organisation of their firms allowing tax avoidance and flexibility in decision making; the structure and management of firms based on kinship and island ties; their connections to Greek international networks providing information about the markets, and from related support within the Greek political environment.[1]

The importance and prestige of shipping in the culture of Greece, a country of only ten million people, is almost as true today as it was during the nineteenth century, when the Greek industry began to present formidable competition to the British dominance of international seaborne trade. Many of the successful shipowners from the Greek islands may be termed 'traditional', because after the Second World War they were at least second-generation shipowners who had inherited their positions from their fathers. Only in recent years has mainland Greece also been providing appreciable numbers of shipowners. These 'non-traditional' owners were characteristically defined as having been in another profession before becoming shipowners, and whose fathers were not shipowners before the Second World War.[2]

Today Greece controls in excess of 17 per cent of world total deadweight tonnage – over half of which is flagged outside of Greece, primarily in Panama and Cyprus – and 12 per cent of the world's fleet by number of vessels.[3] The Greek fleet has been shown to be remarkably resilient following periods of significant losses during the First and Second World Wars. In the latter, over three-quarters of the fleet and thousands of seafarers were lost. But the sale of over a hundred vessels in 1946 by the US government to Greek shipowners formed a take-off for the present-day Greek merchant marine. Most of these vessels were flagged out to Panama and elsewhere.

The Origins of Adriatic Tankers

In a generally accepted account the foundation of Adriatic Tankers lies in the tradition of the island origins of Greek shipping. Adriatic's roots have been attributed to a shipping company set up in Cephalonia in the nineteenth century by Andrea Vallianatos who established a fleet of sailing ships trading within the Ionian Islands. It is said that this is from where the 'V' logo on the Adriatic vessels is derived.[4] Accounts claim that it was the transfer of the company to Panagis Zissimatos from his father Andreas (a grandson of Andrea Vallianatos) in 1978, that set Adriatic on its path of meteoric growth.[5]

Panagis Zissimatos, who owned and ran the company, had a seafaring background, serving it is said both on the company's vessels and other ships, and becoming a captain at the age of 25, five years before taking over the company from his father. This background is traditional and brings with it confidence and prestige; however, as will be appreciated later the account of the founding of Adriatic Tankers told around the Piraeus waterfront is somewhat different.

These points are significant because the traditional roots of a Greek shipping company can give credibility in raising finance. This is discussed later under 'Management' in Chapter 6. The traditional family structure in Greek shipping management was also retained within the company with Panagis Zissimatos owning 95 per cent and his young cousin, and vice-president, Panagiotis (Takis) Giakoumatos 5 per cent. Family members were employed elsewhere within the company: a Gerassinion Vallianatos was listed at one stage and another possible relative, Christos Giakoumatos who headed the company's Singapore office, and a Mr Vallianatos emerges as a director of a subsidiary.

But Adriatic Tankers was only partially typical of Greek companies. It operated in unusual isolation from the rest of the Greek shipping community by using many foreign nationals and a high input of non-Greek overseas funding.[6] This has been attributed to the company's involvement in specialised trades, in contrast to the more conventional tanker and bulk carrier business of other Greek owners. Adriatic's difference from the usual Greek community is reinforced by the use of a number of brokers in Norway and London to conduct deals, rather than one or two firms exclusively.

The Growth and Characteristics of the Fleet

The Adriatic fleet grew to a highly diversified mix of vessels incorporating chemical tankers, product/parcel tankers, crude oil tankers, dry cargo vessels, ro-ros, woodchip carriers and a reefer. However, its main business from about 1983 was in the operation of small chemical tankers. This allowed the company to function in a market dominated by Storli and Stolt-Neilsen.[7] The Adriatic small vessels were operated in niche markets on arterial routes delivering small parcels of products to outports which were unable to accommodate the larger vessels of the chemical tanker majors. Adriatic in particular was seen as a major force in the Mediterranean, with ten vessels employed in the carriage of chemicals and vegetable oils.[8] The diverse structure of the fleet in the mid-1990s is depicted below in Table 5.1.

Table 5.1 Composition of the Adriatic fleet in the mid-1990s

Vessel Type	No
Woodchip carriers	4
Chemical tanker	40
Product/parcel tanker	27
Dry cargo	14
Crude oil carrier	8
Dry bulk	7
Tanker	6
Ro-ro	3
Yacht	3
Reefer	1

Source: Based on data published in *Lloyd's List*, *TradeWinds* and *Fairplay*.

The fleet grew to over 80 vessels by the end of 1993, from just two in 1978. This made Adriatic Tankers one of the largest shipping groups in the world owning, at its peak, 111 ships. Adriatic's management claimed that the company had the skills and capacity to manage a larger fleet of between 120 and 150 vessels.[9]

Before 1995/6, when the fleet was at its peak, several significant sales and purchases had taken place.[10] For example, in early 1989 the company sold many vessels to US buyers en bloc, the revenue from which was used to acquire Uemura Kaiun, a Japanese shipping company, which owned chemical tankers. Some of these vessels were subsequently sold on to Danish owners.[11]

Quality of the Fleet

Little can be deduced about the quality of the vessels originally bought, other than by periodic example, primarily when vessels were detained by port-state control authorities due to defects. This cannot be taken as indicative of the overall condition of the fleet – especially since most of the ships were chemical carriers which were expected to be maintained to high standards commensurate with the business of their charterers.

In 1993, the quality management ethos was certainly being promoted by the company. Adriatic tankers reported that it had become the first of the Greek operations to get a quality manual certificate from Det Norske Veritas, which classed around fifty of its vessels, and had benefited from a 15 per cent reduction in its insurance costs from 1992. However subsequently the validity of the quality manual certificate was questioned by Det Norske Veritas which stated that the safety management system had yet to be audited[12] and also that it had tried without success to improve the technical standards of the Adriatic fleet.

Certainly while port-state detentions occurred in the early 1990s, these were the exception. However, the detention of the *Rokko San*, in 1992 in Norway, raised the issue of vessel seaworthiness in accordance with the classification certificate of the vessel. In this instance, the *Rokko San* had been supplied for a time charter with an 'NS' Class certificate – the highest from the Nippon Kaiji Koykai Classification society. The vessel was subsequently alleged to have serious deficiencies both to the hull and pumping equipment onboard.[13] Whilst both sides disputed the issues, the vessel subsequently had engine failure and had to be withdrawn from the contract.[14]

Other material suggests that Zissimatos, as part of his expansion policies, actually bought vessels which were non-operational. This 'fleet in being' rather than 'in trading' is best represented by the *Stainless King* which spent two years in Piraeus awaiting repairs before sailing to Bulgaria again for repairs – where the condition of the ship was subsequently described as 'falling apart'. A letter to the ITF in London from the crew of the *Stainless King* states:

> vessel sailed here to Varna (from Piraeus) 13 days owing to the bad condition of the machinery and hull, and non-working condition of the hull (covered with shells and seaweed's) ... Harbour Master knows about the radar and some other drawbacks and will not allow to sail without the radar ... So you can see that the tech-

nical condition of the vessel is not too good, but we are ready to sail as far as we can (away from Bulgaria, possibly to Turkey) ...[15]

As the financial condition of the company deteriorated, other vessels in shipyards for repairs had their period of lay-up extended by subsequent arrests on behalf of the yards for outstanding dues on repairs, many of which were never completed. Table 5.2 gives examples of vessels which spent lengthy periods in ship repair yards.

Table 5.2   Adriatic vessels held in shipyards

Vessel	Type	DWT	Period in Yard
Stainless King	chemical tanker	3,014	13 months
Stainless Duke	chemical tanker	10,563	14 months
Ionian Sailor	bulk carrier	29,240	17 months

As Table 5.3 illustrates, during 1994–96 in the UK ports alone there was clearly a general decline in the standard of the fleet as typified by out-of-date charts and certificates, the *Ionian Sailor* having its ship's class suspended, in May 1995, because the period under repair had been so long. This ultimately led to the identification, by port-state control (PSC) authorities of some very major deficiencies. The *Countess*, the vessel with the longest record of port-state detention in the UK – eleven months – was found to have both structural and equipment deficiencies with 42 identifiable problems including 14 classified as detainable. The vessel was also described by the ITF inspectors as being 'dirty' and 'extremely dangerous'.[16]

The current world-wide regulation of the industry comes into question, as these vessels were widely trading and were impounded only when they reached a port where PSC was being implemented. Indeed the most significant case of this occurred in June 1992 when the *Stainless Commander*, a chemical tanker with a cargo of ethyldichloride arrived in Wilhelmshaven in Germany; such was the dangerous condition of the vessel with eleven pages of defects, it was prevented from unloading and ordered to be towed away for repairs.[17]

Additional evidence from seafarers and other creditors shows that the problems increased as the trading status of the fleet declined. The vessels which were detained under arrest in ports stopped having even minimum maintenance due to the lack of funds. In Australia, a supplies creditor of the *Ionian Mariner* used Australian law to force the sale of the vessel. They established to the court that the potential capital security of the vessel was eroded, as a direct result of the period of arrest as maintenance had ceased.[18]

Table 5.3   Adriatic vessels detained under UK port-state control 1994–96

Date and Place of Detention	Vessel	Vessel Type	Defects – Main Grounds for Detention
Cory Town 7–10/9/94	*Ionian Glory*	Chemical Tanker	Lifeboat engines defective. Lists of lights and radio signals out of date. Defective gyro compass. Defective fire dampers. Hole in engine room aft bulkhead. Inadequate functioning of main and reserve transmitters. Extensive corrosion in bulkhead between pump room and chain locker.
Liverpool 29/11–2/12/94	*Stainless Wave*	Oil/ Chemical Tanker	No valid load-line certificate on board. No. 5 starboard ballast-tank air-pipe holed at deck level. Air-pipe closing arrangement holed and seized.
Felixstowe 22–30/12/94	*Captain Lucas III**	Chemical Tanker	Defective auto alarm, 2182 watch receiver, VHF receiver and aerial. Charts out of date. Broken rudder stock in lifeboat.
Felixstowe 20/12/94–6/1/95	*Stainless Supporter*	Chemical Tanker	Main steering gear failed. Defective navigation lights.
Purfleet 23/8/95–7/96	*Countess*	Chemical Tanker	No radar transponder on board. Convention certificates expired. Oily water separator inoperative. Boat-deck plating severely corroded. Fire dampers defective.

* Vessel arrested by the USCG in October 1993 for deficiencies including unsafe life rafts, unsanitary conditions and non-compliance with US pollution laws.

Source: Marine Safety Agency (UK), Press Notices of vessels held under PSC detention.

When it came to paying the crew of a ship under poor physical condition, the ITF were advised that under Panamanian Law, Commerce Code, Article (section) 1168, while the master is not permitted to sell the vessel in the normal course of activities, if it is in no condition to pursue the voyage (either through failure or damages impossible to repair), he may petition for judicial sale of the ship. He may also cause the sale of the ship by arresting it for wages owed.[19] This was tried with Adriatic Tankers' ships.

Another indication of the deteriorating quality of the fleet is reflected in those Adriatic vessels which deleted from classification societies. The two main classification societies involved were Det Norske Veritas (DNV) classifying 49 vessel and Nippon Kaiji Kyokai of Japan. Some of the vessels suspended/deleted from classification in the period 1995 are summarised in Table 5.4.

Table 5.4   Vessels removed from class, 1996

Vessel	Built	Type	Size (DWT)	Classification Society
Stainless Maya	1985	Chemical tanker	7,500	Det Norske Veritas[1]
Stainless Wave	1978	Tanker	960	Det Norske Veritas[1]
Southern Navigator	1984	Chemical tanker	6,100	Det Norske Veritas[1]
Rainbow II	1979	Tanker	1,200	Det Norske Veritas[1]
Ocean Wave I	1971	Chemical tanker	1,700	Det Norske Veritas[1]
Cape Spirit	1985	Chemical tanker	7,568	Det Norske Veritas*[2]
Cape Wind	1979	Products tanker	1,662	Det Norske Veritas*[2]
Ionian Breeze	1969	Dry cargo	29,040	Lloyd's Register[2]
Stainless Queen	1971	Chemical tanker	7,925	Lloyd's Register[2]

* Vessels withdrawn from Det Norske Veritas and transferred to Registro Italiano Navale of Italy.

Source: [1]Garfield and Landells (1995); [2] Guest (1995).[20]

Det Norske Veritas specifically pointed to the poor technical standards of vessels, threatening to expel more vessels if standards were not raised. Adriatic's response to this was to imply differences with DNV and to suggest that the company would change the classification society used as they saw fit.[21]

Partly as a consequence of these deletions/suspensions, but also due to the failure to pay instalments due on a $5 million premium, Adriatic Tankers subsequently lost its P&I cover in January 1996. The cancellation related to the 70 vessels entered with the United Kingdom Mutual Steam Ship Assurance Association and the twelve entered with the Liverpool and London Steamship Protection and Indemnity Association – the former exercising the right to deny cover back to the inception of membership. None of the other mutuals within the International Group cartel offered to replace the cover of these vessels.[22]

All these actions followed on from the expulsion of Adriatic Tankers from Intertanko for failing to comply with requirements on safety, the refusal to supply details concerning the classification and P&I cover of vessels and for the non-payment of membership fees over the proceeding three years in May 1995.[23] This meant also that the crews were no longer covered for loss of life and injuries.

The effect on the company was to further reduce the earning capacity of the ships, which, when combined with the arrest of vessels for non-payment, virtually paralysed the fleet. Once the earning capacity had been undermined the only recourse by numerous creditors was through arrest and the subsequent sale of vessels to recoup some of their losses. Figures 6.1 and 6.2 (pp. 90–1) show the locations where arrests took place of one or more Adriatic Tankers ships up until 1996.

The Seafarers

At its height Adriatic employed between 2000 and 2500 men at sea. Initially, the crews were Greek on the two product carriers acquired during 1978–79. As chemical carriers were purchased experienced seafarers for these types of ships were recruited from Korea. Sometimes Greek masters and chief engineers continued, but with the growth of the fleet even more diversity began to enter into crewing.

During 1992 with the fleet of around a hundred vessels, the Russian captains, officers and crew were most prominent, but, in order of numbers, Korean, Vietnamese, Burmese, Yugoslav, Sri Lankan, Filipino, Polish and a few other nationalities were employed, in various combinations, including some British and Norwegian captains, chief engineers and officers.

The first indicator that the company was experiencing problems came from these crews. During the early 1990s, there were complaints being noted by missions and ITF inspectors regarding non-payment of wages. In 1993, letters began to flood in from seafarers on globally dispersed ships complaining about deteriorating food and general conditions, concerns over the safety of the ships, and the non-payment of money to families.

The ITF responded, as will be seen in subsequent chapters, in a non-confrontational way. They did not see any benefit in putting what may have been, as claimed, a temporarily ailing company out of business with the consequent loss of jobs. However, by 1994 evidence of serious abuses brought more action by the ITF, including legal advice to crews, as well as more arrests of ships by creditors.

The Fall

The above outline of conditions leading to the foundering of Adriatic Tankers as a company provides the framework for the later, more detailed analysis of cause and effect. The collapse when it came did so rapidly as a result of the combinations of the related events described above.

Very important in trying to survive financially were the attempts by Adriatic to retain a cash flow by delaying the payment of crew wages and allotments. These actions resulted in hardships, stresses, discontent and loss of morale among the seafarers, and the subsequent victimisation and mistreatment of crews who objected. This in turn led to the further neglect of the ships and their physical deterioration.

By 1994, a number of suppliers of bunkers, stores and equipment were also complaining that they were not being paid, and reports appeared in the press of vessel detentions under port-state control due to deteriorating conditions and non-compliance with international safety regulations. In this period the company cut back further on repair expenditure, even where safety was obviously involved. The company continued to borrow widely in the US, Japan, South Africa, Switzerland and the UK with some success, and issued statements indicating their positive financial and operational attributes. They blamed most of the problems on administrative difficulties and vindictive trade union actions.

By 1995, time was running out. Adriatic Tankers was being avoided by several charterers, the company was expelled from Intertanko, declassified by DNV, and they lost P&I cover, while the news of many bounced cheques was surfacing.

There was a simultaneous race to obtain warrants for the arrest of the ships on behalf of seafarers and other creditors. The banks and financial bodies also acted to repossess the ships as the major mortgagees. The value of some of the vessels on sale was found to be less than 30 per cent of the initial loans. Some ships were as a result totally abandoned. The company was now on the rocks – or so it seemed.

6

Adriatic Tankers II: Management and Finance

The Adriatic Tanker Company clearly grew at an astonishing rate, from two small product carriers in 1978 to over a hundred vessels in 1996. The impressive rise and sudden decline of the company are attributed in many respects to the management style of the owner, Panagis Zissimatos. But the relative ease by which he obtained vast sums of money is even more significant as it tells us a good deal about a somewhat reckless international ship-financing environment which impacts on investors, service and supply companies, and shore and sea-going employees.

Ownership

There are mixed accounts of the origins of Adriatic Tankers and the background of the owner. It will be recalled from Chapter 5 that the official version published by the company places the founding in the late nineteenth century by the great-grandfather of Panagis Zissimatos, one Andrea Vallianatos of the island of Cephalonia. Panagis Zissimatos subsequently inherited the company from his shipowning father Andreas Zissimatos in 1978.[1]

An alternative account and one which reflects more the determined and entrepreneurial character of Panagis Zissimatos is told by some of the shipping fraternity of Greece. He was born in 1948, and, the story goes, his father Andreas, far from being a shipowner, was in fact quite poor. When Zissimatos obtained his master's certificate in 1978, he was employed by a new aspiring shipping entrepreneur (a former principal of a Navigation School) to collect and deliver a 500-GRT products carrier from Japan to Greece. He then repeated this type of delivery job for a second products carrier. Zissimatos became a partner in the company soon after this and carried out several visits to Japan in that capacity to purchase more vessels between 1983 and 1986.

The company was successful in the short-haul Aegean oil products trade by obtaining charters from the major oil companies. The vessels were worked hard carrying small parcels and by 1986 financial returns were good. Profits were derived also from buying ships at low prices in Japan and selling them in a more favourable market. At some stage in the mid-1980s, Zissimatos became the sole owner of Adriatic Tankers and formed very close business relations with a Japanese company, and had access to Japanese finance.

Adriatic found a new market niche in the chemical trade associated with the chemical company Alpchem.[2] Adriatic bought several coastal chemical tankers with stainless steel tanks which had been laid up in Japan. These were obtained relatively cheaply at the time and converted to foreign-going ships. In this period seafarers were recruited by a Korean manning agency for Adriatic. Many of the masters and officers had chemical tanker experience, and in the 1980s and early 1990s their costs along with Korean ratings were still below those of Greek seafarers. In the early 1990s, Russians were also recruited by a Russian agency, primarily for the bulk carriers now purchased by the company.

Flagging Policies

As Table 6.1 shows, the fleet of the Adriatic Tankers Shipping Company was almost exclusively registered under the Panamanian flag.

Table 6.1   Flag states used by Adriatic vessels

Flag	Number
Not Known	9*
Belize	2
Cyprus	1
Great Britain and Ireland	1
Greece	1
Malta	3
Panama	94
TOTAL	111

*Includes tugs resident in Greece and three yachts.

The advantages of the Panamanian in preference to the Greek flag lie primarily with the regulations concerning crewing arrangements. At the time the company was building, Greek law required that the master and officers must be Greek for ships over 1500 GRT and that the crew be drawn from Greece, unless Greeks were not available. By contrast, the Panamanian flag has no such restrictions on crewing. By using the Panamanian flag, crew costs could be reduced by 30–40 per cent compared with the Greek flag. Panama also permits each vessel of an owner to be registered under the name of a different company, thus further ignoring the requirements for a genuine link between owner and flag under the Law of the Sea. This facilitates the protection of the foreign beneficial owner, and this also makes the Panama FOC attractive for crewing.

Analysis of available crew lists shows that by the mid-1990s over 50 per cent of Adriatic's seafarers were Russian, followed by Koreans (11 per cent); very few Greeks were employed other than several captains. A sample of seafarers from half of the fleet in 1993 is shown in Table 6.2.

Table 6.2   Sample of nationalities of Adriatic's crews during 1993

Nationality	Number
Russian	417
Korean	88
Burmese	74
Vietnamese	62
Yugoslav	51
Sri Lankan	34
Filipino	33
Chinese	21
Pakistani	9
Greek	8
Latvian	2
Ukrainian	1
TOTAL	800

*Based on crew lists from 48 vessels.

Management Structure and Style

The company was incorporated in Panama in 1984 as a management firm with its income ostensibly derived from fees and commissions. Each ship was 'owned' by a separate company in Panama thereby avoiding cross-liabilities between ships. Under Greek law, Adriatic was thus a branch of a foreign company acting as agents for the many single-ship companies. Offices of the agency were established in Piraeus, the Netherlands, Singapore, Korea, Tokyo, Houston and London. A holding company (Adriatic Holding) was subsequently set up in the Channel Islands covering the one-ship companies.

The company management in Piraeus grew on an *ad hoc* basis from a few people to about a hundred. Many young Greek men, and some women, were employed. In addition Koreans, Russians, a few South Africans and some others took up positions in the shore management. When the company ran into difficulties in 1995 a financial advisor, the well-respected banker, George Kokkinos,[3] joined, as did unexpectedly, Charlie Milne, formally of the ITF. The latter had until then been negotiating with Adriatic on behalf of the seafarers they employed (see Chapter 8).

The more experienced additions to the management of Adriatic in the mid-1990s came too late to contribute to solving the problems of the company. Until then Zissimatos had run the company in his own style. He was a man to whom success had come quickly. Undoubtedly astute, and variously described as charming, charismatic, egotistical and threatening, he continued to be involved in all aspects of the enterprise during this period of growth. He worked himself and the company hard, former managers described their usual working day as running from 10.00 a.m. to 10.00 p.m. However, Zissimatos was without formal business education, did not share vital information with his staff, but generally fronted, usually with success, meetings with prospective financiers.

Under Zissimatos, finance flowed fairly easily to Adriatic. The perceived favourable family credentials of a Cephalonian maritime heritage may have had much to do with this. Harlaftis writes of the reputation gained by Cephalonian Captain-owners in these respects during the nineteenth century: 'The Cephalonian masters constituted the aristocracy of the profession and were well respected as men of dignity and independent spirit.'[4] Zissimatos was certainly perceived by many in this way as he sought finance for his company around the world. One of his problems was his inability to delegate, but also, as several of his former employees agreed, 'his total disregard for people'.

Commercial Management

There were no problems initially of obtaining charters. South African companies were well disposed to Adriatic, possibly from past favours during the anti-apartheid trade boycotts of South

Africa. Others valued Adriatic ships for regularity in delivering small quantities of high-value chemicals, thus minimising the storage and inventory costs of smaller firms. In these respects, Adriatic had a comparative advantage over the bigger vessels of the larger well-established chemical carrying companies. Most of the chemical carriers were, at least initially, of a good standard – although ageing. The technical management within the company stretched the view of the continued favourable conditions of the ships beyond actuality.

The management of the technical department, along with the commercial managers, also exaggerated the value of the vessels they wished to purchase. Zissimatos claimed 50:50 equities in these vessels; it was seen later when the value of the ships became evident that his real stake was much less. An anonymous asset recovery agent was quoted in *Seatrade Week* in November 1995: 'Adriatic Tankers vessels were valued often at least 30% out and always high.'[5] This cast doubts on the veracity of surveyors and shipbrokers. Several vessels had no real value as ships involved in trading. They were hulks merely obtained to boost the size of a 'fleet in being', and thereby reinforce confidence.

Financial Opportunities

Traditionally, Greek shipowners were known for financing the growth of their fleets out of capital raised in local communities and from profits. They rarely approached overseas banks or other finance institutions for assistance. It was a very closed society with a certain amount of secrecy about it. However, since the late 1950s, there has been a move among some of the shipowning families of Greece to forgo traditional methods and seek funds from international financiers. Tradition is still strong among several Greek owners but the lure of fairly easy finance from banks with high liquidity and other willing lending institutions has tempted some to follow the route taken by the majority of the world's shipowners. Much of the financing of Greek shipping is now provided by foreign banks and an increasing number of these have offices in Greece for this purpose. The local banking community have always played a secondary role, although that role is also increasing. The state-owned National Bank of Greece has built up an impressive folio since the 1960s and a number of smaller banks are showing an interest in the shipping sector – especially in passenger ships.[6]

Investment in shipping is seen by those who are not privy to its unique characteristics as somehow different to investment in other types of industry. It seems almost to have an air of mystery about it, somewhat due to its specific jargon, the mobility of its assets and the cyclical nature of the sector as a whole. This has led bankers who specialise in shipping to believe that their sector has a certain exclusiveness. It certainly requires specific expertise and a long banking professional life.

In a paper in *Seaways*, Professor Costas Th. Grammenos wrote of the need for financial institutions to employ permanent experienced staff for shipping finance. 'The expert shipping banker will be in the middle of his career and will have been in shipping long enough to have experienced one or two full shipping cycles.'[7]

Peter Stokes of Maritime Consultants stated in a presentation to the Admiralty/Finance Forum in New York, that, although the bankers in the sector derive pride from the fact that shipping is unlike other more prosaic industries, they bemoan the fact that the investment community is neglectful and suspicious of shipping. He goes on to say that given the industry's capital requirements in the 1990s, the modest amounts of equity which have been and are being generated internally and the less accommodating attitude of the commercial banks, shipowners clearly need additional sources of permanent capital.[8]

Apart from obtaining funding from the family, the community, retained profits or earnings from ship sales, a ship mortgage was almost the only method open to an aspiring or expansion minded owner for raising capital to fund a fleet, or the expansion of an existing fleet. Some expansion could be funded by a public offering of shares on the open market. This started in 1987 but even now is not a common method. More recently, private debt placement has been seen as an addition to the traditional methods and this is the route that Zissimatos took with Adriatic Tankers to finance the massive expansion that he envisaged for his fleet. Private debt placement was new to shipping but was of rising interest in the industry. One of the advantages of this is that private institutions can lend for longer periods with reduced or no amortisation.[9]

In spite of being acknowledged as relatively risky, the shipping sector would seem to be one in which banks and other lending institutions have an extremely short memory span when it comes to failures. Although some have specialised and used their experience to minimise their exposure in times of uncertainty, others have paid no heed to the lessons learned by those who went before them and have had to learn those lessons again the hard way.

Getting their collective fingers burned apparently leaves no scars because no matter how often it happens they return for more, perhaps because when the profits are good, they are very good.

The shipping industry is well-known as a cyclical one and banks return to it hoping that this time they will re-enter while the market is on a rise. They never seem to have any reservations about investing in the industry. There can of course be good returns, and shipping often has a certain glamour for finance officers compared with more mundane loans. The measure of attraction and confidence which banks world-wide have in Greek shipping in this respect may be appreciated from a survey carried out in 1997 which showed that bank exposure to the industry was as much as $11 billion.[10]

By the 1990s a wave of new lenders, mainly small banks from Europe, the US and the Far East, entered the shipping market competing more intensely with the traditional players.[11] Banks and institutions that had not lent to the industry before were apparently becoming increasingly interested in lending to shipping companies. The purely financial reasons for this were given by Morten Arntzen in a paper at *Lloyd's Shipping Economist*'s 8th Shipping Finance Conference in London in 1995:

- Risks are less today than in the 70s and 80s because growth in world trade has produced a sustainable dry bulk market.
- The oversupply of tankers has been corrected and environmental considerations which are mostly now in the form of legislation, should produce a better tanker market as well as better tankers.
- Technological improvements and on-line information allow today's bankers to be better informed about who they are lending to and therefore manage the risks that they take in a more efficient way.
- Borrowing spreads have fallen less for the shipping sector than other industries so shipping is looking more attractive.
- Shipping companies increased access to equity capital and the growing number of banks active in the shipping sector makes it a more attractive proposition for lending.[12]

Peter Stokes added that a range of knowledgeable and reliable contacts in the shipping industry is the best safeguard against expensive mistakes. Through such a network one can monitor the operating and commercial reputation of companies, obtain early warning of liquidity pressures and identify significant shifts in trade flows and volumes.[13] A number of family-controlled shipping concerns have now evolved into publicly-held corporations, thus improving the risk profile of the industry.[14] All of these factors should set alarm bells ringing in good time to put preventative measures in place or at least to seek some form of damage limitation.

However, the fact remains that the risks that are generic to the industry have altered very little over the years and the shipping market is still unpredictable, volatile and liable to change very quickly. Long-term lending offered by the new lenders has, therefore, no less risk attached to it than previously. In an article for *Lloyd's Shipping Economist* entitled 'Banking on Experience is what Really Counts', Morten Arntzen further stated: 'The main reason that banks are keen to lend to shipping companies is that their extension of credit remains a cornerstone of the relationship between a shipping company and a financial institution.'[15] Banks that do not stick by their clients in lean times risk them not returning when times are good.

This loyalty factor bears out to some extent the reason why the financial institutions were still willing to lend money to Adriatic Tankers when things were clearly going wrong for the company. There had to be some balance between throwing good money after bad in order to keep a customer and the possibility that a further cash injection may enable the institution to see a realistic return on its investment by keeping that investment trading. But the large size of the fleet, the old age of many of the vessels, the banking exposure and the losses that would have to be absorbed if the vessels were sold at very low prices, all conspired to keep loans flowing to Adriatic.

Sources of Finance for Adriatic Tankers

Panagis Zissimatos, although he had started his fleet expansion with ship mortgages through the more traditional, shipping-orientated banks, turned to the private placement debt market in September 1993 when he borrowed several hundred million dollars from US Trust (UST), an institute that represented a number of very large US insurance and pension corporations. The original eight under UST were Aegon, Cigna, Conseco, John Hancock, Kemper, New England Mutual and Northwestern Mutual. Subsequently, he borrowed from about six other companies, including a pension fund. This caused some surprise in the shipping industry as at that time private debt placement was seen as a very unusual way of financing fleet expansion although it did have the advantage of the longer loan periods mentioned earlier. He had in addition mortgages with a number of banks, including Barclays, the Bank of Scotland, the Royal Bank of Scotland, Christiana Bank, CIT, and others (see Table 6.3).

Table 6.3   Adriatic Tankers Shipping Co. SA – Banks and insurance companies involved

Banks	Insurance and trust companies
Banque Cantonal Valdoise	United States Trust Co. (Trustee for the bond)
Bank of Scotland	Aegon
Christiana Bank of Norway	Cigna
Credit Suisse	Conseco Capital Management
Credit Lyonnais	John Hancock Mutual Life Insurance
Barclays	Kemper
De Nationale Investerings Bank	Northwestern Mutual Life
Den Norske Bank	Teachers Insurance & Annuity
Royal Bank of Scotland	New England Mutual
Indosuez	
ING Bank	
National Bank of Greece	
CIT	

An anonymous financial market expert told *TradeWinds* that he was surprised that Adriatic Tankers had been able to raise such a large debt placement. He believed that the large amount of the placement showed that the market was not ready to evaluate a company such as that of Zissimatos. He said that a positive effect of the whole business was that those involved in the loan, that is, the investors, promoters and underwriters, would in the future be obliged to examine cases more closely.[16] However, in a paper given to the American Stock Exchange, Professor Costas Th. Grammenos commented on how few shipping analysts there were among his audience of Wall Street's top investors. He went on to say that there was a need for analyst education with the increasing need for the raising shipping funds.[17]

Besides its numerous ship mortgages, Adriatic Tankers had several major loans. Finance came from Sentrachem, a South African chemical company which made 60 separate loans totalling $15 million to Adriatic Tankers over the first ten months of 1995. This led ultimately to the suspension of the London-based chief executive of Sentrachem's international division who was alleged to have made the loans. His successor in the post, when asked why the loan had been made, claimed that the loans had to do with keeping ships running with Sentrachem's products. The loan was apparently made without the knowledge of the company's senior management because their London operation had been set up to be 'somewhat obtuse' during the era of sanctions against South Africa and had been given leeway to conduct operations that would not have been allowed under normal trading conditions.[18] Sentrachem is thought to have lent Adriatic Tankers a total of $22 million in all.

CIT had an exposure of US$55 million to Adriatic Tankers.[19] CIT describes itself as an asset-based lender which already had some experience with shipping and was into Regency Cruises (see Chapter 4), another troubled company. CIT say they are transaction orientated: 'We have to see whether the transactions works for CIT and for everybody else involved. It must always go through our credit approval committee process' (Ravi Dandapani, Vice President of the CIT group's Capital Equipment Financing Inc.).[20] Mr Dandapani also said that CIT tend not to syndicate loans but do it for their own books and CIT had decided that it was a good time to lend to the shipping industry. He based this decision on the steady stream of forecasts identifying the industry's capital requirements over the next ten years: 'We think that the industry needs lenders who think long term, rather than short term, and we are prepared to do that if the deal has merit to it.' Zissimatos must have presented good prospects in these terms.

The Effect of Zissimatos' Personality on the Loans

The head of Adriatic Tankers was a man who stood alone, away from the general 'family' of Greek shipowners and was once quoted as saying 'With the Greeks we have no common interest.'[21] He tended to shun publicity of any sort, a factor perhaps connected to the lengths to which he would go to avoid bad publicity when his empire began to collapse: at the merest hint of the press getting to know of his crew troubles he would try to clear these up. A number of his crewmen were able to use this to their advantage if they were owed wages – the threat of public disclosure of their plight, sometimes in the early days, brought about payment. He was known to be very charming at face-to-face meetings, and was able to use this on his frequent visits to the US to obtain further finance for his ailing fleet.

Zissimatos was introduced to several bondholders by Thornhill Capital when he had first sought private placement funds. Certainly those who had dealings with him initially were impressed with the presentation that he made. But Peter Craggs of James Marine Services, a UK parts supplier, who went to Piraeus in November 1994 to try and recover a debt of $420,000 owed by Adriatic Tankers, said, 'We were entertained to a bloody good meal, girls all over the place and given cheques for $90,000, we were absolutely guaranteed to get paid.'[22] Craggs was very angry when cheques bounced, the promises were not fulfilled, and only just over half of what was owed was recovered. His appraisal of the top management of Adriatic was that they were 'immature and incompetent'.

Sandford Ship Management, which had a management contract for two of Adriatic's ships, likewise had to fly a delegation out to Piraeus in August 1995 when funds for running the two vessels were not forthcoming. They were more impressed and left speaking of 'extremely constructive talks', having once again been charmed into believing that they would be paid. Sandford's offices were at one time describing the troubles as 'slight timing problems'.[23]

Mary R. Brooks, in her book *Ship Finance, a Banker's Perspective*, quotes a banker who had experienced a loan default, stating that in the shipping finance industry, personalities can be important: 'Greater attention should be paid to the character and tempera-ment of the individuals directing and managing the enterprise. It is often the case that the growth of a company relies very much on the determination of a single strong personality.'[24] Certainly Mr Zissimatos' skills as a persuasive negotiator were not in doubt but his management record with regard to his company was poor, and, in relation to his crews, was abysmal. Many of his staff were said to be extremely loyal to him, but at the same time there was an element of fear in the office.

An observation worth noting comes from *Lloyd's Shipping Economist* (LSE) of May 1992. The Nortankers enterprise in the US had just collapsed at that time.[25] Nortankers was a company that, with its supposed Norwegian expertise in the tanker market, coupled with the rise in that market, had looked a particularly good investment on the surface and had been the subject of a suc-cessful initial public offer in the US. LSE stated that the lessons to be learned from this collapse included paying close attention to the quality of assets and management. Another interesting aspect of that article was that of the top twenty US stockbroking firms ranked for research by the *Institutional Investor*, only one firm had an analyst partially dedicated to shipping. Although this is a reference made about the public sector in the US it may be an indication of how little their private sector, that is, US Trust, knew about the shipping industry when it lent to Adriatic Tankers.

Asset-based Lending on Adriatic's Ships

One of the important aspects of the loans made to Adriatic Tankers is that many of the ships purchased by Zissimatos were said to have been over-valued and certainly over-mortgaged. The fortunes of the ships which were laid up around the world awaiting repairs bear this out. The story which unfolds later shows that unpaid repair bills were an important factor in the arrest of a number of the ships which inevitably prevented them from trading. Some of the worst crew deprivations also arose from shipyards demanding first call on any assets in an arrest, in order to get their bills paid.

Banks have of course criteria for assessing risks on industry loans such as asset evaluation and commercial performance, but few, as shown above with the US stockbroking firms, seem to have a sound knowledge of the criteria required to assess the shipping industry.[26] Peter Stokes stated in *Lloyd's Shipping Economist* in October 1992 that care should be taken if relying on NAV (net asset value) because ship prices are a highly unreliable guide to making a corporate valuation. Shipbroker's valuations of fleets can be inaccurate where older vessels are concerned, and also second-hand ship prices can collapse very quickly indeed.[27] Adriatic's ships were in any case always over-valued.[28]

Questions being asked on the collapse included: were US Trust officials aware that some of the vessels they were financing stood below an acceptable standard due to their condition? Did this mean that the institute had not done its homework when it came to an asset inspection? There would seem in effect to be a trend among the leading institutions to lend money without considering that the loan is properly secured. The eagerness with which the US bankers and institutions lent to Adriatic Tankers may be seen to bear this out. Certainly there was competition between the banks to lend and this may be seen in the pressure to hurry into loan arrangements.

It is interesting in all these reflections that the Christiana Bank had 100 per cent financing on the tanker *Argostoli Bay* and, in 1990, the then head of the bank's shipping office in London, Bjarte Boe, said in *Fairplay* that his bank looked for two of three legs when assessing security for loans.[29] These legs were asset value, secure cash flow and corporate structure, and the bank concentrates on people rather than assets. This latter must have taken precedence since Panagis Zissimatos managed to charm a loan out of them.

Financial Problems Leading to the Collapse

The first clear signs that Adriatic Tankers was in real difficulty came in 1993 when the company had a number of contacts with the ITF over non-payment of crews. These early signals were not appreciated by mortgagees. In any case Adriatic had always been a slow payer of bills.[30] They would generally only pay their bills after some pressure from creditors. Most of the large bunker suppliers ultimately refused to supply the company after experiences of this kind and Adriatic was forced to use smaller suppliers which, without the economies of scale, charged higher for their services. This meant that the company was already running at an operating disadvantage when it came to everyday costs. It is notable when looking at the later arrests of the company's vessels that a great number of those arrests were by bunker suppliers.

The strategy concerning seafarers is dealt with more fully elsewhere but some points need to be noted here. When Zissimatos started using the ever more available Russian crews, he may have come to some agreement with the Russian unions that 10 per cent of a seafarer's salary would be paid during the voyage and the balance would be paid when the men were discharged at the end of their contract time on board.[31] This probably gave the company a false sense of security as it was able to shelve its wage problem until some months into the future. However, come the day of reckoning, Adriatic suddenly found itself having to fund a large pay-off for a whole crew. This would happen at frequent intervals, such was the size of the fleet; then, in order to keep the ships trading, the company would transfer the old crew to a hotel to await payment while putting on board a new crew to sail the vessel. This tactic was merely a delaying move as the funds still had to be found to pay more and more men as the numbers in the hotels built up.

As crew complaints multiplied, and after allegations by the ITF that the crews were working for months without pay, Zissimatos took the unusual step (for him) of meeting with a journalist from *TradeWinds* in his office in Piraeus to defend his company's record and crew payment policies.[32] He was concerned that the dispute with the ITF would lead the industry to think that the company's growth over the previous few years had been over-ambitious and that Adriatic was having trouble keeping up with its crew payments.

Mr Zissimatos denied that there were any cash-flow problems, stating that the company had enough funds to enable it to purchase additional ships if it so wished and that the banks were happy with the operation of the fleet. They would certainly be happy with the operation of the chemical tankers which were earning time-charter daily rates equal to those of a VLCC.[33] New borrowings which were ostensibly meant to service the day-to-day running costs were in fact being channelled into the purchase of even more ships. This naturally enough did nothing to help the cash-flow problems that the fleet was building up. Stephen Serepca, CIT's chief shipping executive, claimed that Adriatic Tankers was trying to run 80 ships with the same amount of cash that CIT would use to run 30.[34]

Panagis Zissimatos returned to the US in the summer of 1994 to try to obtain further loans of $25 million from US Trust in order to ease his cash-flow situation, but by this time the institutions were becoming alarmed and the request was refused. Adriatic's owner blamed bad publicity for scaring off further investment.

As the cash flow worsened, the funds available to maintain the fleet's condition decreased, and as the vessels deteriorated so port state control began to take a greater interest in the ships, detaining them for various reasons and thereby preventing them trading and exacerbating the situation further. At the core of the fleet were its chemical tankers; the condition of these ships was monitored more closely by port-state control and charterers alike due to the hazardous nature of their trade.

Some of this resulted in more negative publicity and inevitably came to the notice of current and prospective charterers who began to look closely at the company with which they were entrusting their cargoes. The delays associated with problems on board the vessels frightened off much of the trade Adriatic Tankers may have hoped for in order to ease its cash problems. It eventually became exceedingly difficult to fix cargoes for the fleet, a decline that accelerated as both the industry and the financial institutions began to lose confidence in the management and the ships.

Creditors started to call more stridently for payment before the inevitable happened. A Suezmax tanker was held by the port authorities in Trieste in January 1995 for allegedly unpaid bills and port dues, though Adriatic's explanation was that the vessel was renewing some of her class certificates.[35] On another of the company's ships the master and chief engineer were paid off three months late while the crew and agents remained unpaid.[36]

In May 1995, a much-publicised agreement between Adriatic Tankers and the ITF looked to be a turning point for the shipping company. Mr Zissimatos himself visited the Federation's London offices after the ITF voiced concern that the lower management of the company did not seem able to work in concert to reach an agreement over the backlog of crew payments. These payments were estimated to be in excess of $3 million involving nearly half of Adriatic's ships.[37]

This meeting was backed up by a further discussion at the company's offices at Piraeus on 1–2 June on how to go about completing ITF-acceptable agreements for the company's vessels through the relevant local unions. It was about this time that Adriatic Tankers, hoping that its image and reputation were taking an upward turn, was asked to resign from Intertanko. This had followed the resignation of the company A.P. Moller shortly before and Adriatic claimed, somewhat illogically, that it was being made a scapegoat. Giakoumatos, the vice-president of the company, also claimed that they were not interested in being members of the organisation any more.[38] This was a marked contrast to his statements of a few days before when he had told *TradeWinds*, 'We cannot understand why they are doing this ... We got questions from Intertanko and we have responded to them, it must all be a big misunderstanding.'[39]

Intertanko claimed that Adriatic Tankers had been tardy in making its membership payments and had not disclosed certain information concerning the classification of ships despite repeated requests. In its defence the shipping company said that Intertanko already had all the information it was asking for and that it was just looking for an excuse to get rid of one of its members to show how far it would go to prove its commitment to openness. Juan Kelly, chairman of the International Chamber of Shipping, made a valid point when he said at the Intertanko annual general meeting dinner that although a member could be a cast out of the organisation, that owner was still there and still trading, a question that the industry had to find a way to tackle.[40]

Re-financing and Re-entry

There seemed to be little done in this very open market to constrain Adriatic from making a comeback. This was in line with the trend among leading institutions towards lending money without considering that the loan was properly secured. The eagerness with which the US institutions, as well as British and other bankers, continued to lend to Adriatic Tankers bears this out.

Competition to lend was well-understood by Zissimatos. Indeed, come 1996, there were strong indicators that he was back in the market raising loans, operating sub-companies, and purchasing ships in their names. Several of these purchased were ex-Adriatic vessels which had been arrested and were up for sale. Zissimatos had now entered into negotiations with banks which had been left holding embarrassingly high exposures in order to buy back the ships 'at a fraction of the original cost'.[41]

There were many advantages for recovering ownership in this way. The 'new' owner could not be held responsible for the abandoned crew or their wages. There was certainly a sudden appearance of new companies when the vessels came up for sale. Ecbatana Maritime of Cephalonia bought several, including the chemical carrier *Cape Sun*, but Zissimatos denied to Lloyd's List that he had any connections with this.[42] The Ionian Transport and Trading Company, also originating in Zissimatos' home island, appeared trading with ex-Adriatic tankers, including *Blue Sky II* (which sank in the China Sea in December 1996) and *Blue Wave* (arrested in Spain). This company collapsed, but rose again.

As is usual in this shadowy world of FOC ownership under one-ship companies, it is difficult to trace transfers of ships, flags, owners and ship names. In 1996 the *Stainless Commander* was auctioned to pay some of Adriatic's debts. It was sold on to Palmas Navigation, 'a company which Zissimatos was representing'.[43] Later Faber Shipping bought the vessel and she quickly achieved the subsequent names of *Capella II* and *Princess of Rotterdam*. Another new company, Chemoil (manager, a Mr Vallianatos) bought several Adriatic vessels, as did Skaugen Petrotrans. Both companies state they had no connections with Adriatic, although Skaugen said it had helped to set up Princess Carriers to operate a ship bought from a company represented by Zissimatos.[44] This may have been the ex-*Stainless Commander*. In an ITF circular of 7 October 1997, there was advice to look out for Chemoil and ex-Adriatic ships now named *Queen of Evian*, *Queen of Achia* and *Queen of Lausanne*: 'You know what you are dealing with', cautioned the circular.

Many of the ships were now in a precarious physical condition. A British captain in an interview described how repairs were curtailed even when vital safety was involved. Amongst many other instances the variously named *Stainless Commander* can be used as an example in this respect. When, in 1996, the ship was in bad need of repairs, money from Den Norske Bank for the repair work was diverted by

Zissimatos for 'office expenses'. The manager in charge of the repairs was then 'forced to rewrite survey reports by Zissimatos to make them look more favourable'. The manager said later (in a court document) that he was particularly concerned about replacing steel plates on the main deck, which were below minimum thickness. Zissimatos 'refused to do so, instead he ordered to cover this up and suggested to leave this to class. My advice was rejected.' The manager had clear instructions from Zissimatos 'to keep my mouth shut and eyes closed about fundamental defects'.[45]

Reactions on the Market

The major injuries inflicted by Adriatic were on the seafarers and their families, which will be discussed later. The banks and other financial institutions clearly suffered losses and prestige. They were big players with diverse portfolios; as the mortgagees they were also preferential lenders and usually had first lien on the vessels and therefore prospects of recovering their investments if the vessel was arrested and sold. In several cases, however, the mortgages were in excess of the value of the ships.

There were at least twelve banks which loaned to Adriatic (see Table 6.3). In terms of the known levels of loans, four of these banks were together in for about $400 million. The amounts from the other seven are uncertain, and precise losses from all are unknown to the researchers. The banks have tended to be secretive in these respects, sometimes evoking customer confidentiality, even to the extent of denying they had ever heard of the ship or the company involved. A few, such as the Bank of Scotland, which had taken more care to loan on the better-quality vessels, would have recovered much of their money; those loaning on the Adriatic rust buckets would not. Fourteen insurance companies were major investors in Adriatic, primarily US based. The investment from eight of the private placement companies was in the region of $235 million, as far as can be established. Losses for this sector were probably higher than those of the banks.

Why banks continued to put money into this, and other dubious Zissimatos companies has been a matter of debate and speculation. Reasons have ranged from over-enthusiastic bankers lacking shipping experience, corrupt loan officials, blackmailed loan officials (after photographs at parties on board Zissimatos' luxury yachts), to those with a misguided trust. After it had attacked the UST for not trying harder to work things out with

Adriatic, Den Norske Bank drew criticism from the US creditors because of what was considered its encouragement of Zissimatos. The director of one of the crisis management companies assisting creditors said, 'I am appalled that reputable people in the industry are not shy about having their names associated with Zissimatos.'[46]

Barclays Bank clearly reacted to these and other events when in April 1996 they replaced their manager in Piraeus. Barclays Bank have subsequently withdrawn from the shipping market after their Greek portfolio was acquired by Midland. Four hundred million dollars in healthy loans were transferred to the latter after Barclays had written off $150 million owed by 'local clients',[47] of which possibly $40 million was Adriatic.

Classification societies and insurers had their problems and some loss of credibility. The ripple effects on this global market were considerable, for example a judicial hearing was set up to determine how to handle the problem of premiums which were returned to brokers R. Mears & Co. when insurers cancelled cover on Adriatic Tankers ships. Mears was concerned that it would be dragged into the Adriatic crisis by upsetting other creditors if it handed the premiums back to the banks. The majority of Adriatic's hull insurance was placed through Florida broker Coastal States Insurance who used Mears to place a significant amount with Lloyd's and the Institute of London Underwriters. More hull insurance was placed in the Italian and US markets.

Although banks took over the payment of insurance premiums when Zissimatos failed to pay them, a number of insurers cancelled the cover when the ships lost their class. This raised the more general question of how many ships were sailing without insurance. Many of these vessels were old and 'owned' by brass-plate companies in Panama, and, being the only visible asset of the company, this represented a serious situation for any insurance claims by third parties.

Some London brokers were nervous. They could have faced legal actions by US creditors claiming that these brokers had assigned values to the ships which were too high.[48] Under the circumstances, however, it may have been argued that ship values had dropped. The US creditors seem in fact to have little appreciation of the cyclical characteristics of freight rates, or the ship sales markets they had moved into, this no doubt would be part of the brokers' defence when and if a writ is served, although in this case the drop in value seemed to have occured on one day!

On the Greek shipping industry side in particular, the Adriatic Tankers problem could have had dire repercussions. Nicholas

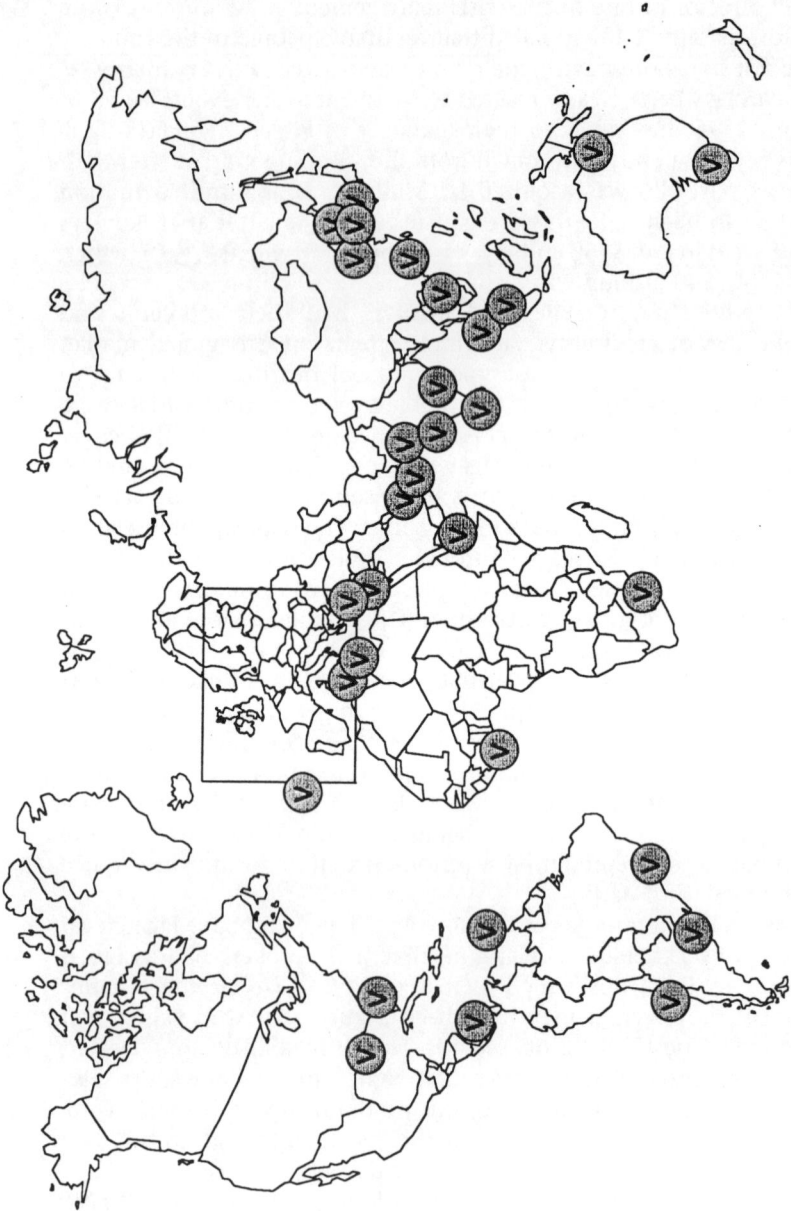

Figure 6.1   Adriatic Tankers Shipping Company SA, Locations of arrested vessels – world

*Figure 6.2   Adriatic Tankers Shipping Company SA, Locations of
arrested vessels – Europe*

Tsakos, one of the forces behind the launching of companies
quoted on the US and Oslo stock exchanges, does admit that the
problems of Adriatic and Regency Cruises, which were in trouble at
the same time, 'don't help' the image of Greek shipping. He went
on to say that these things make US investors uncomfortable.

However, Greek shipping people who approached the US market
soon after the troubles reached their height maintained that the
more sophisticated in the market had not been scared off. In fact
the general consensus was that some of the banks had only themselves to blame and it was the lack of care taken when processing
the loans that had brought about many of the problems.

In addition to the bigger institutions, there were many other creditors such as suppliers of stores, marine spares, small-scale repairers, maintenance firms, hotel owners and ship chandlers, all of whom dealt with many companies and people, and as unsecured creditors lost badly in the Adriatic mess– several never totally recovered.

In 1996, Nic Basilakes, a Greek-born Netherlands ship chandler, got together a group of more than sixty European ship chandlers who were owed US$20 million by Adriatic. He said he was infuriated with the thought that Zissimatos was using Holland as a base for a comeback. The law, he said, was useless and Zissimatos was walking around like a king.[49]

Through interviews, the researchers elicited many such personal reactions from financial players big and small. Bank officials were somewhat philosophical. They were taken in largely because they had 'no reason to doubt the reports from surveyors – there is no reason to question a classification society or shipbroker'. Also, the industry was after all cyclical, and in their company assessments the banks would consider effects of slumps in trading, but 'If it lasts six months and recovers, there is no reason to doubt that should a similar slump occur the company would recover.'

The private placement investors, such as the insurance companies, seem to have had even more lax proceedings. They were, for example, giving ten-year loans on vessels that had less than ten years' life. But the size of investment (a few million dollars) was, they considered, comparatively small in the sum total of their business: 'you win some, you lose some'. Somewhat less philosophical were the many small-business creditors, some of whom lost almost everything – the comments below, recorded from different owners and managers, are typical:

- I cannot believe that they [the banks] were so unbelievably stupid as to lend that amount of money against second-hand tonnage which was in very poor condition.
- They [Adriatic] lied, and lied and lied knowingly, they knew they were not going to pay us ... I had never come across people like that in my life.
- I am not a violent person but I mean I could cheerfully wring his [Zissimatos'] neck, or break his leg, or something.

These small-business creditors were engaged with many companies in relatively small-scale transactions and they could not cover everything by insurance, nor could they, as individuals, arrest ships. Sometimes they could benefit from arrests by others – such arrests were very widespread under many jurisdictions, as shown in Figures 6.1 and 6.2.

7

Adriatic Tankers III: The Tale of Two Ships

Introduction

This is the story of the oil tankers *Lourdas* and *Kyoto1*, and chronicles the impacts of reckless loans, debts, frauds and incompetence on seafarers, and the systematic disregard for their rights and welfare by a typical substandard company interested in seafarers only as expendable assets. Most of the information for this is taken from letters contained in the International Transport Workers' Federation (ITF) files, press reports and interviews with some of the participants

The *Lourdas*

Name of vessel:	*Lourdas*	1994
Original name:	*World Duke*	1975
First name:	*Bright Duke*	1985
Class:	NK	
Date of Build:	1975	
Ship Type:	Tanker	
Length:	321.010 m	
Breadth:	54.030 m	
Draught:	19.862 m	
Gross Tonnage:	122.062	
Net Tonnage:	92.080	
DWT:	238.760	
Propulsion:	Steam turbine	
Flag:	Panama	
Registered Owner:	Sea Confidence	

The first files on the *Lourdas* appear while she was still under the ownership of the Navix Line Ltd, Japan; her name at this stage being *Bright Duke*. A request from the Federation of Korean

94

Seafarers Unions to the ITF London for an ITF Blue certificate was made in October 1993, for the period from October 1993 to 30 September 1994. While under the ownership of the Navix Line, this vessel seems to have had no problem fulfilling its obligation to its seafarers.

During this time, it seems that the vessel was sold to a new company, Sea Excellence, which was founded in Panama in 1994, with the Pallas Shipping Agency of Hong Kong acting as the managers of the vessel. It was at this stage that the name of the vessel was changed to the *Lourdas*. Shortly after this company bought the vessel, she must have been sold once again, to another Panamanian company, Sea Confidence, founded in 1994, whose address was c/o Adriatic Tankers Shipping Company, Piraeus, in Greece.

Adriatic Tankers Takes Over

We begin the tale of the *Lourdas'* long-suffering crews when Adriatic Tankers took over the management of the vessel on 20 May 1994, and a new mixed crew replaced the Koreans. This new crew consisted of 3 Greek nationals (the captain, the chief engineer and the second engineer), 25 Russians, both ratings and officers, and 4 Vietnamese. The employment contracts varied in length, from five to eleven months. The terms and conditions were that all crew would be paid 45 per cent of their earnings each month on board the vessel. On completion of their contracts, the seafarers would be flown to either Rotterdam or Budapest, where the outstanding balance due to the seafarer would be paid. Once paid, the company would then repatriate each seafarer to his home country.

The first Greek captain took command of the *Lourdas* on 20 May 1994. Because the crew's wages were not paid after a month, he contacted the company but was unable to resolve this problem. He was replaced by another Greek captain, in November 1994. This new captain was initially unsympathetic to the crew's pay situation, but it became clear later that he too changed his allegiance in favour of the crew, at which point he too was replaced, on 3 March 1995. The next captain who joined on 3 March 1995, stayed on board until 4 October 1995. He then made a hasty departure with the chief engineer, once the ship returned to the Persian Gulf, and was repatriated by Cosmos Marine, the manning agency employed by Adriatic Tankers. This could only have happened with the permission of Adriatic Tankers. The command of the ship passed to the Russian chief mate. He was not appointed by Adriatic Tankers, rather, it was a case of 'battlefield promotion'. The previous changes in command may reflect the dissatisfaction of the various captains at the treatment of their crew, and their inability to help.

Appeals for Help

The ship arrived in Fujairah, United Arab Emirates, on 2 January 1995. The *Lourdas'* crew had more than enough of Adriatic Tankers' procrastination, and refused to move the vessel after it anchored outside the port limits, unless their demands for payment and repatriation were met.

On 17 February 1995, a fax was sent by eleven crew members to the ITF requesting intervention on their behalf. By then they had been unpaid for nine months. A threat by Adriatic Tankers to blacklist the crew if they turned to the ITF for help had certainly delayed the approach for ITF intervention.

Shortly after the initial contact between the *Lourdas'* crew and the ITF, Mr Fanargiotis, a representative of Adriatic Tankers telephoned the ITF requesting that they ask the crew to move the *Lourdas* into Fujairah in order to load the vessel for a charter worth $1.2 million. The ITF in turn asked Fanargiotis whether Adriatic Tankers was able to pay the crew first; Fanargiotis' reply was that payment of the wages would have to wait until the vessel was loaded. The ITF view was that they would advise the crew not to co-operate until they had been paid.

In response to events the ITF were able to inform a potential charterer, Capital Shipbrokers, of the situation on the *Lourdas*. This resulted in the charter being cancelled. The official reason given by Capital Shipbrokers was that they did not think the vessel could fulfil the time scale of the charter. Further, the ITF told Adriatic Tankers that they would inform all possible clients of the situation of the *Lourdas'* crew, until it was properly dealt with. This threat elicited a promise to have the problems solved as soon as possible.

Although the crew of the *Lourdas* were in intermittent contact with the ITF, they were obviously convinced from past experience that Adriatic Tankers had no intention of fulfilling its promises. The crew informed the ITF on 22 February 1995 that they intended to go on hunger strike, and stop all deck and engine-room watches until their demands for wages and repatriation were met. It would seem that at this point the crew not only did not believe Adriatic Tankers, but also had doubts about the will or capability of the ITF in resolving these issues.

The ITF, for their part, still believed the problem could be solved amicably, and told the would-be hunger strikers of the charter being cancelled and the promise by Fanargiotis to deal with the payment and repatriation as soon as possible. They also advised the crew against taking hunger-strike action.

The situation on board the *Lourdas* was now very tense. This was compounded further by the refusal of Adriatic Tankers to repatriate a very ill crew member. The port doctor had said he should be hospitalised ashore immediately, if repatriation was not possible. Unfortunately, the ill seafarer was not hospitalised, nor did the ITF learn of this problem until much later. The crew, upon hearing of the promise made by Fanargiotis, and the ITF's reaction to their proposed hunger strike, decided not to go ahead with their planned action.

Five days later the crew were once again asked to prepare for sailing, even though no arrangements had been made to accommodate their requirements. On reporting this latest demand to the ITF, and their refusal to move the vessel, the crew also expressed concerns to the ITF about possible blacklisting actions that might be taken against them by Adriatic Tankers. The company now got in touch with the ITF, informing them that there was another charter in the offing, but the ship needed to sail to Kharg Island, Iran for loading, by 3 March 1995. To get the crew to comply, Adriatic promised to pay them by 28 February 1995. Adriatic Tankers was asked by the ITF to confirm this date for the 'full settlement' of wages by telex to both the *Lourdas'* crew and the ITF. When the telex arrived, it did promise 'complete settlement', but the timing of this event had been extended from 28 February to 1 March 'at the latest'. By 1 March, payment had not taken place.

Obviously, honouring its commitments to both its crews and the ITF was not high on Adriatic Tankers' agenda. In spite of its deceit, and probably due to the efforts of a new captain, it persuaded the *Lourdas'* crew to sail to Khor Fakkan. On arrival, on 10 March 1995, she was promptly arrested by creditors. The crew had once again been duped, and no payment was received. They had now been without wages for nearly ten months.

Isolated On Board

Life on board the *Lourdas* now became even more intolerable: the company had ordered the boilers to be shut down, which resulted in the temperature rising to about 35 degrees Celsius, as there was no power for the air conditioning. The crew's families were also very worried, and were contacting ITF affiliates in Russia. This had a negative effect on the morale of the crew: with no payments being made to their families and communication between families and crew difficult, there were grave worries on both sides, which increased the seafarers' feelings of isolation and desperation. To make matters worse, the captain was now claiming that due to the ship's arrest, the crew could not in any case be paid and repatriated as their passports were under arrest along with the vessel. This was only another delaying tactic in order to prolong the payment of wages and the repatriation, and did not have the force of law. The recipe of heat, anger, frustration, worry and desperation that these seamen were forced to endure, through no fault of their own, so easily could have led to violence and destruction.

However, in this potentially dangerous situation, the crew merely 'downed tools', and sent the ITF a press release of their condition, in the hope that the resulting bad publicity for Adriatic Tankers might force a change in circumstances. In the press release, they tell of the physical and psychological stress they were enduring, both as a result of the conditions on board as well as their desperate concerns for their families, who had not received any financial allotments from Adriatic Tankers for over ten months. They also tell of their fears for the seriously ill man still on board, who should have been hospitalised more than a month before on doctor's orders. The article was faxed to *TradeWinds* by the ITF and was published by the journal, which consistently championed the rights of the Adriatic seafarers.

The stress of the situation may have affected the Russian bo'sun, he fell sick with what was diagnosed as myocarditis and ischemia. Now there were two very ill people but no attempt was made by the company to repatriate either, partly because it claimed the ship was outside port limits. However, arrangements were made by Adriatic Tankers to repatriate the Greek second engineer (for unknown reasons). Clearly, through this incident Adriatic Tankers showed either gross negligence towards its crew, and/or a truly racist tendency in the way the different nationalities were viewed. Greeks were in fact often treated better than other nationalities, as Zissimatos may have feared repercussions in Greece, especially from wives of Greek seafarers if they were treated in the same manner as foreign employees. By 27 April 1995, the arrest of the *Lourdas* had been lifted, but the situation remained the same.

The crew had by now stopped working, and were refusing to communicate with Adriatic Tankers, until their demands were met. Adriatic Tankers expressed outrage at this turn of events and contacted the ITF with its complaints against the crew. It claimed that the crew had refused bunkering services until the last moment, and had attempted to shut down the main generator. They had also stolen all the engine-room tools, and were threatening to stop all on-board engines, leaving the vessel powerless, unless their demands were met by 28 April 1995. In spite of all the stress and broken promises, the crew had in fact moved the vessel to Khor Fakkan, and once the arrest was lifted, back to Fujairah, which, under the circumstances, went well beyond the call of duty.

A high-level meeting was eventually arranged in London between Captain Zissimatos and the ITF. Agreement was reached between the two parties whereby Adriatic Tankers promised to repatriate the crew by 1 June 1995, with a cash payment of $3000 on board, with the outstanding balance to be paid within 21 days. In view of Adriatic Tankers' past record of dishonouring agreements, the ITF gave Zissimatos a stern warning that if this agreement was not kept, the ITF would ensure the bankruptcy of Adriatic Tankers within four weeks. The gist of this meeting and its outcome was sent to the *Lourdas'* crew, with a rider that should the crew shut down the main engines, the ITF would no longer be prepared to support the crew's demands. The crew was suspicious of the settlement, and in turn demanded full payment whilst still on board. That the *Lourdas'* crew was unhappy with the agreement was clear by the flurry of telexes and faxes that flowed between the crew and the ITF, in which the crew first wanted full payment on board, and, when that was not possible, the outstanding balance paid whilst in hotels in Europe waiting to go home. The last option finally settled matters, and on 29 April 1995, the crew telexed the ITF to the effect that they had received communication from Adriatic Tankers, confirming their hotel bookings for 2 May 1995.

The crew were eventually paid their $3000 on board and flown to Amsterdam on 4 May 1995. At this stage the crew were ecstatic and very grateful to the ITF, as their telex below of 3 May 1995 shows. All they needed now was the outstanding balance of their wages, which totalled $136,812.66, and a ticket home.

95 – 05 – 03 22:16

8811397ITFLDN G
1331206 JPAN X

TO : I T F LONDON
FM : S/T LOURDAS

DT : 03/MAY/95   TLX/NO.270

DEAR SIRS,
WE, RUSSIAN CREWMEMBERS S/T LOURDAS, WOULD LIKE
TO EXPRESS MUCH GRATEFUL WORDS OF GRATITUDE
TOWARDS I. T. F. STAFF AND PERSONALLY MR. CHARLIE
MILNE, MR. TOM HOLMER AND MR. JAF ABLET FOR THE
HELP AND CO-OPERATION IN THE SOLUTION OF OUR
CONFLICT WITH GREEK COMPANY ADRIATIC TANKERS
SHIPPING CO., WHICH CROWNED FINALLY WITH OUR
WIN.

WE'VE NEVER APPEALED TO YOU BEFORE AND HAVE
KNOWN ABOUT YOUR ABILITIES FROM FRIEND'S
CONVERSATION MAINLY. AND NOW, BY OUR EXAMPLE WE
HAVE SEEN THE REAL POWER OF THE I. T. F IN CAUSE OF
DEFENCE OF INTERNATIONAL LAW AND SEAMEN'S RIGHTS.

GENTLEMEN, YOU CAN BE SURE OF US AS YOU'VE FOUND
EAGER ADHERENTS AND PROPAGANDISTS OF THE AFFAIR
OF CONSOLIDATION OF TRANSPORT AND MARINE LABOUR.
WE'LL RELATE OUR FAMILIAR SEAMEN IN RUSSIA ABOUT
YOUR HONOURABLE WORK.

THANK YOU FOR HELP AND SUPPORT ONCE AGAIN.

FRIENDLY SHAKE YOUR HANDS

SINCERELY YOURS

CH. OFF	AB
3/OFF	P/MAN
R/OFF	OILER
1/ENG	FITTER
3/ENG	COOK

Abandonment Ashore

Fifteen days after their arrival in the Netherlands, two of the crew
were paid and flown home, but only after the ITF had contacted
the vice-president of Adriatic Tankers, Mr G. Giakoumatos. After 28
days, only three of the ten crew waiting in Holland for wages and
repatriation had returned home. The ITF were obviously annoyed
with the way matters were going, as their credibility with the seafarers was also on the line. A fax was sent to Adriatic Tankers from
the ITF, requesting a meeting. The concern expressed by the ITF

was that the repatriation and wage process had come to a halt, and Adriatic Tankers was unable or unwilling to pay the crew's hotel bills. It looked as if Adriatic Tankers was bankrupt.

On 23 June 1995, 50 days after the crew's arrival in Rotterdam, the ITF received a fax from Adriatic Tankers, apologising for the delay in payments and repatriation, and claimed that this was its only delay so far! The promise of repatriation with payment within 21 days of the crew leaving the *Lourdas*, seems to have completely slipped its mind. It now assured the ITF that all the *Lourdas'* crew would be paid and repatriated by 3 July 1995, 61 days after the crew's arrival in Holland, and only 40 days later than the promised maximum length of stay before payment and repatriation was due. It was not until 10 July 1995, over three months later than planned, that all the crew abandoned in Rotterdam were repatriated, although not all were paid. They and their families had been deprived of earnings for over a year.

The Fate of the New Crew of the Lourdas

The ITF was now becoming concerned about the other crews still on board Adriatic Tankers vessels, including the *Lourdas* with its new crew. As satellite communication was not possible with the vessel, due to unpaid Inmarsat bills, other means of communication were resorted to. An attempt was made via Fairdeal, the Adriatic agents in Fujairah, to contact the *Lourdas'* crew. It was unlikely to succeed, and it did not. Another attempt was made to contact the *Lourdas'* crew through the Dubai International Seamen's Club, requesting news of their circumstances. Once again, this proved fruitless, as the location of the *Lourdas* was not known.

On 4 October 1995, news of the second crew of the *Lourdas* reached the ITF via the Russian affiliate, SUR (Seafarers Union of Russia). It transpires that upon anchoring the vessel in the Persian Gulf, the captain and chief engineer quickly left the ship. The *Lourdas* was again deserted by senior officers and short of food, water and diesel. The crew, with no money or chance of repatriation, were in a desperate position, especially as Adriatic Tankers refused any communication with them. Interestingly, it became clear from this first contact with the new crew, that although they were fairly sure that Adriatic Tankers was their employer, officially they were hired by Cosmos Marine, through a manning agency in Novorossiysk, Zoltoy Rog.

The crew gave their position as 19 miles off Dubai, and that they were now in the same situation as the previous *Lourdas* seafarers.

Worse still, the captain had never signed their employment contracts. By this time, one able seaman was dead, because (as previously) no medical advice or service had been made available. The crew had forced the captain to hospitalise a further two seafarers, after an accident which they blamed on the lack of safety equipment. The crew also gave more information about their employment contracts, which they had signed with Ionian Transport and Trading SA, Cephalonia, through Cosmos Marine Management, another front for Adriatic Tankers. The total wage bill owed to the crew at this time was $76,877.65, and the cost of paying the remaining crew each day was $788.27. The main aim of the *Lourdas'* crew contacting the ITF was to insure that the ITF would support them in their demands for pay and repatriation, and to inform the ITF that, without a captain on board and no news from any employer, they were clearly abandoned.

Although Adriatic Tankers was unwilling to deal with the crew's demands and needs, this did not stop it ordering the vessel to Kharg Island in Iran on 16 October 1995. The crew, with ITF backing, refused to move the vessel on the basis that there was little fuel, food or water and no captain, chief engineer or paid crew! Subsequently, the crew did move the ship, on 25 October 1995, but only into UAE territorial waters, six miles off the port of Dubai. The reason for doing this was to enable lawyers in Dubai to arrest the vessel in lieu of the crew's wages as well as to insure that the ITF was able to help the crew with regard to fuel and provisions.

Once the vessel was within territorial waters, the ITF proceeded to make arrangements for bunker fuel, as the acting master (the Russian chief mate) had informed the ITF that there was only enough on board for five days. A few days later, on 31 October 1995, Adriatic Tankers contacted the *Lourdas*, claiming that arrangements had been made to resupply the vessel, and pay the crew within a week, and requesting them to do a short voyage of 20 days to an as-yet-unknown destination, where air tickets would be waiting for their repatriation. The crew's reply, dictated by the ITF, was that they refused to sail unless all the outstanding wages were paid before sailing, including an extra 20 days' pay for the voyage, and that Adriatic Tankers should send written confirmation of the air tickets from the agent at the next port, before a new captain and chief engineer boarded. This communication, repeated on 2 November 1995, was to be the last between Adriatic Tankers and the *Lourdas'* crew.

Adriatic Tankers had now abandoned the ship and the crew to their fate, without money or fuel, and regardless of the consequences to both crew and the ship. The company did face bankruptcy at this stage, and was probably trying to deal with what it had left in the face of very angry creditors. It was prepared to sacrifice the lives of the seafarers and their families to secure some money when the problems were of the owner's own making.

There was now even more concern for the safety of the crew, and especially for the sick seafarer with a heart complaint. As Adriatic Tankers refused to acknowledge any responsibility, the ITF instructed the crew to have the ill man hospitalised. Payment for this would be added to the list of creditors calling for the arrest of the vessel. The ITF also wanted a death settlement of $20,000 made to the widow of the dead seafarer.

The situation was becoming even more critical on board the *Lourdas*, with the generator being run for only five hours a day due to the lack of fuel. As a result, the freezers defrosted and food stocks went rotten. The crew, in desperation again, contacted the ITF to tell them that they could not continue, and that they intended abandoning the *Lourdas* for the lifeboat, and somehow making their way home. The ITF advised the crew not to do this due to the possibility of a jail sentence, as the UAE immigration laws were very strict.

Up until this point, the ITF had been wary of giving too much direct help until the vessel was arrested. However, it was obvious that unless they intervened financially the crew would perish. The ITF decided to act, and arranged for Bridge Oil in Dubai to load 60 metric tons of bunker oil into the *Lourdas*. The ITF covered the bill for this, but only after the acting captain officially requested the ITF to intervene on the basis of the 'Captain's disbursements'. This in turn would allow the ITF to claim the money for the fuel back from Adriatic Tankers at a later stage. The fuel was finally delivered on 13 November 1995, much to the relief of the crew, who now, thankful for small mercies, had enough fuel on board for a further one and half months at anchor. The cost to the ITF for the fuel was $12,657.89.

Throughout this period, the Dubai port authorities had been unwilling to help the *Lourdas'* crew, and refused to allow the crew ashore for any reasons other than repatriation. To be fair to the harbour master, the ship's predicament was not his concern, and while the crew were on board, the problem was in effect contained. In legal terms, the responsibility for an abandoned vessel lies first with the owner of the vessel, and failing that, the responsibility shifts to the country in which the vessel is registered. In the *Lourdas'* case, it seemed clear that neither Adriatic Tankers nor Panama were prepared to act.

The Bankers

On 20 November 1995, the ITF, through a confidential telephone call, received information as to who represented the mortgagees of the *Lourdas*. This was quite a breakthrough as these lawyers were based in London. The ITF at last had someone they could deal with. Adriatic Tankers by this stage was no longer answering any communication from the *Lourdas* or the ITF. The ITF made contact with the lawyers, telling them of the *Lourdas'* predicament. By now, food supplies on board were badly depleted. To their credit, the lawyers reacted swiftly and informed the ITF that they were anxious to co-operate. Further, they told the ITF that after consultation with their client, the mortgagee of the *Lourdas*, it had been decided to either sell or charter the ship, but whatever happened, the crew would be paid. In view of this intention, the lawyers asked the ITF to delay their move to arrest the vessel.

The day after this conversation, the ITF were contacted by the *Lourdas'* crew regarding a Greek man who had boarded the ship. He claimed he was from Kossos Marine, representing Barclays Bank, the mortgagees of the ship. He said that Kossos Marine was now the owner of the *Lourdas*, and the crew should sign new employment contracts or leave the vessel, as the ship was to be moved elsewhere. The ITF immediately contacted the London lawyers, seeking clarification. The lawyers denied the person had anything to do with them, as their client was not Barclays Bank, but rather the Bank of Scotland.

Knowing the identity of the mortgagees was an important step forward for the ITF, allowing the ITF to make a direct approach to the Bank of Scotland on behalf of the seafarers if and when it was needed. The bank's aim was to recover its money as soon as possible, but before any real planning for the future of the *Lourdas* could take place it wanted a proper survey of the ship. Once the bank and the ITF were talking to each other, it soon became clear that the bank knew very little about the condition on the *Lourdas* and the behaviour of Adriatic Tankers. At this first meeting, the bank told the ITF that the UK P&I club was the mutual insurer, and although the bank would settle the crew's wages, the payments due to the dead seafarer's widow were the responsibility of the P&I club.

On 21 December 1995, the two surveyors sent to the *Lourdas* by the Bank of Scotland arrived on the vessel. The surveyors asked whether the crew would be willing to sail the *Lourdas* to either South Africa or Singapore, from where the bank would pay and repatriate the crew. To help the crew's decision, the bank promised a down-payment before the vessel sailed. The crew seemed positive about these plans, but did inform the surveyors that their wages had not yet reached their families at home.

Once again, the fuel situation on board the *Lourdas* was becoming critical, and the *Lourdas'* crew asked the ITF to contact the bank about this problem. The bank again reacted promptly, and immediately a further 20 metric tons of bunker oil were delivered to the ship. The bank also informed the ITF that arrangements had been made to repatriate the ill seafarer and the second mate. This took place on 7 January 1996. Both seafarers were flown home via Budapest, but not paid. Ten days later, the remaining crew on board were paid the promised advance by the Bank of Scotland's representatives, totalling $40,000. Once paid, the bank asked the crew if they were willing to take the vessel to Pakistan, where upon arrival they would receive the balance of their pay and be repatriated. The crew agreed to perform this task, but, still unsure of their changed fortune, asked the ITF to confirm these details on their behalf with the bank.

From January to April 1996, the Bank of Scotland, for reasons known only to itself, left the vessel at anchor in Dubai. The ITF tried unsuccessfully to get the bank to pay the widow of the dead seafarer. The bank's view on this remained steadfast throughout, it was the P&I club's responsibility, not the bank's. The ITF tried repeatably to get the wages for the two repatriated seafarers (a total of $11,491.48), but by May 1996, the payment had still not been made. Besides trying to obtain the seafarers' wages, the ITF was also attempting to retrieve ITF money from the bank for the bunker oil paid for in November 1995. This was received in May 1996.

The end of the Lourdas

An unpaid bunker bill resulted in the arrest of the *Lourdas* on 1 May 1996. This incident seems to have shaken the Bank of Scotland out of its apparent lethargy. Cardiff Marine was appointed to manage the ship. The Bank purchased the ship, sent her to Singapore and paid and repatriated the crew. As previously, more than a year had passed with no money for most of the seafarers and their families.

It still took until November 1996 for the two seafarers repatriated in January 1996 to obtain their money from the bank. A letter of desperation was also received by the ITF in May 1996 from the twelve-year-old daughter of the repatriated, ill seafarer. It was handwritten but is reproduced here:

Dear John Wood
My name is Dima xxxx. I am 12 years old. I live in Novorossisk
(Russia). Please help my Dad xxxx to get money for his work in
ADRIATIC TANKERS SHIPPING CO. on the s/t ,,Lourdas'. He
worked from 10.94 – 04.95. He returned home for he was ill,
first he was sent to Hungary, and then home.

Agent A/O Brig L.T.D. promised to pay money in June 1995:
his money + Basic till the time when he would get them. But it
didn't happen. In october 1995 my Dad asked the ItF to help.
But he didn't get his money yet. I hope you'll help my Dad.
I've read about you in newspapers. My Dad is worring for we
have no money, so he can't leave us. I want to go to the
summer camp, but I have no money to go there. You know I
studied with teachers of English and German, so we need to
400 $. We'll be ashamed if we would'nt pay, for teachers need
money too.
I hope you'll help us. I'll pray for you.

PS: Excuse me please for mistakes.
        I hope I did'nt make a lot of them.
                0.5. 05. 96.
                My Adress is on anvelope.

The *Lourdas* was finally scrapped in Bangladesh in July 1997.

The *Kyoto 1*

Name of vessel:	*Kyoto 1*
First Name:	*Shinwa Maru No.7*
Class:	RI NV(DISK)
Date of Build:	1978
Ship Type:	Product Tanker
Length:	58.960 m (OA)
Breadth:	9.730 m (Ext)
Draught:	4.236 m
Gross Tonnage:	496
Net Tonnage:	335
DWT:	1180
Propulsion:	Oil Engine(s), Direct drive
Flag:	Panama
Registered Owner:	Sea Freedom

The saga of the *Kyoto 1*, its crews and Adriatic Tankers begins with its purchase in April 1994. The ship was bought for $23,400,000 by Adriatic Tankers, using a loan allegedly from Barclays Bank. Trouble between the crew and Adriatic Tankers started almost immediately, although the problems were not brought to the attention of the ITF until December 1994. The crew contacted the ITF from Birkenhead, UK, on 1 December, informing them that they had not been paid for nine months and requesting assistance in obtaining their wages.

Before the ITF could act, the crew were persuaded by Adriatic Tankers to sail the vessel to Vigo in Spain. From there they went to the Netherlands, for repairs, arriving on 10 January 1995, although the *Kyoto 1*'s crew had now been on board and unpaid for ten months (a month longer than their contracts). Adriatic Tankers was telling the shipping world that non-payment of its crews was a thing of the past, and crews were in fact paid regularly and on time.

The ITF had been monitoring the *Kyoto 1* since Birkenhead, and the Dutch ITF were ready when the vessel arrived in the Netherlands. Faced with the arrest of the ship for crew's wages, Adriatic Tankers agreed to pay and repatriate the crew. Adriatic Tankers was, as usual, not true to its word, and it was not until May 1995 that the last seafarer was repatriated, although three were still awaiting their pay in Budapest. A new crew was recruited and embarked, and the *Kyoto 1* sailed from the Netherlands in May 1995.

A New Crew

On 14 July 1995, the crew of the *Kyoto 1* – four Russians and four Sri Lankans – made contact with the ITF from Morocco. Since taking over the vessel three months previously, they had been without pay, and the on-board situation with regard to medicines and provisions was dire. Bound for Rotterdam, the *Kyoto 1* arrived on 26 July 1995, and was immediately arrested by three former crewmen (with the help of the ITF) who were still owed wages totalling $61,000. The incumbent crew refused to discharge the cargo until they themselves were paid. They received their due wages ($23,500 in total) the next day. Although transacted through Adriatic Tankers, it is likely this was more related to the charterers having to pay the wages in order to get their cargo than any obligations by Adriatic Tankers. The company also paid the three ex-crewmen their outstanding wages on 29 July 1995, and the arrest of the *Kyoto 1* was lifted.

A month later, on 30 August 1995, the ship arrived in Durres, Albania, for dry-docking and repairs. On 11 October 1995, the crew reported that the *Kyoto 1* had cleared the dry dock after the repairs had been completed, but was arrested by the shipyard as they had not been paid for the work. The shipyard (jointly owned by the Gdansk shipyard in Poland and by the Albanian state) had previously repaired another Adriatic Tankers vessel, and wanted payment for the work done on both ships. Throughout this period, and since leaving Rotterdam, the crew were not paid nor were provisions supplied, so necessitating the contact with the ITF.

On 14 October, the ITF received a fax from the Sri Lankan complement of the crew to the effect that the Russians were selling what diesel remained and plant equipment to local fishing trawlers and traders. This fax clearly showed that there was disharmony amongst the crew, which under the circumstances is not suprising. The Sri Lankans were aggrieved as they were not beneficiaries to any of the cash from these sales, and further, they felt that the Russian crew were abusive to them, especially after drinking. Their life was further complicated by the refusal of the Russian cook to prepare their food.

Unfortunately, the situation on the *Kyoto 1* had grown to such proportions that the Sri Lankans told the ITF that they felt their lives were in danger from both the Russian crew and their Albanian friends. Multi-ethnic shipboard life is not easy at the best of times, but in periods of great stress, particularly when cooped up in port, with nothing to do and no money, as the *Kyoto 1* crew were experiencing, it is not suprising at all that disputes between the crew had arisen. The ITF immediately faxed the captain of the *Kyoto 1* to try to resolve the arguments, and find better ways to manage the mixed crew, which he agreed to try.

On 27 October 1995, the crew again faxed the ITF, reiterating their wage position, and asking for information regarding the financial and future prospects of Adriatic Tankers. The ITF told them about surveyors being sent by the various mortgagee banks to which Adriatic Tankers owed money in preparation for these vessels to be sold. The ITF asked the crew if they could find a local lawyer to represent them, and that they should make contact with their respective embassies and inform them of the situation.

Three days later, the crew notified the ITF that the agent's and shipyard's lawyer might be an acceptable choice. The crew were particularly interested in getting ITF approval for their choice of lawyer, as they needed the ITF to act as surety for the prospective legal bill. On 5 December 1995, an already bad situation for the crew was made worse by the refusal of the agent to supply any further provisions and water, due to Adriatic Tankers' non-payment of previous bills. To make matters worse, the shipyard informed the crew that their court case for the arrest of the vessel was to take place on the following day, and that the shipyard had no legal interest in the crew with regard to helping them recover their wages. The yard went so far as to say that should they gain possession of the *Kyoto 1* the crew's wages would not be paid.

The crew were naturally even more worried by this decision, and felt that, other than the ITF, the shipping-related industry had not the slightest interest in offering help and support. The crew, in a type of a retaliation, decided that if they ever did get their wages, they would not pay the recruiting agency, Brig Ltd, the 10 per cent of their wages as per their contracts. Under the circumstances, this would seem fair considering the problems the crew were having receiving their pay, with no help from Brig Ltd.

Legal Action

On 8 December 1995, the shipyard, via the Durres court in Albania, had the vessel arrested for the repair debt of $40,000. The shipyard did not actually gain possession of the *Kyoto 1* in lieu of the debt, which for the crew meant there was still a possibility of receiving their wages whilst they still controlled the vessel by their presence on board. Further, the agent who would no longer supply provisions to the crew suggested another Albanian lawyer, who might possibly be able to get their case for wages against Adriatic Tankers dealt with in the Albanian courts.

The new Albanian lawyer, Ilir Misa, was in many ways the only glimmer of hope on a rather bleak horizon. He stated his terms of a no-win, no-fee basis to the ITF, as well as informing them of the sorry and inadequate state of Albanian law when it came to dealing with foreign shipping and their crews who were having problems. According to Ilir Misa, in Albania there was no legal code relating to maritime law. The only codes available related to civil and labour law. This meant that it was most unlikely that the crew would be able to lodge a maritime lien against Adriatic Tankers and the *Kyoto 1* for their wages in Albania. In spite of this, Ilir Misa was prepared to attempt this course of action, although, this being the first case of this kind to be heard in Albania, it was unlikely to succeed.

The crew could do little in the ten months between December 1995 and October 1996 but wait and hope that their case might be heard by the court in Durres. During this long fruitless period, they were visited by numerous anonymous shipping representatives, who would come to the *Kyoto 1* to ascertain its condition with a view to buying the vessel. The crew were first made aware in March 1996 by the Dutch agent of Adriatic Tankers, Lindmar Shipping (who were also AT's in-house brokers), that Adriatic Tankers now intended to auction the *Kyoto 1*. In April 1996 they learnt of a meeting that took place between the Durres-Gdansk shipyard and Zissimatos. What actually transpired was not revealed to the crew, but the stream of visitors to the vessel for the purpose of buying her indicates that the sale of the ship and clearing the shipyard's debt would probably have been high on the agenda, although it's fairly certain that the plight of the seafarers was of no consequence in this discussion.

By May 1996, the situation remained much as before. The ITF wrote to both the president and the prime minister of Albania, informing them of the circumstances of the crew and requesting intervention on behalf of the seafarers. However, by now the political situation in Albania was already beginning to spin out of control, and these two people no doubt had more important problems on their minds than abandoned seafarers. The ITF received no answer.

In order to survive, the crew were selling whatever they could in order to buy provisions, water and gas. The stress of the situation was, however, taking a toll on all the seafarers. This was illustrated in late May 1996, when the crew contacted the ITF with regard to the mental condition of one of the Russian crew members. They asked the ITF to send funds to repatriate the man, as he was a danger to himself and other crew members. They also asked the ITF for funds for provisions, as they were fast running out of anything to sell.

When the ill seafarer was told of his imminent repatriation, he immediately phoned the ITF, pleading with them not to send him home. He said that he would 'rather die'. To return home without his wages meant that the 'nasty guys' who had loaned money to his family on the basis of his due wage, would demand repayment on his arrival. Without wages he could not repay the debt, and would end up losing his home, and perhaps his life, or worse, incur injuries to his family. After discussion with the crew, it was agreed with the ITF that the seafarer would not be repatriated at this time. His illness would be appraised daily, and should the crew feel that his staying on board was too detrimental, only then would he be repatriated. The money already sent for this intended repatriation was spent on provisions. By the end of May 1996, the crew and their families had been without any income for ten months.

In June 1996, Ilir Misa and the shipyard and agents lawyer believed they had found good grounds for the crew to lodge an appeal, simply on the basis that as the shipyard and agent had been successful in arresting the *Kyoto 1*, so should the crew's claim be successful. This process resulted in the crew's appeal being given the date of 10 October 1996 for a hearing at the Durres court. This was good news for the seafarers, as there was now hope of justice.

A Time of Desperation

Two days before the court hearing, on 8 October 1996, the crew were visited on board by two unknown men. They said the crew would lose their case in an Albanian court then the *Kyoto 1* would be auctioned and the crew would be forcibly removed from the ship without pay or repatriation costs. The feeling, unproven, was that these men were probably sent by Zissimatos in order to stop them getting a lien for their wages, as this would make the ship's sale even less attractive to prospective buyers. Whatever the reason for the visit, it did not intimidate the crew and they remained determined to have their day in court.

On the day before the hearing, the crew were quite optimistic. This view was short-lived: the court would not allow them to speak, and within five minutes of the beginning of proceedings the court had thrown out the appeal on the grounds that Albania had no jurisdiction over wages on a Panamanian-flagged vessel. Their legal view was that the crew should lodge their claim in Panama. This ruling was a crushing blow to the crew who by now had been on board the *Kyoto 1* for 18 months, the last 14 spent in virtual captivity in Durres, awaiting a favourable ruling. During this period, the news from the seafarers' families had got progressively worse. Some of the Sri Lankan families had recently lost their homes due to the debts they had incurred while waiting for the seafarers' wage dispute to be settled. Extracts from one of their letters to the ITF are reproduced:

Hon. President
ITF House
49–60 Borough Rd
London

From:
The Crew
MT *Kyoto 1*
Durres Gdansk Shipyard
Durres ALBANIA

Dear Sir
Our terrible case and our family problems stimulate us to write you continuously. Also there is no other places to inform or to write about ours and our families dearth cituations ...

To help our families whoes cituations are more harder than us
over here. Because of this companys scoundrelism. We and our
families facing this hard movements. We no send even a dollar
for their expenses for a period of 15 months ...
Our families are very poor. Impossible to do anything without
our help. The people who lend money for high interest rates
also stopped helping. After came to know our situations and
pressing for repayments. If not the lender will remove all
belongings by forcely from house. Because without our help.
So much money was borrowed from the lender ...
We can read all these hard red lines written through our wifes
and elders ...
Much of us are married people in this ship. More much
worrying for our childrens educations. No money for to pay
college fees. Some of them are in college hostel. Our childrens
future will be spoiled too.
The crew
MT *Kyoto 1*
19–10–1996

The choices facing the seafarers after the ruling of the court can
only be described as stark. On the one hand, they might be paid via
a successful Panamanian claim, although the ITF informed the
crew that this was a last-ditch option which, as it had never been
attempted before, was unlikely to succeed. The other option was
for the ITF to repatriate the crew, but without wages they would
then have to face irate money lenders and suffer some awful consequences to themselves and their families.

Their real hope lay in ignoring the arrest and moving the ship
to another country, which would uphold their lien under maritime
law. This was something which other Adriatic Tanker ships had
done, but the main problem was that the ship had no fuel or provisions. In desperation the crew turned to the ITF, and asked them
to supply the money so that they could make 'a run for it'. The
costs of reaching the various destinations chosen by the crew were:
$25,000 to Poland, $6000 to Greece or $5000 to Italy.

The ITF could not sanction this course of action with an arrested
vessel. They continued to propose that the wage claim be lodged in
Panama, and would publicise the crew's predicament in the hope
that this might mobilise public sympathy (and the conscience of
the British bank mortgagee). The *Kyoto 1* story did reach the press,
with both *TradeWinds*[1] and *Lloyd's List*[2] publishing articles about
Adriatic Tankers and the consequences being suffered by the *Kyoto*

1 and other Adriatic Tankers crews. *Lloyd's List* said that mortgagee banks should bear some responsibility for abandoned crews on their vessels. Unfortunately, this attempt to publicise the *Kyoto 1*'s saga had no tangible impact.

The crew were by now desperate for money, for their families more than for themselves, and were deeply depressed, as the extracts from one of the now-recurring pleas to the ITF show:

FROM: The Crew
        M.T. *Kyoto 1*
        Durres Gdansk Dry Dock
        Durres
        Albania
        Fax:–355 52 22249
        17 – 10 – 1996

TO: The Hon President
     I.T.F House
     London
Ref: May Day
     (S.O.S)
Dear Sir
On behalf of eight crews. We together sending this letter to you ...
We had been concerned with our case in Albania Law Court. We are afflicted and really bamboozled. Nothing can't do in this country. Now nearly 15 months we are in this port. Just dreaming when we will get clear from here. Only God knows. The day and the date ...
Some of our crew members are overburden with so many family problems. So we beg you for help, and please help us. Thank you Sir.
Yours faithfully
We remain
The crew
M.T.*Kyoto 1*
Durres
Albania

The Albanian lawyer, Ilir Misa, was also unhappy about the experience he and the crew had suffered at the hands of the Albanian judiciary. Despite this, he still felt that there was a way around the decision. He proposed that an Albanian national should take on the debt of the crew's wages, which would in turn allow for that person to arrest the *Kyoto 1* for the debt for the wages he had incurred against Adriatic Tankers. The flaw in this plan was finding an Albanian that would be prepared to risk so much on a dubious venture, and who could afford to pay the crew their wages. The ITF initially gave Ilir Misa the go-ahead to attempt this new plan of action, but after a short period the obstacles to the success of this were soon apparent, and the ITF requested Ilir Misa to halt this quest. In the meantime, the ITF had begun the process of registering the crew's wage claim in the Panamanian courts through the ITF's Panamanian lawyers. By putting a lien on the *Kyoto 1* in the Panamanian courts for the crew's wages this, in theory, would mean that the vessel could not be sold or moved off the Panama registry until the wage debt was paid.

Repatriation by the ITF

Whilst these legal wranglings were in motion, the Russian chief officer received a desperate message that he was needed at home as soon as possible because his daughter had contracted a serious kidney infection. Having no money, he appealed to the ITF to repatriate him and the ITF agreed. The crew too were in dire straits and asked the ITF for $1000 for provisions for the next two months. The ITF sent $2000 for the repatriation of the chief officer on 6 November 1996, and the request for money for provisions for the rest of the crew was also agreed.

Clearly, the continued presence of the crew in Albania was serving no purpose, for apart from there being no hope of a wage settlement, the civil strife was a real danger to the crew. On 14 November 1996, the ITF concluded that the best course of action would be to repatriate the crew as soon as possible, at the ITF's expense. This of course did not solve the crew's problem of returning home without wages. After much soul-searching, the ITF decided that in view of the crew's money problems at home, it would offer each seafarer a payment of $5000 on humanitarian grounds, plus their repatriation costs.

The 'soul-searching' that took place within the ITF was due to a real fear that these humanitarian payments might be setting a precedent which could easily be abused by other unscrupulous shipowners of Zissimatos' calibre. The ITF were loathe to send a message to scoundrels and incompetents that the ITF would not only repatriate their abandoned seafarers, but pay them wages as well. The ITF offer was faxed to the *Kyoto 1*'s seafarers on 19 November 1996. Both the Russian and the Sri Lankan crew accepted the offer, and both groups asked for the offer to be extended to the repatriated chief officer. The Sri Lankans asked for the offer to be increased to $6000, understandable due to their predicament, but unrealistic under the circumstances. The humanitarian payment, for the record, was not increased, but was extended to include the repatriated Russian chief officer. The ITF was hoping to get the men home in time for Christmas 1996, but the 'Jonah' syndrome attached to the *Kyoto 1* was still alive and well.

The captain and first engineer were told by the authorities when the ITF offer was made that they would not be allowed to leave the vessel until the arrest of the *Kyoto 1* was lifted. This development would in fact mean that the captain and first engineer were in an even worse position than state prisoners, even though they were on board the *Kyoto 1*. The Albanian state was not prepared to pay them to caretake the ship, nor to supply provisions, nor to work ashore: this meant that they would starve, which, but for the help of some local people and the ITF, might well have been the case.

The money for repatriation and the humanitarian payment arrived in Albania on 10 December 1996. Because the captain and first engineer could not leave, the ITF stressed that their share of the money should not be used to maintain themselves on board the *Kyoto 1*, but should be sent to their families. The ITF emphasised that the payment was of a 'one-off' nature – it would not be repeated. The ITF, in wishing the crew good luck for the future, warned them that when they next sought employment, to watch out for a company called Ionian Transport, as the ITF believed this to be a new Zissimatos company. They had information to the effect that Zissimatos was once more successfully raising bank loans and was involved in the shipping industry. They advised the crew to check with them about any possible employer should they have the slightest doubts.

The money from the ITF had been sent via the ship agent in Durres on 12 December 1996. However, the crew informed the ITF that the agent was refusing to pass on the money as he wanted to recover his debts for the provisions he supplied in the past. After a brief talk with the ITF, the agent agreed to pass on the money to the crew, but also asked the ITF to pay Adriatic Tankers' provisioning bill. The ITF refused to do this for a number of reasons, but mainly on the grounds that the agent, unlike the crew, had recourse to Albanian law to arrest the ship and recover his debts. By 31 December 1996, to everyone's relief, the four Sri Lankans and the Russian cook had been repatriated. The captain and first engi-

neer, due to Albanian law, remained on board with little to look
forward to.

Escape of the Ship

In early March 1997, fighting broke out in Albania, and the airport
came under rebel control. The ITF were concerned for the *Kyoto 1*'s
captain and the first engineer still aboard the ship. On 14 March
1997, the *Kyoto 1* finally made headline news as a ship bringing
refugees from Albania to Italy. The Italians were not sympathetic
and designated the refugees as illegal immigrants, and a new crew
of the *Kyoto 1* as 'terrorists'! The captain and the first engineer were
arrested as terrorists in the port of Brindisi, even though the
captain had documents from the shipyard in Durres addressed to
the Italian Coast Guard which claimed that the shipyard had
requested him to move the ship to Italy in view of the unrest in
Albania. Ironically, they were also charged with sailing an unseaworthy ship.

For the ship to have taken fuel on board in Albania, there must
have been a degree of complicity with the shipyard and port
authorities. This had offered the captain the best chance of escape,
with refugees paying the bills. It has subsequently been alleged that
each refugee paid $800 for the voyage to Brindisi, and estimates of
the number of refugees on board varied from 300 to 800! The
captain also pointed out, however, that it was the people who came
on board with guns who collected the money and instructed him.
The 'new crew' were described by the Italian authorities as
Albanian and Turkish 'guerrillas' and were hastily deported from
Italy (no doubt with their profits secure), leaving the captain and
first engineer alone and under ship arrest. They were once more
prisoners on board, and were facing imprisonment terms of two
years and/or a fine of two million lire. They were in a desperate
state and it was some time before the authorities would even allow
supplies of oil and food to be brought aboard. The weather was by
then wet and cold.

In March 1998 ITF and Italian legal representation were successful in getting criminal charges against the master and the chief
engineer dropped. They were now free to return home, but without
wages, and after two years and eight months of hardship.

The story of the *Kyoto 1* and the horrific neglect of its crew by
the owners, Adriatic Tankers; the lack of interest by the flag state
and the port state, and disregard by the bank mortgagees was
allowed to go on for over two years. In 1998 their suffering was still

not over. The best hope is that in future the crew of *Kyoto 1* will get their hard-earned pay and that some lessons are learnt in law, especially by wealthier people who finance ships and ought to know better.

8

Seafarers and Their Families and Allies

With Adriatic Tankers, as in all other cases of abandonment, the most frequently recurring pleas from the seafarers were for their families. Many seafarers borrowed from money lenders to pay manning agencies, sometimes as a bribe to an individual. Several had to borrow money for fares to join vessels, and then borrowed again to keep the families going until the first allotment was received. When this was not paid, and months passed, it was necessary for the family to raise further loans. There are thick files of independent letters to the ITF and messages to the missions trying to convey the fears sailors have for the welfare of their families. Two of the senior crew of the *Assos Bay* wrote on 17 October 1996:

> One of us ... is the only breadwinner in his family ... The company has left his family without any means to support itself since it does not pay him his earnings. This has led to him having to borrow money subject to high rates of interest in order to support his family, as a result of which he has suffered financial loss in the sum of $3,000.

This letter was written just prior to the completion of an eight-month contract, in which time the family had received only $550 out of total allotments due of $7560. In this case Fairwind Shipping managed to take possession of the ship for the mortgagees, paid the crews off and repatriated them.

The Burmese crew of the *Oceania I* were faced with more complex problems, as a letter to the ITF demonstrates:

> We are not possible to get back to Mynamar without money. If we cannot pay our taxes to the military government (on return) he will keep our passports and seaman books and never give them back to use. If we have no passport and seam book, we can not join another ship ...[1]

The seafarers found themselves in impossible situations, either living in hotels awaiting payment on the promises of Adriatic, or on board the vessels unable to leave. If they did so, the ship could have been declared abandoned, which would have drastically reduced their ability to recover wages owed. This waiting caused, in many cases, further concern when problems were experienced at home. For example it necessitated immediate repatriations due to hospitalisation of seafarers' wives from the *Thunder I*, *Stainless Hawk* and *Ionian Star*. Such was the desperation that the first engineer of the *Cape Breeze* resorted to selling the ship's emergency radio to fund his passage home, following his daughter's injury in a car crash.

Instances of hardship were further evidenced not only by families waiting in vain for wages, but by the lack of compensation to the family for loss of life of a seafarer while serving aboard Adriatic's vessels. One-off compensation payments were sometimes received in the course of time, but the facts are the company or their agents were often responsible for deaths in the first place as a result of neglect. This is not often revealed in enquiries. Examples of deaths on board several of these vessels are shown in Table 8.1.

Table 8.1 Seafarers' deaths aboard Adriatic Tankers vessels

Vessel	Circumstances of death
Fiskardo Bay	Captain died of a heart attack due to lack of medical assistance. Agents refused to provide emergency assistance and it was only due to Fairwind's intervention that the UK Club landed the body. $60,000 in compensation received by widow through ITF assistance.
Lourdas	Widow of ex-AB paid $20,000 in death compensation following death from meningitis, this was secured through ITF efforts.
Maistros I	Court awarded $50,000 to mother of seafarer who had died on board. The compensation cheque from Adriatic Tankers bounced.
Nova Progress	Widow of seafarer seeking help from the ITF in obtaining compensation for husband's death.
Stainless Queen	Seafarer died of a heart attack with the widow receiving no support from Adriatic Tankers in any matters concerning her husband's death. In July 1998 this ship was still trading in Nigerian waters, out of reach of creditors.
Starlight	Adriatic Tankers considering a claim for $60,000 for loss of life of a seafarer.

In the case of the *Stainless Queen*, the following has been extracted from a letter from the New Russia Marine Workers' Union to the ITF in London dated 15 February 1996 concerning the seafarer's widow:

> ... her husband ... passed away from heart attack 31.12.95. Nothing was heard about the deceased since that time.
>
> Actually, nobody is aware of the details of the accident. The representatives of Adriatic Tankers Co. do not undertake anything in investigating the case and in granting assistance to the relatives.
>
> Especially, I was frustrated by the great indifference and irresponsibility of these people and the fact that the company does not even contribute to deliver the body of the deceased to the relatives.[2]

The company frequently prevented ill seafarers from receiving medical and dental treatment. One able seaman on the *Assos Bay*, as a direct result of non-treatment of a chronic gum disease, subsequently required dental treatment worth thousands of dollars to rectify the situation. There were more tragic consequences for families with the suicide of the chief officer aboard the *Stainless Supporter* and the deaths of three crew members from the *Ocean Breeze I*, following attempts to desert the ship.

Many of the seamen and their families were very confused as well as desperate. The Russian seafarers in particular were often initially disorientated. In the old Soviet system, a sea-going career was desirable and sought after. The ships had totally Russian crews, leave was predictable, and although wages and conditions were well below those of western seafarers they received some payments in foreign currency, and were able to see the world and to buy consumer goods not available in the USSR.

The first taste of free enterprise capitalism on ships like those of Adriatic Tankers (and to some extent on their own newly privatised vessels) came as a shock. As letters show, there was anger and also concern for families dependent on a new breed of money lender in Russia.

Letters from Third World seafarers are often more pathetic, as in the plea from a Pakistani sailor who says he does not want a campaign for what he is entitled to, he just wants his basic pay and to go home.

Now sir,

In these more than 6 months in my house for my children and wife there is nothing they want money. Also my wife is sick and hospitalised. How can I wait more two months. I don't want I.T.F. wages, I don't want my overtime money or extra job money. I only want my basic wages and want to go home. WHO WILL HELP ME FOR GETTING MY MONEY.

There was always great relief when the seafarers were able to let their families know that they had left these ships and were now in hotels about to be paid and repatriated. There was often an anti-climax to this. It is difficult to know just how many of these crews were left for long periods in hotels extending from Singapore to Budapest, but Table 8.2 gives some indication over the period 1995–96.

Table 8.2   Adriatic crews stranded in hotels 1995–96

Vessel	Details
Annapurna	Crew in Budapest
Assos Bay	Crew in Budapest
	Crew in Rotterdam
Atheras Bay	Crew in Budapest for one month
Camellia	Crew members deported home from Rotterdam after refusing to accept offer put forward. One repatriated by ITF.
	Russian crew members unpaid in Singapore. Fined $200 per man for overstaying their visas.
Cape Spirit	Ex-crew members in Rotterdam
	Russian crew members unpaid for five months in Rotterdam
	Crew members in Budapest
Dolicha Bay	Crew members in Rotterdam unpaid for 3–6 weeks
	Crew in Budapest awaiting wages
East Wind	Crew transferred from *Princess of Adriatic*. Used as a hotel for Vietnamese while awaiting wages.
Eastern Navigator	Crew members in Rotterdam, repatriated by ITF
Fiskardo Bay	Russian crew members in Amsterdam hotel awaiting eight months' wages
	Crew members in Budapest for up to three months

Vessel	Details
Fuji	Crew in Budapest for 2.5 months. Crew repatriated from hotel over eight months
Hegg	Charter for vessel offered in payment for hotel in Rotterdam, charter failed
Hikari I	Crew waiting for wages in Budapest
Ionian Breeze	Yugoslav crew in Singapore waiting for wages, one not paid for eight months
Ionian Challenger	Relief crew stuck in Madras with Visas running out, vessel in Madras outer anchorage
Ionian Eagle	Crew members in Rotterdam and Budapest. Budapest complaining about hotel bills. Crew members repatriated at ITF's expense
Ionian Glory	Crew members in Rotterdam awaiting payment
Ionian Jade	Crew members in Rotterdam, partly paid and repatriated
Ionian Light	Russian crew members in Budapest for 2.5 months awaiting nine months' wages
Ionian Master	Ex-crew members in Rotterdam, deported home
	Crew members in Rotterdam hotel
Ionian Prince	Crew members in Seoul
	Crew members in Singapore for three weeks
Ionian Sky	Crew in Budapest for over three months
Ionian Sprinter	Crew members in Piraeus awaiting several weeks' wages
Ionian Wave	Crew paid at Rouen and repatriated
Irene VII	Crew in Budapest for two months
	Crew in Budapest for nine months
Kyoto I	Ex-crew members in Budapest awaiting payment
Lourdas	Ex-crew members in Budapest and having to go to Rotterdam to await outstanding wages
Maistros I	Ex-crew members repatriated home from Rotterdam
Muroran	Crew in Rotterdam awaiting wages
Myrtos Bay	Crew in Budapest awaiting payment
Nova Progress	Ex-crew members repatriated after five months waiting for payment in Amsterdam

Vessel	Details
Ocean Sky	Crew in Piraeus awaiting wages
Oceania Glory	Russian crew in Amsterdam awaiting wages
Otaru I	Ex-crew in Piraeus awaiting wages
Poros Bay	Ex-crew in Budapest for three months awaiting wages
Ro Ro Runner	Ex-crew in Budapest
Ro Ro Sprinter	Ex-crew in Budapest for 2.5 months
Southern Navigator	Crew awaiting wages in Amsterdam for 50 days
Sprinter	Ex-crew members repatriated from Rotterdam by ITF
Stainless Bird	Ex-crew in Budapest awaiting payment
Stainless Commander	Ex-crew in Piraeus awaiting payment
Stainless Fighters	Ex-crew in Piraeus awaiting wages
	Ex-crew in Budapest awaiting wages
Stainless Hawk	Crew members repatriated home from Rotterdam
	Crew in Budapest for 2.5 months
Stainless Hyogo	Crew in Rotterdam awaiting payment
Stainless Kobe	Ex-crew members repatriated home from Rotterdam
	Ex-crew in Budapest
Stainless Pride	Crew in Budapest awaiting wages
Stainless Queen	Ex-crew repatriated from Rotterdam
	Ex-crew in Budapest
Stainless Shield	Crew member in Piraeus awaiting payment
Stainless Supporter	Ex-crew in Budapest
Stainless Sword	Master in Rotterdam hotel awaiting payment
Starlight	Ex-crew in Budapest awaiting payment
	Ex-crew in France awaiting payment
Thunder I	Ex-crew in Budapest awaiting pay and repatriation

Source: ITF records.

The seafarers concerned were not the only people to suffer. In Rotterdam, at least six hotels were left with unpaid bills of nearly $400,000 by the end of August 1995.[3] In one instance, Rotterdam hotels were offered the proceeds of a vessel charter in payment of outstanding bills – the charter subsequently failed but Adriatic's agent in Rotterdam did not inform the hotels of this. The ITF inspector in Rotterdam gave the ITF a financial claim and an example of problems experienced by one particular hotel.

> ... claims of the crew from the *Stainless Kobe*, who were accommodated at hotel KLARENBEEK. This is the small family hotel who suffered financial trouble due to the fact that Lindmar did not pay the accommodation for the crew. It is (enclosed) a handwritten statement from Miss Klarenbeek and the company still have to pay f27,647.00.[4]

The Seafarers' Allies

Those assisting seafarers and their families include the International Transport Workers' Federation, the various Christian missions to seamen, local charities and individuals world-wide. There were several organisations whose tasks were to recover abandoned ships on behalf of mortgagees, including Fairwind Shipping and Marine Risk Management. They were able to move ships to suitable jurisdiction where arrests could take place and ships sold. These were commercial agencies, but co-operation between them, the lenders and the ITF enabled seafarers to obtain back-wages and be repatriated.

The International Transport Workers' Federation

The ITF is involved globally on behalf of abused and abandoned seafarers. They focus primarily, but not exclusively, on the issues within the FOC sector and help is often given to seafarers whether or not they are members of an ITF-affiliated union.

Not all seafarers in difficulties are able to contact ITF. Under some regimes, trade unions are banned; in other cases seafarers have had to sign contracts prohibiting contact with the ITF or unions, and there is always the underlying threat to families and of blacklisting if these 'agreements' are violated. The ITF in turn have to be careful they are not accused of inciting mutiny, or endangering ships, in giving advice to seafarers about actions which they can take on board the ship.

On the other hand, ITF have maintained that they have no wish to be unfair to shipping companies which are trying their best in difficult economic circumstances. In a letter to an affiliated trade union which had criticised ITF for being too lenient with Adriatic in not getting more vessels arrested, the head of the Special Seafarers' Department (SSD) wrote:

> The reality is however that this approach, if continued to its logical conclusion, would have resulted in: a) the bankruptcy of Adriatic Tankers and b) as a result, the loss of over 2,000 seafaring jobs. This is clearly not in the long-term interests of these seafarers. We took the view that it would be better to allow Adriatic vessels to trade on the clear understanding that they pay all the outstanding claims within a given period. Our reason was simple logic – when the ships trade they make money, the company pays the seafarers, otherwise everyone loses. (25 June 1995)

Another area in which ITF had to be careful was with possible bogus complaints. The SSD regularly receive communications direct from seafarers (or through inspectors) about grievances of every description. Some they can reject as trivial, or clearly bogus. Or it is a communication they have seen before – a standard letter which comes as a matter of course from some sailors (the so-called 'sea lawyers') who move between ships.

Not all seafarers belong to unions affiliated to ITF, nevertheless complaints from all are dealt with. It is also a fact that unions have been suspended from affiliation to the ITF for not representing members properly. Some unions which emerged from the old institutions of eastern Europe and elsewhere have inheritances as government agencies, and still tolerate bad conditions on vessels under national flags. There are cases also of corrupt officials acting as paid job agents. According to the general secretary of the ITF, David Cockroft:

> We know that not all our affiliated unions are perfect either, and one aspect of our policy review is that we shall be providing technical assistance to ensure that all our unions have the capacity to properly represent their members. And we are insisting on financial transparency from all ITF affiliates together with minimum standards laying down the services which seafarers have the right to expect from their unions.[5]

But most complaints to the ITF are real, and when complaints are received a procedure is put in place. Usually the shipping company is contacted, an explanation asked for, and the complaint verified in other ways. After that initial exchange a considerable amount of time, effort and cost is likely to be incurred by the ITF on behalf of the seafarers. This is one of their main functions, but not entirely so as an international organisation. A brief outline of the ITF and its wider functions may be useful before dealing with the role as allies to the seafarers employed by Adriatic Tankers.

The Wider Functions of the ITF

The international Transport Workers' Federation, whose head office is in London, has 398 affiliated unions in 105 countries. It has a membership of over 4.3 million of which 680,000 (16 per cent) are in seafarer unions. With a significant percentage of sea-faring members, a considerable amount of the ITF's work deals with relationships between shipowners and crews.

The Federation has run a campaign against flags of convenience for fifty years, a campaign which adjusts its aims along with the changes that take place within the industry itself. It lays down its own scale of minimum wages and minimum safe crewing. These levels are contained in a series of agreements produced by the ITF as its acceptable standards for seafarers. A shipping company or manning agent which accedes to these agreements is then issued with a 'Blue Certificate' for each ship which indicates that the vessel is in compliance with the ITF standards. This certificate is an important part of the ship's documentation.

The reason for the ITF's campaign against FOCs is due to the lack of regulation from a number of these states concerning the welfare of the seafarers working under their flags. UNCTAD's failure to achieve adequate regulation of shipping registers has contributed to a growth in the number of obscure maritime flags.[6] This growth is accompanied by a parallel increase in the number of complaints received from seafarers concerning conditions and pay aboard sub-standard ships. Safety standards are another victim of lax regulations and the pollution risk to an environmentally conscious world is consequently increased.

The ITF trains inspectors who are members of affiliated unions throughout the world. These inspectors board vessels in their own areas to inspect the working conditions and to ensure that any agreements in force are being adhered to. If they discover that the shipowner is not in compliance with any aspect of the agreement then they attempt to negotiate. If these negotiations are unsuc-cessful, the inspectors will attempt to instigate a boycott against the vessel by using their links with the dock-workers, tug crew's unions or pilots.

The objective of the ITF boycott is to prevent the ship from continuing her voyage if pay and conditions are below ITF standards. To avoid disruption, many charterers and terminal operators prefer, or even insist, that a vessel is in possession of a Blue Certificate before they will have dealings with it. Several FOC owners have ITF agreements and are more able to compete with less scrupulous owners as these are not deterred from entering ITF-strong areas by fear of detention. Partly as a result of this some FOC vessels compare well with those of certain national flags.

As well as recommending minimum standards, the ITF requires a shipowner who has signed an agreement to contribute to the ITF Seafarers' International Assistance, Welfare and Protection Fund. The investment of these funds support the ITF Seafarers' Trust which was established in 1981. This Trust has charitable status and is dedicated to the spiritual, moral and physical welfare of seafarers; it contributes to many schemes benefiting seafarers throughout the world. It has made contributions to missions for seamen, funded the establishment of the Seafarers' International Research Centre at the University of Cardiff, donated to the World Maritime University in Sweden, and funded the secretariat for the International Committee on Seafarers' Welfare, amongst several other projects and many donations.

The ITF also plays a humanitarian role. The Federation, through its affiliates, keeps a close watch on ships of all flags and the conditions in which the crew live. They stand as advocates for seafarers with grievances – the Special Seafarers' Department deals with daily complaints from vessels in port and at sea. It is one of the busiest sections within the ITF.

Within the SSD is the Actions Unit, which is the point of contact with the seafarer – a number of different language skills are required to deal with the incoming calls. Once contact has been made, a file is opened on each vessel and the case followed through. The SSD may then communicate with the shipowner, manning agent or management company, although strict confidentiality is kept where the complainant's identity is concerned.[7]

Relations with Adriatic Tanker Company

A number of Adriatic Tankers' vessels had ITF agreements and were issued with Blue Certificates, but, by mid-1993, reports came into the ITF's offices in London of crews unpaid for months. Most of these reports claimed that the company was four to five months in arrears. It was then that the crews decided it was time to obtain ITF help.

There had been smaller disputes with the company before this but most had been fairly quickly cleared up. They apparently arose from temporary cash-flow problems and difficulties with currency exchange. These were accepted by the ITF as minor issues and there was no hint in 1993 of the major problems that lay ahead.

Some of the complaints received from seafarers indicated that they were close to the end of their contracts and they did not trust Adriatic Tankers to pay them when the time came for crews to sign off. The company's answer to these criticisms was that the contracts signed by the seafarers, stipulated a method of payment which was being adhered to and that there was no substance to the complaints. Zissimatos claimed that 'complaints from some individual crewmen are inevitable, given that Adriatic has up to 2,000 seafarers on its ships at anyone time'.[8]

It was apparent also that the company's debts were building up in other areas with complaints from agencies in various ports about insufficient funds being allocated for stays in port. The ITF maintained that over thirty Adriatic vessels were in dispute with either crews, bunker suppliers, ship chandlers or a combination of these.[9] By March 1995 it was common for the company to be eight months or so behind in the payment of its seafarers and those who had left ships with the promise of payment after repatriation or while waiting in hotels, were owed as much as a full year's wages. Despite this, Adriatic was still buying vessels to join the fleet and recruiting crews for those ships, knowing that it would have difficulty paying them.

In late April 1995, Panagis Zissimatos visited the ITF offices in London to negotiate an agreement to prevent Adriatic Tankers from being included in the ITF blacklist of shipowners. The ITF had considered arresting the entire fleet but in May they stated that 'undertakings given by Adriatic at the meeting were being met and ships which were under arrest, or the subject of industrial action, were sailing'.[10]

The ITF claimed that Zissimatos had agreed to allow them to work with the company's senior management to resolve the various crew disputes because, in the words of an ITF spokesman: 'We got the impression we were not dealing with the right people at Adriatic, we needed to go to the top. I don't want to criticise the management but I think they did not know what each other was doing. We have a commitment that claims will be dealt with.' He said that promises had been made and broken in the past.[11]

It was clear at this time that the Federation's negotiators cautiously believed this agreement would resolve the crew payment disputes, which by then amounted to $3 million and it looked as if Adriatic Tankers had the intention of clearing up its debts and creating a better working relationship with them. The company also felt that the deal would improve its image in the market generally; however, this suffered another setback shortly afterwards when the company was expelled by the independent tanker owners' group, Intertanko.

On 1 June 1995, a two-day follow-up meeting was held in Adriatic's offices in Piraeus at which a discussion took place concerning future employment agreements between the ITF and the company. Adriatic agreed to put ITF agreements on 80 of its ships and a schedule was to be agreed to decide how to solve those disputes still outstanding while keeping the ships trading. However, a spokesman at ITF's offices in London said that a decision whether or not to include Adriatic in their blacklist would be taken after monitoring the company's June performance.[12]

By the first week in July, the agreed settlements made at the two meetings had only been partly carried out, as there were still a number of vessels in Europe and the US with unpaid crew members aboard and the ITF was considering renewed action against Adriatic. The company had surprised observers of the dispute by poaching the ITF official who had led the talks between the two parties. Zissimatos may have tempted Captain Charlie Milne, a former ship manager, by offering him a free hand to do what he could to lift the company out of its current doldrums,[13] while Zissimatos went off to try to secure further funding. Whatever the reason, Milne departed for Greece with an intimate knowledge of the ITF's strategy in dealing with rogue shipowners and was soon displaying a high profile in the dispute, but this time against the ITF and the seafarers rather than for them. This defection led to some seafarers becoming cynical about external support for their cause, as may be appreciated by a letter from the officers and crew of the *Ionian Sailor*:

m.v. 'IONIAN SAILOR'   TULCEA July 26th, 1995

To: ITF LONDON
Att: SSD, Action department
Fax: 44 71 407115/   71 3577871

FM: OFFICER & CREW OF m/v 'IONIAN SAILOR'

Dear Sirs,
Please be advised that this morning allready passed 144 hors
that We are in HUNGER STRIKE against our company which
keeps our families hungry more than 15 months.
We very hoped in Your full support in this desperate try to save
our famalies, but until today (in last 20 days) We didn't receive
anything from ITF. We have only ADRIATIC'S empty promises.
Charlie Milne's case consolidates us in our certainty that We
must not believe to anybody, any more.
Please be advised that our health condition getting worse and
worse from minute to minute.

We hope that you believe us that We shall not stop this strike
until We receive our full salaries. This is our strong decision
and nobody can change it.
In hope that We shall get Your full support,
    BEST REGARDS

cc: Mr. Mihailciociu/Constanca

Following the Milne affair, the ITF's patience ran out, and towards
the end of July it gave Adriatic a deadline to pay all its outstanding
wage bills or face 'all-out war'.[14] This was the second deadline that
had been set and the Federation was no longer willing to allow more
time or to listen to any more lies from the company. Adriatic
claimed to be trying to obtain further loans to see it through the
period and to enable it to pay off waiting crews, but no results were
forthcoming.

The *Ionian Sailor* hunger strike was on, while there were over
seventy of the company's crew members waiting in Budapest
hotels for payment from their last voyages. Rotterdam too had 28
Adriatic seafarers awaiting payment and that number was increasing as more seafarers were sent in from other company ships.
Adriatic was relieving them on board their ships with other crews,
and promising them payment and repatriation after they arrived at
the hotels. An ITF inspector sent out to hotels in Budapest warned
'These seamen in Budapest were on 7 to 12 month contracts and
with the period spent in the hotels they have been away from
home for more than a year, they are becoming suicidal.'[15]

Adriatic Tankers placed a statement in *Lloyd's List* claiming that
it had 'kept its agreements and deadlines in all respects'.[16] The ITF
replied to this with a press release of their own denying a corporate
campaign against the company and claiming that its efforts to co-

ordinate legal action against Adriatic stemmed from requests from crew members who had been 'underpaid, unpaid and faced with a trail of broken promises by the company over a period of many months'.[17]

In fact the ITF were still being patient because a third deadline had been set for 31 July for final crew payments to be made, but this again passed with no progress. The Federation found that it was devoting a great deal of time, money and staff to this company, which was putting a terrific strain on ITF infrastructure.[18] The ITF issued another press release announcing a public meeting in Rotterdam for the seafarers stranded there. These men were coming under pressure from the local authorities who considered that they were now in the country illegally because some of them had been there for months.

It was due to deportation threats that the ITF considered repatriating the men at the ITF's expense while continuing to fight for their wages. Whereas the best chance that a seafarer has to get his back wages is to stay with his ship, in this case there was nothing to be gained by leaving the crews in the hotel, except for the pressure by hoteliers on Adriatic agents to pay the accommodation bills, which was frequently futile. The cost to the ITF was over $1 million.

Help from the Christian Missions

The Christian missions most involved in the Adriatic Tankers case were the Missions to Seamen (Flying Angel) and the Apostleship Of the Sea (Stella Maris). Both of these societies, along with those shown in Table 8.3, and some others, give assistance to seafarers and their families throughout the world.

Table 8.3   Charitable organisations directly involved with Adriatic seafarers

Association Marseillaise des Amis des Marins
Casa Del Marino
Greek Red Cross
The Apostleship of the Sea
The Flying Angel
The International Sailors Society
UK Burmese Support Group
The British Sailors Society
The Norwegian Seamens Church

Source: Mission and ITF records.

The port chaplains of different Christian denominations have as their main objectives the spiritual and material interests of seafarers and they often work in concert and coordinate their experiences and knowledge through the International Christian Maritime Association (ICMA). Since the Adriatic debacle the International Committee on Seafarers' Welfare (ICSW) has also stepped up its activities to facilitate communication between seafarers and supporting bodies.

Without the help of the charitable bodies and individuals, the plight of the seafarers would have been even more intolerable. Yet the missions emphasise the Adriatic case is not unique – they are regularly called upon to support seafarers stranded in ports around the world. However, the scale of the Adriatic Tankers collapse was unique, with so many mission centres called on simultaneously to provide assistance. Table 8.4 gives several of the locations of the missions where such support was given to the ships listed.

Table 8.4   Some Christian missions supporting Adriatic seafarers

Location	Vessels Involved
Melbourne, Australia	*Ionian Mariner*
Pusan, Korea	*Sapporo*
Rotterdam, Netherlands	*Ionian Prince*
	Ionian Glory
Tilbury, UK	*Countess*
Falmouth, UK	*Stainless Hawk*
Rouen, France	*Stainless Glory*
Dubai & UAE coast	*Annapurna*
Felixstowe, UK	*Ionian Eagle*
Durban, South Africa	*Stainless Hyogo, Stainless Kobe, Anchen, Cape Spirit*
Rouen, France	*Stainless Glory*
Dunkerque, France	*Starlight*
Kobe, Japan	*Stainless Supporter*
Larnaca, Cyprus	*Seiko*
Barcelona, Spain	*Captain Lucas II*
Many other vessels received support through the offices of the Mission, for example	*Fiscado Bay* *Lourdas* *Assos Bay* *Myrtos Bay* *Argostoli Bay*

Source: Mission correspondence

The mission is often the first place of call for a seafarer going ashore. Frequently, the mission is established close to the port gate and offers a quiet place for seafarers to relax and obtain information about the port. They can also get personal advice, make telephone calls home and socialise. Although Christian religious services are offered in the mission's chapel, it is stressed to visiting seafarers that all denominations and religions are welcome to use the facilities and to seek a wide variety of advice and support from the resident chaplain.

In practice, the open-door mission works extremely well. A visit to any mission throughout the world will show seafarers of many nationalities and diverse beliefs using it as a haven away from shipboard life. Competitions are often organised between ship's teams for football or other games, and a mission will regularly show films and videos in the evening as well as offering a bar, games and sometimes a swimming pool.

The missions all offer both moral and spiritual support to seafarers in trouble, which is why they played such an important part in the care of distressed seafarers abandoned, unpaid, and ignored by Adriatic Tankers. As charitable organisations, they act as a catch-all for those forsaken through acts of unscrupulous shipowners. Without realising it, the Adriatic company helped the missions in this task by tending to group ships which were waiting for orders in specific ports, thereby allowing certain missions to care for a number of vessels at the same time. Unfortunately this put a much greater load on some chaplains but that seems to have been borne cheerfully and efficiently.

One of the ways in which pressure could be brought upon Adriatic Tankers was by threatening it with bad publicity. In the early days of the company's problems, if there was any chance of a potential charterer or buyer being scared away by a story of an unpaid crew on an Adriatic vessel, then the office would usually quickly try to solve the problem. The missions played an important role in this way by publicising the observed and reported abuses to seafarers. However, in most large ports around the world, the authorities are very security-conscious and are unwilling to allow journalists and camera crews into port areas to interview ship's crews about reported problems. As the missions tried to publicise the plight of cheated seafarers on Adriatic Tankers' vessels in this way, these port restrictions caused a further complication.

The chaplains try to visit many ships and are of course welcomed in most port areas. They are careful not to abuse that welcome by interfering with the working of the ship or the port.

This care also extends to the use of the media in combating the abuse of seafarers. Local press may be persuaded to carry articles on a crew's plight but local sensitivities also need to be taken into consideration. These include security, political and religious matters. An Islamic country might not wish the work of a Christian organisation prominently displayed in a local journal if it outlined any deficiency of its authorities, and it may sometimes be difficult to explain that the mission's concern was for seafarers of any nationality or religion.

A number of the missions were engaged in purchasing food, water and even some diesel oil to keep Adriatic ship generators running. To do this, they often used the Samaritan Fund which is contributed to by a number of organisations specifically for the well-being of seafarers, for example:

> In Dubai, the *Annapurna* has been under arrest for five months and the Russian and Sri Lankan crew are not allowed out of the port. Some food has been put on board by the agents, but mission chaplain Trevor Hearn has been supplementing their provisions. And when the fuel ran out he started supplying gas cylinders so the crew could at least cook some hot food. But as important as the material help being given by our chaplain are his regular visits to their ship to provide a listening ear and a reassuring presence. (The Revd Canon Glyn Jones, Feb. 1996)[19]

Chaplains were also able to persuade some agents and suppliers that they had a charitable duty to those seafarers and that they would subsequently be paid through the eventual sale of the vessel at judicial auction, for example:

> The Tanker *Captain Lucas II*, at Barcelona
> (Crew 12 Koreans, 5 Burmese, 2 Chinese)
> ... Stella Maris in Barcelona together with Coritas and a ship chandler provided them with food and tobacco. After dealing with the Port authorities, the vessel got fresh water and also gas oil for the refrigerator and the kitchen ... The ship was dirty and rusted. It was a hard time for the crew. The fact they belonged to different countries caused some distrust between them. (extract from letter from Ricardo Rodriguez-Martos, Apostolado Del Mar, 1 August 1997)[20]

In supplying basic necessities to vessels, the mission had to be careful not to give Adriatic Tankers the idea that they no longer had any responsibility towards their own men. A company as poorly run as Adriatic would gladly have abandoned even more ships if it thought that someone else was footing the bill for keeping the crews alive; the company had already done enough harm to its employees without being given an excuse to do more.

There were cases where the mission actually housed some crew members. When the *Countess* was detained by port-state control in Tilbury, the two remaining crew members left on board (the captain and the bo'sun) were housed in the Stella Maris Centre because the conditions on board the vessel were described by the chaplain as 'a disgrace'. The mission even took it upon themselves to pay hotel bills in cases where all other possibilities had been exhausted.

There were instances when a mission chaplain would have to travel considerable distances to visit vessels that were in holding anchorages or in remote ports. Contact with the ships at anchor was often difficult as on most of them the communications systems were discontinued due to unpaid bills. A master described a voyage in which one shore radio station after another was denied for communication purposes as the unpaid bills mounted. This of course led to increasing frustration among the seafarers as they did not know what was going on either with the company or at home. Being out of touch meant that many of them were unaware for a long time that their salaries were not being paid.

On many ships the only means of communication left was VHF radio and as this was a short-range medium, it was only of limited use. Fortunately, there was a certain amount of sympathy for the seafarers among several ships' agents and suppliers and some of them were kind enough to let the Adriatic crews and the mission chaplains use their facilities to contact unions and homes. Phones and fax machines were made available for incoming messages enabling the missions and the ITF to advise and inform the otherwise isolated ship's crew. On ships with very little fuel, even the VHF radio was not available and one ship was using hand-held radios until their batteries ran out.

Those seafarers lucky enough to have direct access to the missions themselves found a sympathetic ear for their problems. Many of them were uncertain of what was happening to their ships and themselves and were worried about their families because they suspected that their allotments had not been paid. This led to a great deal of anguish and a considerable need for counselling from the missions, but they could not reach everyone. On one of the ships in Varna, the bo'sun, under mental stress, became a danger to the rest of the crew – after initially refusing repatriation, he was eventually persuaded by the master that it was better for all concerned if he went. On the *Stainless Supporter*, which had been at anchor off Kobe for three months under arrest, one of the officers took his own life seemingly in a fit of depression.

In a rather strange case in South Africa, Adriatic Tankers' lawyer threatened a court injunction against one of the local missions because the chaplain had informed the crew of their rights under the law. The Piraeus office called this 'inciting distrust and anguish' and claimed that the crew would have plenty of time to lodge their complaints and claims against the vessel after the sale was confirmed by the court. The injunction threat was ignored.

The psychological problems increased as did the need for counselling as ship arrests dragged on for months. The crews were still for the most part unsure of whether or not they would be paid in the end, and the vessels were becoming increasingly hard to live on, due to their deteriorating condition and the lack of facilities aboard. Depending on the jurisdictions under which the ships were arrested, the process of disposing of the vessels was often painfully slow. Many individual seamen expressed their thanks for the mission:

Naing Oo was overwhelmed that they should have taken so much trouble for him. For a short time it took his mind off his considerable difficulties. He is one of eleven Burmese, Russian and South Korean seafarers who have been stranded without pay on board the chemical tanker *Stainless Glory* in Rouen since last May. For eight months they have been dependent on the Missions to Seamen, the international seafarer's centre, and gifts from individuals for all their food and other necessary supplies. (Andrew Marche, Chaplain Rouen, 1996)[21]

There were cases of ships working at private berths where even the chaplains were denied entry, and as a result it was not possible to observe the problems. Sometimes it was necessary for sailors to slip ashore and find someone at the mission to whom to tell their story; just as there were similar, arranged dock-gate meetings between ITF inspectors and seafarers. Occasionally, captains obstructed mission access to their ships, as in the case of the intrepid Karen Lai who was called to help an abused Honduran seafarer in a US port:

This man was being refused medical treatment, he hadn't been paid for several months and all he wanted was to go home ... By the time I got to the ship the gangway was partially raised ... I climbed a piling and carefully pulled myself up to the bottom step of the gangway that was hanging across the water. They were suprised. Really suprised! Once on deck I asked to see the captain.

The captain finally agreed to the company paying the man's ticket 'just to get rid of that garbage'. As I walked down the stairs of three decks, I was greeted by many of the crew who heard what took place. Every one of them said thank you.

Out on deck I saw that the gangway had not been lowered. Several officers came out to watch me go down. At the bottom I safely jumped to the dock and turned round and waved.[22]

Adriatic threatened more than one crew member that if they spoke to the mission, or anyone else, about their pay problems they would be sacked and blacklisted. The mission chaplains took it upon themselves to inform embassies and governments of their nationals' problems on board Adriatic's ships to induce them to take some responsibility. Some embassies showed no interest whatsoever in the plight of even their own national seafarers.

The missions did very good work during the fall of Adriatic Tankers, much of it far beyond the usual set of responsibilities and expenditures expected of them. Many seafarers were able to benefit from the moral and spiritual guidance provided by chaplains worldwide and without doubt this relieved many of the intolerable burdens that had been placed upon them by an uncaring company. The considerable financial costs to all the missions cannot be quantified with any accuracy, and through their influence they were able to find willing support from the port community:

> Four of these ships are at anchor and the crews are unable to get ashore. While the Missions to Seamen has been visiting and caring for them throughout, a very special effort was made to ensure that they had a good Christmas. With the help of everyone in the port from tug crews and pilots, to port police and customs officials, a fund-raising concert was held in the town enabling Christmas trees, food and presents to be bought and delivered. (Flushing mission, the Netherlands, 1996)[23]

Actions by the Seafarers

Whatever advice and help they received, it was also up to seafarers to take action. Many were confused, helpless and passive; others took industrial action by refusing to move the ship, while some went on hunger strike. Others were intimidated by blacklisting, threats to families, and by the arrival of 'new crews', described as 'very heavy' and 'none under 6 feet', who saw they left the ship before yet another crew was sent by an agency.

Some of the Greek captains of Adriatic acted in defence of their crews, but were soon replaced. The British captain of one of Adriatic's vessels eventually managed to get himself and his crew (British officers and Polish ratings) paid after several months by sheer persistence with the agents, the officers' union (NUMAST), the British High Commission and the charterers of the ship; as well as through the wives of the British officers who badgered the UK agents: 'The second mate's wife was particularly upset because of the financial difficulties she was in ... she was tending to get the office girls when she phoned ... they did not have much idea about what was going on.' The captain said it was a different matter with his wife – she succeeded in obtaining information from agents by sheer persistence and more experience.

The captain of this ship was very professional in his attitude to the situation and when the agent at Singapore arrived with some money from the charterers, he noted: 'There was a group of officers who wanted to leave the vessel as soon as they were paid, but I insisted that I would not pay them off till everybody had been paid and we would all leave together ... I was worried that the British Officers would leave the Poles to fend for themselves' (Interview, 15 January 1997).

But even these senior officers had to give up defending their crews in the face of confusion, isolation and sometimes rising conflict between the nationalities on board who were all under stress. The Russian chief officer of the *Kyoto 1* wrote to the ITF after he finally returned home expressing his sorrow at not being able to defend his crew:

I kept them all the time in good relations, assured them in good end in our victory, spent so much my effort to arrange everything for my crew but I lost, I couldn't, circumstances were against me ... I wish to thank you and everybody who was in our matter again and will pray God for your health. (Letter, 25 November 1996)

9

The Legal Rights of the Abused and Abandoned Seafarer

Introduction

Despite the demise of Adriatic Tankers, there is nothing to stop an affair of that scale happening again. Crews are still regularly being abandoned without pay, food, water or medicines in ports throughout the world, and substandard ships operate regardless of the law. In 1996, the Organisation for Economic Co-operation and Development published a report which stated: 'Given the present legal framework, penalties applied to substandard vessels are, if they exist at all, relatively low compared to the advantages obtained from non-observance of international rules and standards.'[1]

The Sources of International Maritime Labour Law

Perhaps the finest ever attempt at a definition of the relationship between people and work is that which begins the Declaration of Philadelphia of 1944 which is annexed to the Constitution of the International Labour Organisation:

> All human beings, irrespective of race, creed or sex, have the right to pursue both their material well-being and their spiritual development in conditions of freedom and dignity, of economic security and equal opportunity ... The attainment of the conditions in which this shall be possible must constitute the central aim of national and international policy.

The International Labour Organisation (ILO) was created by the Peace Treaty of Versailles in 1919 alongside the League of Nations, of which it was an autonomous part, with the aim of helping to fulfil the hopes and aspirations born of the technological revolution and the social upheavals of the time by working to promote social progress, without which it was generally felt there could be no harmonious economic or social development. It is the principal international lawmaker, along with the International Maritime Organisation (IMO), as regards the working and living conditions of seafarers serving on board ocean-going vessels.[2]

Today some 168 member states subscribe, ostensibly, to the principles written in the Constitution of the ILO. They co-operate in its work, which they also finance, and are represented at all levels of the Organisation by government, worker and employer delegates who confer together on the basis of equality.

The International Maritime Organisation, on the other hand, began its life as the Inter-Governmental Maritime Consultative Organisation (IMCO). It was born of a Convention adopted at the United Nations Maritime Conference in Geneva of 1948 and was devoted entirely to shipping matters. Due to differences of opinion as to whether IMCO's role should be limited to merely technical matters or embrace commercial matters also, it was not until one decade later, in 1958, that the 21 states (of which seven had to have at least one million gross tons of shipping each) necessary to bring the Organisation into being, had ratified the Convention. In 1982 IMCO became the IMO, a specialised agency of the United Nations whose membership included not only traditional maritime states but also those which relied heavily on the shipping services of other countries.

One of the main aims of the IMO is to provide the machinery for co-operation among governments concerning regulations and practices that have related to all kinds of technical matters affecting shipping. The IMO also functions to encourage and facilitate the general adoption of the highest practicable standards in matters concerning maritime safety, efficiency of navigation and the prevention and control of marine pollution from ships as well as to consider any matters concerning shipping and the effect of shipping on the marine environment. Major conventions adopted by the IMO include the International Convention for the Safety of Life at Sea 1974 (SOLAS), the International Convention on Standards of Training, Certification and Watchkeeping for Seafarers 1978 (STCW) and the International Safety Management Code for the Safe Operation of Ships and for Pollution Prevention 1993 (ISMC).

The work of the ILO overlaps, to some extent, with that of the IMO. It adopted what is known as the 'International Seafarers' Code' covering a set of minimum standards on all aspects of seafarers' employment conditions. On 16 January 1959, an Agreement between the IMO and the ILO provided for co-operation and con-sultation, reciprocal representation, joint committees and the exchange of information and documents. To a certain extent the work of the IMO in turn overlaps with that of the United Nations Conference on Trade and Development (UNCTAD), particularly in the areas of maritime liens and mortgages, arrest of vessels and other sanctions, and registration of rights in respect of ships under construction. After several meetings between the IMO and UNCTAD, an understanding was reached on 2 March 1983 con-cerning the demarcation of work between the two organisations. It was decided that the IMO would take responsibility for technical or ship-related matters (with co-operation from UNCTAD as and when necessary) and UNCTAD would take the lead in commercial or trade-related issues (with reciprocal co-operation from the IMO when required).

The *Comité International Maritime* (CMI) also works very closely with the IMO and UNCTAD, and has permanent representatives at both these agencies. The CMI is composed of 54 affiliated national maritime law associations and has as its main aim the harmonisa-tion and improvement of maritime law globally. The CMI National Associations are composed of both maritime lawyers and other pro-fessions engaged in the maritime trade and the CMI itself has been active in drafting conventions for the legal committees of the IMO and UNCTAD on, *inter alia*, wreck removal, arrest, electronic data interchange of bills of lading, off-shore craft and structures and maritime liability insurance.

Though the work of the many organisations involved in inter-national shipping is laudable, and despite the comprehensive legislative regime they have created concerning standards and con-ditions for the worker at sea, the reality of the sector of seafaring described in this book involves virtual slavery, appalling living conditions, starvation rations and criminal exploitation. The ques-tion is, why is the law so deficient and ineffective?

The Role of the International Labour Organisation

Since the creation of the ILO, questions relating to the employ-ment and working conditions of seafarers are normally considered by special maritime sessions of the Conference devoted exclusively to them. The second session of the Conference that was held in Genoa in 1920 was the first maritime session and it adopted the first three conventions and two recommendations for seafarers. Over the next 67 years, 36 conventions and 26 recommendations concerning seafarers would be adopted (see Tables 9.1 and 9.2).[3]

Table 9.1   ILO Maritime Labour Conventions[4]

No.	Title	No. of ratifications as at 26 Dec. 1993
7	Minimum Age (Sea) Convention, 1920	50
8	Unemployment Indemnity Shipwreck Convention, 1920	57
9	Placing of Seamen Convention, 1920	37
15	Minimum Age (Trimmers and Stokers) Convention, 1921	67
16	Medical Examination of Young Persons (Sea) Convention, 1921	76
22	Seamen's Articles of Agreement Convention, 1926	56
23	Repatriation of Seamen Convention, 1926	43
53	Officers' Competency Certificates Convention, 1936	32
54*	Holidays with Pay (Sea) Convention, 1936	6
55	Shipowners' Liability (Sick and Injured Seamen) Convention, 1936	16
56+	Sickness Insurance (Sea) Convention, 1936	18
57*	Hours of Work and Manning (Sea) Convention, 1936	4
58	Minimum Age (Sea) Convention (Revised), 1936	50
68	Food and Catering (Ships' Crews) Convention, 1946	22
69	Certification of Ships' Cooks Convention, 1946	34
70*	Social Security (Seafarers) Convention, 1946	7
71	Seafarers' Pensions Convention, 1946	13
72*	Paid Vacations (Seafarers) Convention, 1946	5
73	Medical Examination (Seafarers) Convention, 1946	40
74	Certification of Able Seamen Convention, 1946	26
75*	Accommodation of Crews Convention, 1946	5
76*	Wages, Hours of Work and Manning (Sea) Convention (Revised), 1949	6
91+	Paid Vacations (Seafarers) Convention (Revised), 1949	23
92	Accommodation of Crews Convention (Revised), 1949	39
93*	Wages, Hours of Work and Manning (Sea) Convention (Revised), 1949	6
108	Seafarers Identity Documents Convention, 1958	52
109*	Wages, Hours of Work and Manning (Sea) Convention (Revised), 1949	15
133	Accommodation of Crews (Supplementary Provisions) Convention, 1970	25
134	Prevention of Accidents (Seafarers) Convention, 1970	26
145	Continuity of Employment (Seafarers) Convention, 1976	17
146	Seafarers Annual Leave with Pay Convention, 1976	12

No.	Title	No. of ratifications as at 26 Dec. 1993
147	Merchant Shipping (Minimum Standards) Convention, 1976 and 1996 Protocol	29
163	Seafarers' Welfare at Sea and in Port Convention, 1987	10
164	Health Protection and Medical Care of Seafarers Convention, 1987	6
165	Social Security for Seafarers Convention (Revised), 1987	2
166	Repatriation of Seafarers Convention (Revised), 1987	4
178	Labour Inspection (Seafarers) Convention, 1996	not yet in force
179	Recruitment and Placement of Seafarers Convention (Revised), 1996	not yet in force
180	Seafarers' Hours of Work and the Manning of Ships Convention, 1996	not yet in force
Total		953

* Conventions which did not receive the requisite number of ratifications.
+ Conventions which are closed to ratification.

Every member state of the ILO is required within a given time of the ratification of a convention or recommendation by the ILO (usually two years) to submit the same to the competent national authority for a decision as to the action to be taken on them, and to report to the ILO at regular intervals on the action that has been taken to implement ratified Conventions. Two special bodies – the Committee of Experts on the Application of Conventions and Recommendations and a tripartite Conference Committee – evaluate these government reports. Member states are also required to report on the extent to which unratified conventions and recommendations specified by the governing body have been put into effect or how it is proposed to put them into effect.

As we shall see, however, this is one respect in which the ILO, despite all the efforts of the organisation, is not always successful. Let us take as an example a convention and a recommendation which *should* address the two major problems facing seafarers serving on board substandard ships. The Seafarers' Wages, Hours of Work and the Manning of Ships Recommendation 1996 contains, *inter alia,* provisions as to the seafarer's right to wages. The Repatriation of Seafarers Convention (Revised) 1987 contains detailed provisions regarding the shipowner's duty to repatriate seafarers serving on board their ship when the seafarer's contract comes to an end or the vessel ceases trading.

Table 9.2   ILO Maritime Labour Recommendations[5]

No.	Title
9	National Seamen's Codes Recommendation, 1920
10	Unemployment Insurance (Seamen) Recommendation, 1920
27	Repatriation (Ship Masters and Apprentices) Recommendation, 1926
28	Labour Inspection (Seamen) Recommendation, 1926
48	Seamen's Welfare in Ports Recommendation, 1936
49	Hours of Work and Manning (Sea) Recommendation, 1936
75	Seafarers' Social Security (Agreements) Recommendation, 1946
76	Seafarers' (Medical Care for Dependants) Recommendation, 1946
77	Vocational Training (Seafarers) Recommendation, 1946
78	Bedding, Mess Utensils and Miscellaneous Provisions (Ships' Crews) Recommendation, 1946
105	Ships' Medicine Chests Recommendation, 1958
106	Medical Advice at Sea Recommendation, 1958
107	Seafarers' Engagement (Foreign Vessels) Recommendation, 1958
108	Social Conditions and Safety (Seafarers) Recommendation, 1958
109	Wages, Hours of Work and Manning (Sea) Recommendation, 1958
137	Vocational Training (Seafarers) Recommendation, 1970
138	Seafarers' Welfare Recommendation, 1970
139	Employment of Seafarers (Technical Developments) Recommendation, 1970
140	Crew Accommodation (Air Conditioning) Recommendation, 1970
141	Crew Accommodation (Noise Control) Recommendation, 1970
142	Prevention of Accidents (Seafarers) Recommendation, 1970
153	Protection of Young Seafarers Recommendation, 1976
154	Continuity of Employment (Seafarers) Recommendation, 1976
155	Merchant Shipping (Improvement of Standards) Recommendation, 1976
173	Seafarers' Welfare Recommendation, 1987
174	Repatriation of Seafarers Recommendation, 1987
185	Labour Inspection (Seafarers) Recommendation, 1996
186	Recruitment and Placement of Seafarers Recommendation, 1996
187	Seafarers' Wages, Hours of Work and the Manning of Ships Recommendation, 1996

The Seafarer's Right to Wages and Repatriation under ILO Instruments

It is in the nature of a tripartite organisation such as the International Labour Organisation that when representatives of shipowners, seafarers and flag states are all involved in the drafting of a convention or a recommendation each party will need to make concessions in order for there to be any hope of reaching a final text. This is perhaps the first thing we should note about the international law governing an abandoned seafarer's right to wages and repatriation. Hence the ILO conventions and recommendations do not go anywhere near as far as the seafarer's representatives would have liked. Dilution is an inevitable prerequisite to agreement.

The ILO's Recommendation Concerning Seafarers' Wages, Hours of Work and Manning of Ships

This very comprehensive ILO Recommendation 'lumps together' the *minimum* standards concerning wages, hours of work on board ship and manning and so would not prejudice an agreement between a shipowner and seafarers, such as the *ITF Standard Collective Agreement*, which is more favourable than the conditions contained in the Recommendation. It was passed by 197 votes to 11 (there were 16 abstentions) at the 84th (Maritime) Session of the International Labour Conference in Geneva on 22 October 1996. The Recommendation states:

3.   For seafarers whose remuneration includes separate compensation for overtime worked:
(a) for the purpose of calculating wages, the normal hours of work at sea and in port should not exceed eight hours per day;
(b) for the purpose of calculating overtime, the number of normal hours per week covered by the basic pay or wages should be prescribed by national laws or regulations, if not determined by collective agreements, but should not exceed 48 hours per week; collective agreements may provide for a different but not less favourable treatment;
(c) the rate or rates of compensation for overtime, which should be not less than one and one-quarter times the basic pay or wages per hour, should be prescribed by national laws or regulations or by collective agreements; and
(d) records of all overtime worked should be maintained by the master, or a person assigned by the master, and endorsed by the seafarer at regular intervals.
4.   For seafarers whose wages are fully or partially consolidated:
(a) the collective agreement, articles of agreement, contract of employment and letter of engagement should specify

clearly the amount of remuneration payable to the seafarer and where appropriate the number of hours of work expected of the seafarer in return for this remuneration, and any additional allowances which might be due in addition to the consolidated wage, and in which circumstances;

(b) where hourly overtime is payable for hours worked in excess of those covered by the consolidated wage, the hourly rate should be not less than one and one-quarter times the basic rate corresponding to the normal hours of work as defined in Paragraph 3; the same principle should be applied to the overtime hours included in the consolidated wage.

(c) remuneration for that portion of the fully or partially con-solidated wage representing the normal hours of work as defined in Paragraph 3(a) should be no less than the applic-able minimum wage; and

(d) for seafarers whose wages are partially consolidated, records of all overtime worked should be maintained and endorsed as provided in Paragraph 3(d).

Article 6 goes on to list the principles that must be taken into account when adopting national laws and regulations or collective agree-ments based upon this Recommendation. These principles include equal pay for equal work regardless of race, colour, sex, religion, political opinion, national extraction or social origin; freedom of information concerning wage rates; payment in appropriate legal tender and payment at regular intervals directly to the seafarer or their designated bank account. Article 6(e) states that: 'Adequate penalties or other appropriate remedies should be imposed by the competent authorities where shipowners unduly delay, or fail to make, payment of all remuneration due.' No deductions can be made from a seafarer's pay in respect of obtaining or retaining employment and member states are required to ensure that, after consultation with shipowners' and seafarers' organisations, appropriate and ade-quate procedures are put in place to investigate complaints relating to any matter contained in the Recommendation.

Articles 8, 9 and 10 deal with minimum wages and the minimum monthly basic pay or wage figure for an able seaman. The Recommendation provides for the participation of representative organisations of shipowners and seafarers in determining minimum wages for seafarers with due regard to international labour standards as well as the nature of maritime employment, the cost of living and the needs of the seafarers. A system of supervision and sanctions must be set up to ensure wages are not paid at less than the rates fixed and that, if they are, there is 'an inexpensive and expeditious judicial or other procedure' by which the seafarer can recover the amount by which he or she has been underpaid.

The basic pay or wages for a calendar month of service for an able seaman cannot, it is recommended, be any less than the figure set by the Joint Maritime Commission or another body authorised by the Governing Body of the International Labour Office. Upon a decision of the Governing Body, the Director-General of the ILO shall notify any revised amount to the Members of the International Labour Organisation. As of 1 January 1998, the amount set by the Joint Maritime Commission was $435 for an able seaman.

The ILO's Repatriation of Seafarers Convention

This convention is stated to apply to every seagoing ship, whether publicly or privately owned, which is registered in the territory of any member state for which the Convention is in force and which is ordinarily engaged in commercial maritime navigation as well as to the owners and seafarers of such ships. A 'seafarer' is defined as any person who is employed in any capacity on board a sea-going ship to which the Convention applies. Article 2 of the Convention states that:

1. A seafarer shall be entitled to repatriation in the following circumstances:
   (a) if an engagement for a specific period or for a specific voyage expires abroad;
   (b) upon the expiry of the period of notice given in accordance with the provisions of the articles of agreement or the seafarer's contract of employment;
   (c) in the event of illness or injury or other medical condition which requires his or her repatriation when found medically fit to travel;
   (d) in the event of shipwreck;
   (e) in the event of the shipowner not being able to continue to fulfil his or her legal or contractual obligations as an employer of the seafarer by reason of bankruptcy, sale of ship, change of ship's registration or any other similar reason;
   (f) in the event of a ship being bound for a war zone, as defined by national laws or regulations or collective agreements, to which the seafarer does not consent to go; or

(g) in the event of termination or interruption of employment in accordance with an industrial award or collective agreement, or termination of employment for any similar reason.

Clearly then the Convention provides for repatriation following a broad range of incidents. Article 3 states that the destinations prescribed for repatriation shall include the place at which the seafarer agreed to enter into the engagement, the place stipulated by collective agreement, the seafarer's country of residence or such other place as may be mutually agreed at the time of engagement. The seafarer has the right to choose from among these prescribed destinations the place to which he or she wishes to be repatriated. Most importantly of all, Article 4 provides that it is the shipowner's responsibility to arrange for repatriation by appropriate and expeditious means, normally by air, and that the cost of repatriation is to be borne by the shipowner. This cost includes airfare, accommodation, sustenance, wages and transportation of 30 kilograms of personal luggage as well as any medical treatment required.

The shipowner is prohibited from demanding any sort of advance payment from the seafarer at the time that he joins the ship that is to go towards the cost of repatriation, nor can the shipowner recover the cost of repatriation from the seafarer's wages. If the shipowner fails to make arrangements for or to meet the cost of repatriation of a seafarer then responsibility falls upon the country of registration of the vessel, who may then recover the cost of repatriating the seafarer from the shipowner.

The Repatriation of Seafarers Recommendation of 1987 states that whenever a seafarer is entitled to be repatriated in accordance with the Repatriation of Seafarers Convention but both the shipowner *and* the flag state fail to meet their obligations then either the state *from* which or the state *to* which the seafarer is being repatriated (where that is the state of which they are a national) shall arrange for their repatriation and recover the cost from the flag state who can in turn recover from the shipowner. This of course never happens in practice.

The 1926 Convention came into force on 16 April 1928, and the revised Convention on 6 July 1991. However, a close look at the number of ratifications shows that the revised Convention has had only four ratifications – from Hungary, Luxembourg, Mexico and Spain – compared to the 43 ratifications of the much less comprehensive 1926 Convention.

Why don't these ILO Instruments have Appreciable Effect on the Substandard Sector?

The provisions set out above would appear to constitute clear rules of international law for ensuring that abandoned seafarers, or seafarers whose contracts of employment have come to an end, will be returned home quickly and for free, and receive the wages that they are owed. But tragic stories such as that of the *Lourdas* show that this is patently untrue. There is still a significant minority of shipowners of the same ilk as Adriatic Tankers, who essentially leave their crew for dead when one of their vessels has to cease trading. So why, despite the existence of ILO conventions and recommendations, is this terrible exploitation and abuse of fellow human beings still taking place? Have flag states enacted the necessary legislation to give effect to the ILO convention and recommendation, whether ratified or not?

The answer to this is a very qualified 'yes ... sort of'. For all the major flag of convenience states have in fact given effect to all the main ILO instruments through their national legislation. But what is equally true is that these countries have engaged in what can only be described as 'creative legislating', enacting in some cases only the most basic of the ILO rules. Moreover, while many flag states have left sufficient loopholes in their national law for a reasonably resourceful shipowner to avoid ILO minimum standards, many states have legislated not for the benefit of the seafarer but for the benefit of their registries, creating onerous rules which attract shipowners to register under their flag but which have harsh consequences for workers at sea.

The table in Appendix 3 gives a breakdown of the national laws created by the main FOC states with respect to repatriation and wages.[6] If someone were to briefly examine this table they might be tempted to conclude that the FOC states have, to all intents and purposes, enacted sufficient national legislation regarding repatriation and wages to protect the seafarer employed on board a ship registered under that state's flag. But take a close look with an analytical eye and you begin to see how each country has added to or subtracted from the provisions of the ILO recommendation and convention to the extent necessary to keep their registries attractive to international tonnage. There are several ways of accomplishing this.

(i) Vague or ambiguous wording
The use of vague or ambiguous wording, capable of several different interpretations, is illustrated well by Article 145 of the

Panamanian Labour Code. This Article gives the seafarer the right, through 'judicial proceedings', to claim the establishment of a fair wage where 'the wages the seafarer receives are remarkably unfair in comparison with the average wage for his or her job in the maritime industry'. But how is this comparison to be made? How is the industry's 'average wage' calculated? What is the definition of 'unfair'? What *sort* of judicial proceedings are involved and how does the seafarer obtain access to and representation at such proceedings? Under Panamanian law the seafarer is entitled to wages earned during 'the last voyage'. Lawyers representing owners and financial institutions holding mortgages on their ships have been successful in arguing this point: a victory, one would think. But in reality seafarers who succeed in obtaining *some* wages have gone home with a small fraction of the total wages they are owed. The law as it presently stands in Panama, therefore, is interpreted in such a way that it can be used to give seafarers sufficient monies for them to get home, but no more. Once repatriated, more often than not it is impossible for the seafarer to recover their remaining back-pay without (and sometimes even with) the assistance of the ITF. The swift repatriation of seafarers by a shipowner from an arrested or abandoned vessel without their full outstanding wages is usually a strategic move, not a compassionate one.

The questions raised about the nature of Panamanian 'judicial proceedings' are not answered at any point in the text of the Labour Code: to do so, of course, would be contrary to the best interests of those registering under the Panamanian flag who don't *want* their crews to be aware of their legal rights for fear that they will cause trouble if they are not paid sufficiently or repatriated on time.

Keeping seafarers in the dark regarding their employment rights is an important part of the rogue shipowner's larger policy of maintaining a docile and obedient crew. This has been well-illustrated in this book and also by cases in Chapman (1992).[7] 'Blacklists' and 'ITF Warnings' are too often the consequence of seafarers trying to find out about their rights or actually trying to enforce them. These blacklists are distributed among port manning agents. The seafarers listed are 'guilty' of contacting the ITF when the shipowner on whose vessel they worked fails to pay them or to repatriate them at the end of their contracts. The fact that they have been blacklisted can mean that they may never be able to work at sea again – and herein lies the crux of the issue. If this kind of very strong disincentive is associated with contacting the ITF, imagine the consequences for the seafarer of contacting a lawyer.

(ii) Putting a time limit on the claiming of legal rights
Section 342(3) of the Liberian Maritime Law and Regulations states that a seafarer will lose the right to repatriation if he or she fails to request it within one week of the time they are eligible for repatriation. This single clause renders any other provisions relating to repatriation superfluous. In this one sentence, the Liberian legislature has created a fluid and infinitely elastic law that can be used to deny the seafarer rightful repatriation at the shipowner's whim.

This section not only assumes that there is a contract in existence with an expiry date that has been clearly agreed between the seafarer and the shipowner, but that this date is known by the former and will be duly respected by the latter. However, the reality for many crews serving on board FOC vessels is that there is no contract or, if there is, that the seafarer is at best unable (through illiteracy or language barriers) to understand the contract or, at worst, never even made aware of the details of their own contract of employment.

Indeed, the ITF has documented many instances of two contracts being signed – one which records the seafarer's real wage (substantiality below the ITF minimum wage) and one which records an 'official' wage. It is the latter contract that is shown to ITF inspectors. The scope therefore exists for seafarer's contracts to be unilaterally amended, simply lost or kept safely away from the seafarers, in the master's safe.

(iii) Referring disputes to an inaccessible third party
In relation to wages, Section 327(3) of the Liberian Maritime Code states that the master of a vessel must pay a seafarer half of their earned wages when they ask for them at any port in which the ship loads or unloads cargo before the end of the voyage. He may do this only once every ten days but if the master does not pay, *and he is wrong*, the seafarer has the right to be paid their full earned wages – which of course begs the question: just *who* is to be the judge of whether or not the master is wrong? Given the near impossibility of a seafarer being able to hire a lawyer, discussed below, let alone bring a legal action for repatriation or wages anywhere near a courtroom, this provision is not worth the paper it is written on.

(iv) Discouraging industrial action
The Norwegian Seamen's Act of 30 May 1975 states that, on board ships sailing under the Norwegian International Registry flag, the seafarer is not entitled to wages for any period during which they unlawfully refuse to work. In a similar vein, the Bahamian Merchant Shipping Act states at Section 153(3) that if the seafarer

decides to cease working on the ship before the end of their contract the owner will not be responsible for paying their repatriation expenses. These provisions, while appearing fair to employers, have the practical effect of heavily penalising – and hence effectively preventing – industrial action by seafarers who are dissatisfied with their working conditions, be it wages owed, poor standards of hygiene and safety on board or actual mistreatment at the hands of the master or officers. Where conditions are so desperate, therefore, that seafarers try to leave a ship when she calls at port and present themselves to the port authorities, they run the risk of becoming disentitled to repatriation by the shipowner. There may also be a very real danger of the port authorities, reluctant to have to accommodate and repatriate such seafarers themselves, refusing to take the claims of these people seriously.

The Case of the Glory Cape

A recent case in Australia which highlights the mistreatment of seafarers is that of *Yulianto & Ors* v. *The Ship 'Glory Cape'*,[8] which has already been cited in this report. In a court action the crew recovered damages for their mistreatment and it was held that personal injuries suffered by a seafarer as a result of mistreatment on board a vessel may well be grounds for arresting the vessel pursuant to the Admiralty Act 1988. It should be remembered, however, that this happy conclusion was largely down to luck: the seafarers were abandoned in a jurisdiction with an enlightened and responsible attitude towards seafarers' human rights. One wonders how the crewmen might have been treated had they jumped overboard in the port of a less friendly jurisdiction.

The Problem of Enforcement

So far we have considered the way in which FOC states have enacted just two ILO Conventions into their national law. And although we have seen a number of lacunae in what purports to be a thorough application of international law, there are further and much more important reasons why seafarers are unable to avail themselves of the law. The first is the near impossibility for a seafarer of securing legal advice and representation and the second the ineffectiveness of almost all forms of legal action due to the failure of many states to put into place proper safeguards to ensure the application by registered shipowners of their obligations towards their crews.

(i) Obtaining legal representation and enforcing a lien

Many flag and port-state jurisdictions provide for the creation of a maritime lien. A maritime lien is a claim against a ship which can be enforced by means of her seizure, arising from non-payment of, for example, salvage charges or the master's and crew's wages. The practical consequence of attaching a maritime lien to a ship is that the ship will be arrested and cannot be removed from the court's jurisdiction until the debt has been paid or security for the debt lodged. It exists quite independently of the possession of the object over which it is claimed, but is attached to it in the sense that it is unaffected by a change of ownership. It is therefore called by lawyers a right *in rem* – a right enforceable against the whole world. The priority given to the different types of debt for which a maritime lien is available, as between each other, varies from jurisdiction to jurisdiction. For instance, in Panama, Article 1507 of the Mercantile Code states:

> The following charges against the ship will have priority, and will complete regarding their respective amounts in the order set out in this Article, viz.:-

1. Judicial costs incurred in the common interests of the maritime creditors.
2. Expenses, indemnities and salaries for assistance and salvage due for the last voyage.
3. Salaries, payments and indemnities due to the Master and members of the crew for the last voyage.
4. Salaries and fees due to stevedores and wharf-hands directly engaged by the owner, fleet owner or Master of the ship for loading or unloading it at its last point of arrival.[9]
5. Any indemnities arising for damage caused by fault or negligence.
6. Amounts due in respect of contributions towards damages suffered in common.
7. Ship mortgages.
8. Sums due in respect of contractual commitments for the needs and fitting-out of the ship.
9. Sums taken on bottomry on the ship's hull and gear for stores, supplies and making ready, if the contract was concluded and signed before the ship left the port where such obligations were undertaken; the insurance premiums for the last six months.

10. The salaries of experts, and watchmen, and the costs of maintenance and safety measures for the ship, its gear and its stores after the last voyage and entry into port.
11. Indemnities due to shippers and passengers for non-delivery of items loaded or for damage to these attributable to the Master or crew during the last voyage.
12. The price of the last purchase of the ship and the interest due during the last two years.

There are several international conventions which have attempted to create a uniform legal framework for liens. The first two of these – the *International Convention for the Unification of Certain Rules Relating to Maritime Liens and Mortgages 1926* and the 1967 Convention of the same name which was intended to replace the earlier version – have not been widely ratified by the more powerful maritime nations. A third attempt resulted in the *International Convention on Maritime Liens and Mortgages 1993*.

The lack of success in attracting more widespread international support for a uniform system of liens might be said to reflect the varying national laws which go more to the nature of the claim for which the lien is sought than the actual characteristics conferred by a 'lien'. Moreover, the failure to find consensus on the conflict-of-laws principles that will govern the creation and operation of maritime liens has led to the possibility of a lien being attached to a ship but then lost if she sails from one country to another. As the 1993 Convention presently stands, a vessel must be arrested in order to ensure the enforcement of a maritime lien and this is where the great difficulty lies for a seafarer who is seeking to recover significant back wages as against his employer. There are three main reasons for this.

First, few seafarers are aware of their legal rights, indeed many are not even aware of the terms of their contract. Poor levels of numeracy and literacy among seafarers from developing countries are a major factor in this.

Second, ships often stay in port for only a very brief period of time and may only be visited by the port authorities and shipping agent. Neither of these parties would want to see the berth congested by an arrested ship. Moreover, a seafarer will most probably find it impossible to obtain information about where to find a lawyer in a country whose language he or she does not speak.

Finally, to hire a lawyer costs money and very few countries have any sort of legal aid scheme that would enable a seafarer to obtain free legal advice or representation. In the UK a lawyer would be unlikely to take a maritime labour case on a *pro bono* basis, and if a lawyer was to accept a case on a contingency-fee basis the claim is unlikely to be big enough to induce the lawyer to take the case on. Moreover, lodging documents in court may incur fees and a court may well require that a bond be placed in the court prior to arrest; the bond could be as high as the alleged debt itself or based on the expense of keeping the ship in port. A seafarer simply would not have this kind of money. Even if the seafarer was able to arrest the ship, what good would this do if the vessel has been abandoned anyway? In such circumstances ships often lie moored at a berth for months on end, with the seafarers relying upon the help of the ITF and the generosity of local communities and Christian missions to obtain food as they await repatriation.

Where the shipowner has become insolvent and there is no chance for them ever to take possession of their ship, or to discharge the lien (even if they wanted to), the mortgagee bank, if there is one, will often step in as beneficial owner. Most ships are mortgaged and sometimes the bank will decide to take charge of a crew while they plan to recover their asset, namely, the ship. But banks will naturally only take responsibility for abandoned seafarers where repatriating the crew will enable them to take possession of the ship. There are many cases on record of the mortgagee bank cutting its losses by simply denying any responsibility towards the crew and the ship.

(ii) The genuine link concept – fact or fantasy?

The second major problem is the lack of control exercised by FOC states over their shipping. When the issue of flags of convenience was reviewed by the International Law Commission during its preparation of draft articles on the Law of the Sea (which were to be considered further by the first United Nations Conference on the Law of the Sea in Geneva in 1958) they took the view that a state should accept certain restrictions in the case of ships which were neither owned by it nor the property of a nationalised company. They concluded that:

> ... national legislation on the subject must not depart too far from the principles adopted by the majority of States, which may be regarded as forming part of international law. Only on that condition will the freedom granted to States not give rise to abuse and to friction with other States. With regard to the national element required for permission to fly the flag, a great many systems are possible, but there must be a minimum national element.[10]

However, the Commission did not describe, in anything more than the very vaguest of terms, what this 'minimum national element' should be. Although the draft article eventually formulated stated that, 'Nevertheless, *for the purpose of recognition of the national character of the ship by other States*, there must exist a genuine link between the State and the ship', the middle, italicised part of this sentence was deleted from the Convention that the United Nations Conference eventually agreed upon. Hence Article 5(1) of the Geneva Convention stated: 'There must exist a genuine link between the State and the ship; in particular, the State must effectively exercise its jurisdiction and control in administrative, technical and social matters over ships flying its flag.'

Article 91(1) of the United Nations Convention on the Law of the Sea changed this to an even simpler formula:

Every state shall fix the conditions for the grant of its nationality to ships for the registration of ships in its territory, and for the right to fly its flag. Ships have the nationality of the state whose flag they are entitled to fly. There must exist a genuine link between the state and the ship.

Hence, even though Articles 94 and 217 of the same Convention expand the duties of the flag state to exercise jurisdiction and control in administrative, technical and social measures and ensure safety at sea in matters relating to manning, seaworthiness, collision prevention, construction and crew qualification in conformity with generally accepted international regulations, procedures and practices, the inclusion of these duties in a completely separate article and the absence of any link between Article 91(1) and Article 94 makes it very difficult indeed to argue that the failure by a flag state to perform its duties under the latter article would provide evidence of the absence of a genuine link between it and the ship concerned.

So although the United Nations Conventions clearly sets out flag state obligations, the concept of the genuine link and what it means is not explained or defined. Indeed, many of the obligations that are defined in the Convention are vague, ambiguous or imprecise. M.L. McConnell, in her article 'Darkening Confusion Mounted Upon Darkening Confusion: The Search for the Elusive Genuine Link', states: 'It is difficult to believe that failure of a flag state to comply with the requirements of Article 94 could render national registration a nullity or that this was the intent of the conference without further statement in the Convention.'[11]

Arguably the member states of the United Nations Conference on the Law of the Sea did not at any stage intend to change the existing international law regarding FOC registration, much less add a new requirement that there should be a genuine link between ship ownership and the country of registration. But even if one does accept that the UN Convention adequately defines a genuine link (which given that some 116 states have ratified it would mean such a concept has now been absorbed into international customary law and is therefore binding even upon non-signatories) it is clear that there is a major problem of implementation with this Convention, as well as with the ILO recommendations and conventions identified above.

The United Nations Convention on Conditions for Registration of Ships 1986 does provide for participation by nationals of the flag state in the ownership, manning and management of ships, stating at Article 10(1):

The State of registration, before entering a ship in its register of ships, shall ensure that the shipowning company or subsidiary shipowning company is established and/or has its principal place of business within its territory in accordance with its laws and regulations.

But in the very next paragraph this provision is almost completely diluted by the caveat that where this condition is not met registration may none the less proceed if the flag state 'ensures' that there is a 'representative or management person who shall be a national of the flag State or be domiciled therein': one of the three conditions required for there to be a genuine link. It should not be surprising therefore that the loose and flexible language of this Convention – like so many others that have emerged from Conferences that were opened with fine speeches and great intentions but concluded by a desperate search for consensus at any cost – makes it of little practical benefit to seafarers. Moreover, the ratification of not less than forty flag states representing 25 per cent of the world's gross tonnage is required before the Convention can enter into force. This has not yet happened and does not seem likely ever to happen.

The Search for a Solution – Compulsory Insurance

At the International Labour Organisation's Tripartite Meeting on Maritime Labour Standards in 1994, the seafarer members of the

Committee on Placing Seamen proposed that responsibility for abandoned seafarers should fall squarely upon the shoulders of the manning agents by forcing them to contribute to something in the nature of a guarantee fund. No agreement was reached but the Committee did agree to propose an amendment to the Placing of Seamen Convention 1920 (No. 9) to be considered by the 84th (Maritime) Session of the International Labour Conference in October 1996 which stated:

> The competent authority shall ensure that a bond, guarantee fund or similar arrangement is maintained to compensate seafarers and shipowners having incurred a monetary loss as a result of the default of a recruitment and placement service.

And as if this amendment was not diluted enough from the original, the actual outcome of the Conference was even less satisfactory. For although the subsequently revised Placing of Seamen Convention requires that a competent national authority must supervise closely all recruitment and placement services, particularly with respect to meeting legal requirements and staffing of the agencies with adequately trained personnel, with respect to abandonment it states only that placement services must 'adopt measures to ensure, as far as practicable, that the employer has the means to protect seafarers from being stranded in a foreign port'.

Although the revised Convention now requires that private placement services are 'in conformity with a system of licensing or certification or other form of regulation' and that ratifying member states must ensure that 'no fees or other charges for recruitment or for providing employment to seafarers are borne directly or indirectly, in whole or in part, by the seafarer' many might feel that a golden opportunity has, once again, been missed. Without any solidly enforced system of regulation and penalisation by dedicated government inspectors, there seems no reason why manning agents will not, in practice, still be able to appear and disappear in the same way that they have been doing for the past decade or so.

But whilst the idea of a guarantee fund (successful in the case of oil pollution) might have gone some way towards protecting seafarers it would, even if it had been incorporated without dilution, only have approached the problem from one direction. The manning agents are just the tip of the iceberg – it is the shipowners themselves that must be compelled to accept their obligations under international law. To talk about obliging manning agents (who may in any case be employed by shipowners) to set up compulsory guarantee funds is otiose when the real source of the problem is the failure by shipowners to accept responsibility for *their* employees, working aboard *their* ships, that *they* abandon in foreign ports because of *their* culpable mismanagement. Could the answer be the compulsory insurance of shipowners against the cost of repatriating seafarers and paying them their accrued wages when they are abandoned due to the arrest or judicial sale of a ship?

Traditionally seafarers have not been allowed to insure their wages, the rationale being that to allow them to do so might somehow discourage full diligence in the 'preservation of the voyage'.[12] At a time when any sea voyage involved a high degree of risk, freight was 'the mother of wages': if no freight was earned then there would be no fund from which wages could be paid. But this principle was abolished in 1854 when the shipowner became statutorily bound to pay wages up until the loss of the ship although, naturally, a loss would still be incurred if this happened since the seafarer would not receive any wages for what would have remained of the voyage. Section 3 of the Marine Insurance Act 1906 states:

(1) Subject to the provisions of this Act, every lawful marine adventure may be the subject of a contract of marine insurance.

(2) In particular there is a marine adventure where – The earning or acquisition of any freight, passage money, commission, profit, or other pecuniary benefit, or the security for any advances, loan, or disbursements, is endangered by the exposure of insurable property to maritime perils.

'Pecuniary benefit' includes a seafarer's wages, which are dependent upon the well-being of the ship (the 'insurable property') and Section 11 reinforces this by stating: 'The master or any member of the crew of a ship has an insurable interest in respect of his wages.'

However, conventional marine insurance underwriters have not, historically, indemnified shipowners against every liability to which they are exposed. Liability for crew's wages in some situations is indemnified under hull policies or allowable in general average. For instance, Clause 16 of the Institute Time Clauses (Hulls) states:

No claim shall be allowed, other than in general average, for wages and maintenance of the Master, Officers and Crew, or any member thereof, except when incurred solely for the necessary removal of the Vessel from one port to another for the repair of damage covered by the Underwriters, or for trial trips for such repairs, and then only for such wages and maintenance as are incurred whilst the vessel is under way.[13]

Nominally, though, accrued wages and the costs of a seafarer's repatriation are not insured under the hull policy but by mutual insurance. This has much to do with the fact that the traditional insurance market, since the case of *De Vaux* v. *Salvador*,[14] has only provided cover for three-quarters of the expenses (up to the insured value of the vessel) arising as a result of damage done in a collision with another ship. Hence the shipowner was left uncovered in respect of the remaining one-quarter of the expenses, the excess liability above the value of the ship, and also in respect of liabilities for death, personal injury and damage to fixed and floating objects falling outside the definition of a vessel. It was these extra risks, as well as the possibility of incurring liability to cargo-owners that conventional insurance would not cover (for example, because the vessel had made an unjustifiable deviation from its agreed route or had been lost due to negligent navigation) that provided the catalyst for shipowners to form mutual hull underwriting associations, the forerunners to the modern Protection and Indemnity ('P&I') clubs:[15]

> To say that the clubs cover everything not covered by some other policy of insurance would not be too wide of the mark, and to say that the clubs were a receptacle for all risks unplaceable elsewhere sounds disparaging, but nevertheless reasonably describes the position. A true enough brief description of a P&I insurer is that he covers shipowners (or whomever) against their legal liabilities to third parties.[16]

Under P&I club cover, a member can insure against costs or expenses incurred because of the terms/contract of employment and arising directly from them and which would not otherwise have been incurred. Such costs, though, are only recoverable if the terms of employment had received the prior approval of the club managers. These costs would include the wages of a seafarer during hospitalisation or treatment abroad, or while awaiting or during repatriation, and reimbursement of expenses incurred in sending substitute crew abroad or repatriating a substitute necessarily engaged abroad. Repatriation expenses are also recoverable if the reason for the repatriation is not that the seafarer is ill or needs home treatment but is essentially required to attend a spouse, child or, in the case of a single person, a parent who has fallen ill. So why then are seafarers abandoned when the cost of repatriation can be adequately insured against? There are a multiplicity of reasons.

First of all, because P&I insurance is a form of *mutual* insurance, the quality of a vessel's management will have a great influence on whether or not a club will accept it and a club's underwriter will require to be informed of the experience of the vessel's management, the level of crew training, the shipowner's previous loss record, the nationality of a ship's crew and evidence of the ship's continuing maintenance. In order to minimise their risk exposure, mutual insurance associations must ensure that the quality of their membership stays reasonably high. Hence many ships in the sub-standard sector will always be excluded from the possibility of P&I insurance, or will only be able to insure at a very high premium. Indeed, one anonymous P&I source estimates that as much as 5 per cent of the world's tonnage does not have P&I club cover. Approximately 2 per cent can be accounted for by the small group of shipping concerns that are big enough and solvent enough to be self-insuring. The remaining 3 per cent are in the substandard sector.

Second, P&I clubs do not allow recovery for losses arising out of irrecoverable debts or out of the insolvency of the shipowner, or indeed any person. Whilst the exact rules in this respect will vary from club to club, it is generally the case that when a company goes under but its ships continue trading, the insurance lapses and the crew on board are left totally unprotected against sickness or injuries whilst on service, since the insurance company or P&I club has the power to withdraw its coverage retroactively. This is what happened in the case of Adriatic Tankers.

In January 1996, *Lloyd's List* reported that failure to comply with classification society requirements and to pay due instalments on a $5 million premium had led to Adriatic's two key mutual insurers terminating their cover.[17] About seventy vessels were entered with the United Kingdom Mutual Steam Ship Association and a further twelve with the Liverpool and London Steamship Protection and Indemnity Association. Adriatic had been one of the UK club's larger members for over a decade but this didn't stop the club from exercising their right to retrospectively cancel cover as far back as the inception of membership. Rule 31 of the UK club's *Rules and Bye-Laws* states:

> Where an owner has failed to pay, either in whole or in part, any amount due from him to the Association, the Managers may give him notice in writing requiring him to pay such amount by any

date specified in such notice, not being less than seven days from the date on which such notice is given. If the Owner fails to make such a payment in full on or before the date so specified, the insurance of the Owner ... in respect of any and all ships referred to in such notice and entered in the Association by him or on his behalf shall be cancelled forthwith without further notice or other formality ... The Association shall with effect from the date of cancellation cease to be liable for any claims of whatsoever kind under these Rules in respect of any and all ships in relation to which the insurance of the Owner has been cancelled ... irrespective of whether such claims have occurred or arisen or may arise by reason of any event which has occurred at any time prior to the date of cancellation, including during previous years.

The third reason is perhaps the most important one in terms of understanding why P&I club insurance does not protect seafarers and it is best understood by looking at the very nature of this kind of insurance. Most P&I club rules state that it is a condition precedent to recovery that, since the policy is one of indemnity, it is necessary that a shipowner member should have discharged his liabilities prior to seeking reimbursement. The clubs undertake only to pay that amount which the shipowner has in fact paid out. For instance, Rule 5A of the UK P&I club states: 'Unless the Directors in their discretion otherwise decide, it is a condition precedent of an Owner's right to recover from the funds of the Association in respect of any liabilities, costs or expenses that he shall first have discharged or paid the same.'

This is an essential part of the concept of indemnity insurance to which there are only two exceptions: where the club committee exercises its discretion to waive strict compliance of this general rule – for example, where the club has taken control of the handling of a claim and settles directly with a claimant, and where the club has given a letter of undertaking. Thus when a shipowner finds himself with a cash-flow crisis on his hands, even if he manages to avoid his P&I club cancelling his insurance, he must still pay the cost of a crew's repatriation and remunerate them any accrued wages himself before he can turn to the club for indemnification: he must 'pay to be paid'. It should not be any surprise to learn, then, that paying a crew and repatriating them come fairly low down on a shipowner's list of priorities in times of crisis. It is an obligation that is, as we've shown, very easily avoided. So it is. But what about borrowing money? Could a shipowner's liability be discharged by someone else paying off the repatriation expenses and owed wages if the shipowner is not able to do so? There is certainly some case law authority for this. In *Arthur L. Liman* v. *American Steamship Owners Mutual Protection and Indemnity Association Inc.*,[18] a US court held that, where a member's liability was discharged by a third party, the club's rule that it was a condition precedent to the right to recover from the club that a claim had been paid *was* satisfied.[19] However, take a look at a P&I club rule-book today and you will see that the utility of this decision is now almost completely lost. A typical clause states:

> In the case of a liability, actual payment (which shall be made out of moneys belonging to the member absolutely and not by way of loan or otherwise) by the member of the full amount of such liability shall, unless the committee otherwise decide, be a condition precedent to the right of a member to recover and the obligation of the club to satisfy and make good.

Some older authorities have often been cited in support of the proposition that equity will allow a person to seek indemnity prior to payment where to make such a payment would otherwise render him insolvent.[20] Surely a court of law, appraised of the need to pay and repatriate a group of abandoned seafarers, would allow a shipowner to avail themselves of this equitable jurisdiction? Sadly, in the cases regarding the *Fanti* and the *Padre Island*,[21] the House of Lords held that equity cannot be used to override the express provisions of the contract of indemnity and that, moreover, on the ordinary and natural meaning of the P&I club rules in question, members were not entitled to be indemnified by the club unless and until the members themselves had first discharged liabilities in respect of which they sought an indemnity from the club – payment of the claim by the member was a condition precedent to reimbursement of the member of the club.

Their Lordships, however, did not rule out the operation of the equitable principle where club rules did not have a clearly worded 'pay to be paid' rule. In such a case, the contract of indemnity between member and club could be performed at the suit of the member (or a third party) prior to payment by the member to the third party claimant. It was also held that the member in question, having not paid the claim, had only a contingent right against the club and it was that same contingent right which was transferred to the third party (under section 1(3) of the Third Parties (Rights Against Insurers) Act 1930[22]). The third party was not to be put in any better position as against the insurer than the assured himself would have been and hence their Lordships also confirmed that an insurer with a good defence against the original assured would have the same good defence against a claim being advanced by a third party.

Thus it would seem that, when times are hard, direct action by a shipowner against his P&I club for the funds necessary to repatriate a crew will only be possible where there is no 'pay to be paid' provision in the club rules. But in modern mutual insurance practice, the absence of such a provision is almost unheard of. Does the answer lie in a club committee's discretion to waiver this condition precedent? In the *Fanti* and the *Padre Island* cases, Lord Goff warned the P&I clubs that they should not use the 'pay to be paid' rule as a means of 'hiding' from their responsibility to pay victims or their next of kin in cases of personal injury or death. His Lordship stated that, were they to do so, the legislature could promote remedial legislation.[23]

It could be argued therefore that, by implication, where there are sufficiently pressing humanitarian or compassionate grounds, a P&I club might be convinced to indemnify a member without requiring him to pay anything out first. Assuming that Lord Goff's warning has been taken seriously by the P&I clubs – and there seems no reason to suppose that it hasn't, for the alternative would surely be for the clubs to lose a great deal of their autonomy and discretion in such matters – there is the very real possibility that a club might feel sufficiently moved by the plight of a group of abandoned seafarers to repatriate them. Such a solution assumes, however, that the nature of the repatriation is such that it is covered in the first place, that mutual insurance has not lapsed for any reason and that premium payments continue to be made on time. There is a big difference between repatriating seafarers whose employer has gone 'belly up' and seafarers who were working on board a genuine casualty. Given the draconian manner in which most P&I clubs interpret their rule-books it is submitted that for the former group this is a not a solution of any great utility. The better view, it is submitted, is that compulsory insurance could work, but not if it is required to coexist with the 'pay to be paid' rule.

Conclusions

The international legal framework that is supposed to protect seafarers is a messy business. The tripartite structure of the ILO means that however well thought-out and however badly needed legislation on an aspect of maritime labour law and policy might be, it may be so diluted when it is finally adopted that the Unions will soon cry out for a new instrument and the process will begin all over again. As we have seen, flag states can and do avoid properly implementing ILO instruments and even when adopted into national law, shipowners can and do avoid their obligations, often by using the lacuna that the flag state itself has created. Shipowners will not get serious about their legal obligations towards their employees until flag states get serious with them. But who's going to get serious with the flag states? If anyone does, some shipowners may leave for friendlier shores.

While pressure is slowly being brought to bear on the substandard sector by port-state control and the respectable mainstream of the industry, it cannot be denied that this has less to do with an interest in human rights than with the unfair competition that the substandard sector and its ultra-low overheads present to the bona fide shipowner. Those within the shipping industry feel sure that the industry will eventually force out the substandard sector. But they are equally sure that doing so will be a long haul and will depend upon co-operation and transparency in the application of conventions and codes such as SOLAS, STCW and the ISM Code.

It has always followed that the media pressure which often catalyses the enforcement of conventions like STCW and the ISM Code has been based upon protecting the marine environment, not on improving social conditions for the human beings working on board substandard ships. The two elements have seldom been perceived as connected.

Hence improving conditions for the seafarers will inevitably have to go hand-in-hand with media education and the modernisation of business practices in the shipping industry generally. As long as everyone involved in the industry – shipowners, brokers, manning agents, marine underwriters, P&I clubs and maritime lawyers – continue to cultivate a climate of antiquity and secrecy, closed off from the outside world and inaccessible to the seafarer, then making people take responsibility for the human beings who go to sea to earn a living will not be attainable. There is clearly a need for a critical review and revision of the system in a new globalised era.

10

Towards Global Governance in Shipping

In 1996 Captain Panagis Zissimatos was sentenced by a Greek court to three years in prison, and a fine of $20,500 was imposed for passing dishonoured cheques.[1] This sentence was never carried out (his appeal has yet to be heard). Meanwhile Zissimatos is living in Switzerland and is back in the shipping business.

Assignment of Blame

The purpose of discussing Zissimatos was not simply to give wider exposure to an unscrupulous shipowner. More importantly it was to trace the failure of his company, the illegal methods and legal loopholes he found, and the misfortunes that befell his seafarers against the background of unacceptable practices towards ships' crews more generally. These, since the early 1970s, have characterised the substandard sector of world shipping. Adriatic and other shipping companies explain away neglect and abuse by referring to the force of economic circumstances, unfair actions by trade unions, a malevolent maritime press, panicking creditors and bad luck.

While some of the excuses may have a little validity, it is in fact the chaotic financial procedures, employment conditions and flag states with no genuine interest in shipping which allow companies like Adriatic to function in their reckless pursuit of profits, while denying that they have any responsibility for the seafarers they employ. These companies work within virtually unregulated international markets when it comes to raising finance and the employment of seafarers. It is therefore not only the greedy Adriatic-type owners who are culpable.

Traditionally, the modern free market system has depended on a certain amount of integrity and business ethics. But with a substandard sector in shipping there has been a degeneration into at best a general disregard for crews which are often drawn from the poorest countries, and at worst, complicity in their abuse on the part of many of the institutions of shipping. Assignments of blame have therefore to include dubious surveyors, over-competitive classification societies, P&I clubs and underwriters which do little to promote high standards, negligent loan officers in banks, imprudent investment managers, brokers who conceal the truth, flexible accountants, careless charterers, corrupt crewing agencies, imposition of unfair contracts by labour-supplying countries, denials of responsibility by flag states, and a few self-serving national trade unions, over-protective shipowners' associations, weak maritime administrations and outdated concepts and legal instruments.

Some of the problems which can be assigned to states and institutions singly and collectively include the major features of a world surplus of ships and the low freight rates that charterers now expect. This has led to owners directing economies on to crew wages and conditions and avoiding tax on earnings. Other defects which are currently tolerated include: class-hopping by national and FOC ships which are in poor physical condition, failed companies and rogue owners which reappear and obtain further loans, mortgagees who tolerate for long periods the destitution of seafarers on board ships under their mortgages (and even deny knowledge of such ships on which they have loaned), the ease by which owners can change flags and names of ships, tolerance of uninsured vessels, laws and contracts which are blatantly unfair to seafarers, and all the other legal loopholes available to FOC states which allow the continuation of disgraceful conditions under their flags.

There are also national flag ships with bad conditions, unpaid wages and abandoned seafarers. But in these cases, some crews can resort to national courts and owners are identifiable. Abuses have been identified on Russian, Ukranian and Romanian vessels under national flags. Some of this is attributable to administrative chaos, corruption and lack of finance; only time will tell if compliance will be forced on new owners by the flag state.

There are of course individuals in shipping companies, maritime administrations and banks with social responsibility. But the large corporate organisations and institutions to which many belong, and the separation of ownership by distant deregulated management companies, often remove them from accountability and the realities of the crew. Bruyn defines social responsibilities in this sense as 'the conscientious efforts to take account of these who are adversely affected by corporate policies'. Social responsibility, he says, refers to a structure 'that makes certain that those who exploit are answerable to the exploited'.[2] The law should take care of this, but it clearly does not always in a global environment with only national enforcement of international legislation.

Defects in the Present International Regulatory System

As outlined in Chapter 9 (and in Appendix 3) there are in fact many international conventions and state regulations which should prevent most abuses. But the UN conventions are not ratified by some key flag states, or, if they are, they are not implemented, or are subtly distorted.

The UN agencies of the ILO, the IMO and UNCTAD have undoubtedly worked assiduously over the years facilitating and steering these conventions through committees and diplomatic meetings in order to protect the welfare and safety of seafarers. They could not prevent dilution and they have no powers of enforcement, which rest with flag states. These have, as sovereign nations, always been considered the primary regulators of vessels flying their flags.

Many flag states have clearly not done what was required of them in relation to ships on their registers. Consequently the best hope for implementation of international regulations has now shifted to port-state control (PSC) exercised within states that have ratified conventions or have equivalent legislation. These states now have the authority to enforce international regulations on foreign flag vessels in their ports. But PSC has its drawbacks. Ships spend only a short time in port and it is difficult for surveyors to check on every aspect – they seldom reach the social and welfare categories. For example, the convention which offers most potential for the health and safety of seafarers is ILO 147 (1981). Over half of the world fleet by tonnage has not ratified this convention after 16 years. Nevertheless port-state officials in places where ratification exists have the powers to detain all ships violating the convention whether they have ratified or not, and regardless of flag. They have only done so on the social and health aspects in a limited number of occasions at a few ports, and usually only subsidiary to the arrest of vessels for other defects.

Not every port has PSC, and for some of those that have, there can be a reluctance to detain too many ships because of an underlying awareness that ports compete for ship calls. In any event PSC officers take most actions in relation to the major IMO safety con-

ventions such as SOLAS (dealing with life-saving, fire and navigational equipment, etc.) and MARPOL (pollution prevention of the
marine environment). This is often because of shortages of adequately trained inspectors, pressures of time and a lack of
prescriptive international standards in welfare and social respects.

However, at EU level, PSC is undoubtedly moving in the direction
of quality shipping by the enforcement of both technical safety
measures and adequate social conditions, not only on EU flag ships,
but on all vessels calling at EU ports. In this respect an editorial in
Lloyd's List in 1995 observed: 'the enthusiastic new European
Commissioner Neil Kinnock could make an immediate impact by
declaring an exploitation free sea area where ships in inter European
trades are required to employ seafarers at European conditions'.[3]

Another line of approach is selfregulation by the shipping industry. The International Chamber of Shipping (ICS) and the
International Shipping Federation (ISF) have produced a Code of
Good Management Practice in Safe Ship Operation.[4] It is 'intended
solely for voluntary use'. While most of the Code relates to technical management ,there is general guidance drawing attention to
relevant ILO and IMO conventions on seafarers. The ICS/ISF Code
is likely to be observed by decent shipping companies, indeed it is
based on the best practices within these. However, being voluntary,
there are no requirements for monitoring its implementation, or
for taking action against members that do not observe the Code.
The assumption in self-regulation is that competing interests will
co-operate for the public good by not seeking economic advantages
through cutting safety and social corners. Many ICS/ISF members
would do this but a formal system of accountability would help
persuade the others.

It is true that the trade body Intertanko expelled Adriatic
Tankers from that club. But this did not stop Adriatic from obtaining charters, nor did the cancellation of Adriatic's insurance cover
by its P&I club prevent the ships from trading uninsured.

Uninsured Seafarers and Ships

The last observation is another serious defect in the regulatory
system which has widespread implications. The absence of insurance not only removes any vestige of guaranteed protection for
seafarers and their families in the case of accidental injuries and
deaths, it exposes third parties (ships, ports, coastal communities
and the environment) to the consequences of ship disasters, with
little possibility of any liabilities being covered. The maximum rec-

ompense for third parties would be the value of the ship (or what was left of it), and only that one ship, as this may be the only visible asset of the owner.

The loss of insurance is relevant also in relation to the abandonment and the arrest of vessels in ports. A ship may have dangerous cargoes and fuel on board. At best it will have an unpaid and demoralised crew with little interest in the vessel. In most ports an abandoned ship (which is not yet arrested) and an owner who has disappeared may fall under the jurisdiction of the Harbour-master, although in practice there will be little he can do unless an accident occurs. Even then he could find himself sued for damages to the ship by a reappearing owner as a result of his intervention.

Of even more concern are substandard vessels abandoned outside of the territorial sea with inadequate crewing, low in fuel and without proper communication systems. It is possible that the charterers as the owners of the cargo would be liable for any pollution and other damages that occurred should something happen to the ship.

Because of lack of insurance for the crew, it will be appreciated from previous chapters that it is left to commercially uninvolved parties, especially the ITF and the missions, to take responsibility for the abandoned seafarers, and to help them get home. Neither the port state nor the flag state will accept this task despite what is laid down in international conventions. The P&I clubs will only act on claims if a shipowner has paid his premiums and has paid the liabilities: P&I work on the principle of 'pay to be paid'. The mortgagees in turn may pay the crew only if the ship is worth arresting and selling. For these reasons major efforts have been made to introduce compulsory insurance covering crew wages and repatriation, and a mandatory international system of third-party insurance. These matters are being considered by IMO/ILO working groups involving many interests and are subject to negotiations, agreements, ratifications and enforcement.

Human Rights

Another general international dimension which is highlighted in the report involves the many violations of basic human rights of seafarers. Seafarers under FOC have lost their rights as citizens of homelands. They come under flag-state laws on the high seas, which, if they are protective, can be conveniently ignored. They receive only partial protection under PSC. The human rights of seafarers should clearly not be a matter of flag, either national or FOC.

These are indivisible rights regardless of race, nationality, culture, location, or whatever. Human rights are, according to the 1948 UN General Assembly, the Universal Declaration of Human Rights and the Vienna Declaration of 1993, rights by virtue of being human. The instances of violation of human rights run through the previous chapters ranging from prohibition of freedom of association to physical and mental abuse.

New Developments in International Legislation

The mid-1990s has seen a rising awareness of the unsatisfactory conditions of ship safety and the treatment of seafarers under some national and FOC regimes. This is reflected in amended and new pieces of legislation. Several of these discussed in the previous chapter are of particular significance for future improvements if they are passed unadulterated into national laws.

But, as always, it is the flag state which is required to implement international conventions. During 1997, the IMO drew up guidelines for flag states and how best to do this. The IMO also encouraged port-state inspection programmes to co-operate on a regional basis: several EU and other states have already been doing this since 1982 under a Memorandum of Understanding.

Very often it has been the captain of a vessel who has been prosecuted for non-compliance. Accountability has now been extended through the International Safety Management (ISM) Code which has been introduced as a chapter of SOLAS to enter into force at various dates extending from 1 July 1998 to 2002. This puts more accountability for defects and non-compliance with regulations on the shipping company. However, the responsibility for ensuring compliance and issuing documentary proof still rests with the flag state. In this case though, the ISM code is likely to be applied more searchingly by PSC, especially in the EU and the US. The management and directors of the company, and the required 'designated person' under the Code, can all be prosecuted.

No doubt there will be further amendments to international conventions and the tightening of the gaps between regulations. However, this policy of continuous updating, while needed, misses the main problem. That is, it fails to recognise explicitly that the political and economic structure of the shipping industry has changed qualitatively. It is now truly global in every respect, but the primary authority for implementing regulations still rests with the individual flag states of registry. It is argued that only when this contradiction is resolved will unsafe vessels and the disgraceful treatment meted out to seafarers in a significant sector of the industry be adequately removed. The concluding sections of this report deals with this fundamental point.

The Legal Fiction of Flag and Territory at Sea

The structure of the shipping industry is now built around ships financed internationally, crews which are multi-national and beneficial owners who may reside elsewhere than the state of registration. There is, as has long been recognised, often no genuine link between the ship and the flag of registry. Yet it is that state of registration whose laws apply and whose administrations are supposed to exercise control. The state has sovereign rights over the ship and seafarers as part of its territory. This is now a form of political sophistry in the global industry. The flag state is in control *de jure*, but only theoretically; in practice the *de facto* authority lies with the foreign-based beneficial owner (via the master), who can dictate procedures and conditions on board regardless of the flag of the ship.

Similarities have often been made between the modern globalised shipping industry and transnational corporations which move capital and activities between countries in response to differentials in the cost of labour. There are important differences between these global companies and international shipping. The activities of the transnationals lie squarely within the geographical territories of the host states. They can, and do, exert pressures on the state but ultimately they are subject to the laws of that state. The transnationals employ local labour and resources, and sometimes stimulate indigenous entrepreneurs, and there are OECD and ILO guidelines relating to their behaviour.

The analogy with shipping breaks down quite quickly. The beneficial shipowners of FOC have no real contact with the flag they choose to fly on their ships. They do not normally move capital or management of the company to the state of registry, nor do they employ local people. They employ labour from world-wide sources, and the ships seldom if ever call at the flag state. There is no justification for the pretension that the ship is a floating part of a sovereign territory by virtue of flying a flag that the shipowner has hired for a small rent.

This legal fiction is one of the elements that facilitates abuse. Seafarers under this system cannot easily reach accountable sources. They become, as Lane puts it, 'disenfranchised'.[5] The FOC states take no action against pirate attacks on ships which are nevertheless regarded as floating parts of their territories, nor do they act in protection or rescue of seafarers on their flag ships trapped by civil war or other upheavals in foreign ports.

Only when the ship enters the jurisdiction of a foreign state where there are responsible administrations and teams of surveyors (or vigilant NGOs) do FOC vessels come under the scrutiny of a truly legal regime. Even then, as has been repeatedly pointed out, PSC is not world-wide, nor does it always extend to protection of the social and health conditions on ships.

The existence of globalised shipping with its substandard sector clearly represents unfair competition to decent shipping companies. But it is more socially pervasive than that. Because of competitive pressures, some FOC ships (in the absence of an ITF Blue Certificate) can induce a downward levelling in the conditions of seafarers under all flags by undermining the economic viability of socially responsible owners. In this respect there is some analogy with the transnational corporations, whereby governments in some developed countries argue that the choice of their country for the location of transnational enterprises will be successful only if pay and working conditions are competitive with alternative locations in the Third World.

It is argued in the concluding remarks that the more responsible owners, investors and seafarers need better global jurisdictional processes as countervailing power to owners of substandard ships who find refuge predominantly in FOCs. The powers of the flag state in this respect are becoming increasingly inappropriate in such a globalised industry.

Transition to Global Governance in Shipping

There are already distinctive changes taking place in the relationships between sovereignty of nation states and international interests. Castells, in his concluding third volume on the millennium, goes as far as predicting that the 'nation states will survive, not so their sovereignty'.[6] Certainly in recent years there has been what is termed a process of 'suturing' taking place, that is, the 'policies and practices of states in distributing power upwards to international levels and downwards to sub-national agencies'.[7] This has been most evident in the socio-political context of the European Union whereby member states of the EU have ceded a certain amount of authority over common interests (trade, agriculture, fishing) to the supra-national EU. Although, in the case of ship registration, the attempt to introduce a 'EUROS' flag for member-state vessels has not as yet been successful, largely because of the attractions of FOC for the industry. There has also in the EU been a downward devolution of centralised state power from, for example, London and Madrid to Scotland and Catalonia. Voluntary nation-state suturing is going to continue, and is likely to be more evident in the reduced authority of flag states compared with the interest of the international community in world shipping.

Some authority has already been wrested by PSC from many flag states (both FOC and national) because of their inability and unwillingness to implement acceptable global safety regulations. The port states have been sanctioned by the international community via the IMO to enforce rules over ships in what has hitherto been the almost exclusive province of the nation state. In effect, nation-state territorial sovereignty is beginning to be perceived as confined to their circumscribed geographical territories. In other words, state sovereignty rights may not in the future be attributable to a ship by virtue of its flag. So far this transition is only apparent when a ship enters a foreign port, although, in the territorial sea of a foreign state, all ships regardless of flag must comply with the rules of innocent passage, and on the high seas merchant ships can be intercepted by government vessels of any state if they are suspected of specific criminal activities.

The rules applied by PSC and at sea have been formulated and approved at international forums, including the International Maritime Organisation and the International Labour Organisation. The rules over ships and territorial rights are also embodied in the 1982 UN Law of the Sea Convention, which was adopted by an assembly of world governments as binding on all nation states.

Furthermore, directives of the European Union require member states to enforce these regulations in EU ports and sea areas (as well as EU regionally specific rules) with respect to ships of all flags. Similarly, the United States has extended the territorial reach of several international maritime conventions beyond PSC to the US Territorial Sea and Exclusive Economic Zone.

Another important feature of the erosion of sovereign immunity of merchant ships lies in how regulations are made. In determining the content and scope of international treaties binding on ships, it is not only consensus of nation states which is involved. Other international bodies, which are non-governmental (NGOs), exert pressures in the formulation of the conventions. These include the International Chamber of Shipping, the International Shipping Federation and related organisations, and the International Transport Workers' Federation, Greenpeace, Friends of the Earth, Amnesty International and other organisations with global scope, including the US Center for Seafarers' Rights, the UK-based Seafarers' International Research Centre and the many religious affiliated bodies.

Several of these NGOs have consultative status with the UN international agencies. But they not only enter into the making of conventions, they conduct and present research results, monitor procedures, pressurise enforcement and take direct actions against non-compliance, including holding ships in port and intercepting vessels at sea in cases of dumping toxics, and matters such as illegal whaling. Government representatives at international meetings now take more account of such pressures.

What we are witnessing is the evolution of an international 'governance' as countervailing power to what has become globalised economic activities, safety avoidance and labour conditions which shelter behind nation-state rights and immunities and poor international enforcement mechanisms. By governance is meant 'a function that can be performed by a wide variety of public and private, state and non state, national and international institutions and practices'.[8] Governance has already partly evolved at the IMO and the ILO but the resulting regulations from these bodies need to be closely integrated. Hirst and Thomson, in their study *Globalization in Question*, argue that:

> The different levels and functions of governance need to be tied together in a division of control that sustains the division of labour. If this does not happen then the unscrupulous can exploit, and the unlucky can fall into the 'gaps' between different agencies and dimensions of governance.[9]

The point being made regarding governance in general and the gaps between agencies of governance in particular is very apposite to the structure of regulating international shipping. Because, for example, PSC is legitimated by IMO resolutions (embodied in the influential SOLAS convention) the port-state control officers in their training and functions tend to focus on ship safety and pollution prevention: whereas conventions from the ILO regulating, say, hours of work receive less attention. Labour is in fact inadequately represented amongst IMO delegations. There is consultation between the IMO and the ILO but there are gaps in their respective legislations through which the interests of seafarers, and therefore of safety, can slip. Governance as distinct from government means a formal coordination of the various public, private and international bodies and the methods of proper enforcement by them.

Governance of global activities also entails the ability to deal with problems arising from contracts and other legal issues which affect multi-national crews but are embodied in flag-state agreements. However, seafarers may never go to the flag state, neither will they have tangible human links, as the owners, managers or charterers of the ships can all reside in different countries from those of the seafarers.

When disputes come to law, it is a matter of chance for the crew if a particular national court acknowledges, shall we say, the natural justice of awarding seafarers the wages they have contracted for. Alternatively a judge may simply decide, after a wait of many months, that they must take the case to Honduras, or wherever. Because of differences in interpretation and procedures of courts, mortgagees frequently contract with specialised companies to get an abandoned ship taken to a 'friendly' jurisdiction where they will be able to recover some of their investments on arrest and sale of a vessel (as the mortgagee in possession), and pay and repatriate the crew. But owners or the flag state may well 'persuade' the crew not to sail there. International governance, it can be argued, needs some form of global judiciaries, as for example the International Tribunal for the Sea (established in Hamburg under the 1982 Law of the Sea Convention), or a more easily accessible arbitration system, independent of nation states, where seafarers can obtain justice. The problem with the Tribunal in Hamburg, is that under Article 292 of the Convention it is the flag state which has recourse to the Tribunal, and several will simply not bother when it comes to abandoned foreign seafarers.

There would be understandable reluctance for private business to accept more regulation or enforcement at international and supra-national levels. The shipping industry was enthusiastic towards deregulation after 1973 in order to reduce costs, and they succeeded in doing this. However, maintaining the present system of making shipping conventions at international forums and relying on flag-state implementation and enforcement has proved chaotic. It opens the way to the abuses detailed in this book and it may undermine the competitive position of decent companies operating in the global market.

Conclusion

The open labour market for seafarers globally is based primarily on lowest costs, and the supply countries compete on this basis. There are no integral economic mechanisms in such a market system which can ensure decent levels of social welfare for seafarers. Indeed, the poor conditions under many FOC vessels exert downward pressures on national flags. These pressures can only be resisted if flag states are made to comply with international standards. Furthermore, the crews of ships drawn from the poorer countries and sailing under flags which are not their own have no basis for obtaining social justice when vessels are arrested in foreign ports. Of even more concern, if they are abandoned in a region of political and military upheaval (as in the example of the *Kyoto 1*), the crews are exposed not only to the hardships of abandonment but immense dangers. There are no international rescue provisions for these crews, and flag states and the institutions of shipping take no interest in them.

In the above respects, international legislation has clearly not kept pace with the changes in the structure of the industry. What in effect has happened over the past three decades is a growth in the gulf between the components of shipping embodied in seafaring labour, finances, sectoral representation (ITF and ISF) and lawmaking (the IMO, the ILO and UNCTAD), all at global levels, and the enforcement of international regulations at nation-state levels. Some of these states, and particularly FOC countries, have no proper maritime administrations, and are interested only in registration fees. Compliance with regulations is thus left to individual beneficial owners. These vary from those providing good conditions and ITF rates, tolerable conditions and ILO minimum wages, to the totally unacceptable substandard owner with poor on-board conditions and very low wages. The latter consider ships and crews as exploitable assets to be abandoned when they cease to make money, and have little regard for the environmental and human consequences of their operational strategies. The present system allows them to do this with impunity.

The loopholes through which the unscrupulous owner can make rich pickings are many. They do so through the banks and other financial institutions, avoidance of payments to seafarers and their abandonment. When need be, they go bankrupt and reappear again to obtain further loans while keeping most of their earlier gains. As new owners (often of the same ships), they thereby have no obligations towards former seafarers or creditors.

There are short-term and long-term solutions to improve the position of seafarers in the new era. The former can include more 'naming and shaming' of negligent companies like Adriatic, better vigilance by mortgagees and some discarding by them of 'customer confidentiality' and 'non-interference with customer business' caveats, when made aware of the maltreatment of people on the ships they finance. Similarly, cargo interests should take more notice of evidence produced by the ITF and the unions about substandard owners and crew conditions on ships they are chartering.

Some of the P&I clubs can be less than scrupulous when it comes to seafarers from poorer countries and their families. The best, such as GARD, pay medical and compensation claims promptly, but some others deliberately delay and make one-off offers below contract agreements. This is not acceptable. Indeed, it is well past the time when shipowners should have compulsory deposition of funds for the repatriation of seafarers through P&I or other means. Certainly, there should also be a process whereby a vessel without proof of P&I cover or other third-party insurance, would be excluded from ports and even from the territorial sea of a coastal state. Underwriters, it is argued, should in any event refuse to insure these vessels (even at high premiums) and this should be transparently evident to coastal states and charterers.

When a substandard vessel is in port it is certainly expected in the EU that port-state control surveyors will in the future look more closely at the condition under which seafarers live and work. This has as many implications for ship safety as has defective equipment.

The need to be considered in the longer term is for the separation of the unequivocal rights to the registrations of ships from all flag states. The international community (embodied in, for example, the IMO) could reasonably lay down requirements for a registry and list states that meet these at economic, safety and social levels. This would represent further erosion of nation-state sovereignty, although it would also raise respect for flags and would provide administrative procedures which correspond to the global structure of modern shipping. It is in line with trends towards governance over global activities in a new era and it may culminate in an international registry. Governance in this way will, it is argued, require even greater integration between agencies such as the ILO, the IMO, UNCTAD and the public and private organisations dealing with trade, finance and employment.

There is no doubt that in this new era, shipping is more than ever essential for the international division of labour, but it is being provided too cheaply, partly at the expense of seafarers. The system, and especially the usage of the flag of convenience, encourages rogue owners, pressurises others into reducing further the levels of working and living conditions, and seriously damages the public image of shipping and seafaring The substandard sector has to be eradicated in everyone's interest. There are no good reasons why this should not be tackled by the International Shipping Federation and the International Transport Workers' Federation together, as it represents threats to the interests of both.

As this report may be taken as a criticism of shipowners generally, the last word is given to someone expressing the views of the more socially responsible owners. Mr E.M. Everard, of the old established company of F.T. Everard of London, has this to say: 'It is up to us to make sure ships and the people who sail on them have the highest possible reasonable standards of equipment, inspection, training, etc. As a ship operator we have to examine our own consciences and personally, I like to go to sleep at night.' He goes on to advise:

There is no simple solution to the problem for rogue ships. These ships set the lowest common denominator as far as the market is concerned. Charterers rightly want their goods carried at competitive rates. If standards are brought up on all ships they will achieve this and get a better quality of services.[10]

Notes

Chapter 1

1. Lubbock, Basil (ed.), *Barlow's Journal 1659–1703*, Volume 11 (London: Hunt and Blakelt Ltd, 1934) p. 90.
2. Kverndal, Roald, *Seamen's Missions: Their Origins and Early Growth* (Pasadena, CA: William Corley Library, 1986) p. 384.
3. Anon, 'Pondering the Adriatic Riddle', *TradeWinds*, 28 July 1995, p. 2.
4. Chapman, P.K. *Trouble on Board* (USA: ILR Press, 1992).
5. Commonwealth of Australia, *Ships of Shame*, inquiry into ship safety (Canberra, 1992).
6. For expansion on this process see Couper, A.D. 'The Crisis Decades', *Maritime Policy and Management*, vol. 25, no. 3 (1998) pp. 207–11.
7. For references to these other companies, see ITF, *The Top Twenty Worst Shipping Companies in the World* (London: ITF, 1998).

Chapter 2

1. Kendall, L.C., *The Business of Shipping* (London: Chapman and Hall, 1986).
2. Hope, Ronald, *A New History of British Shipping* (London: John Murray, 1990).
3. Stopford, Martin, *Maritime Economics* (London: Unwin Hyman, 1988).
4. Couper, A.D., 'Maritime Jurisdictional Zones', *Times Atlas of the Oceans* (London: Times Books, 1983) pp. 220–3.
5. Hirst, P. and Thomson, G., *Globalisation in Question* (Oxford: Polity Press, 1996) p. 1.
6. Stopford, Martin, *Maritime Economics*.
7. UNCTAD, *United Nations Review of Maritime Transport 1997* (Geneva: UNCTAD, 1998) p. 29.
8. Ibid., p. 29.

9.   Shell Briefing Service, *The Tanker Industry in the 1990s* (London: Shell, 1989).
10. Marcadon, Jacques, 'Refrigerated Transport', in Couper, A.D. (ed.), *The Shipping Revolution* (London: Conway Maritime Press, 1992) pp. 33–41.
11. Couper, A.D., 'Cruise Ship Design and the Seafarer', in Gouielmos, A.M. (ed.), *Essays in Honour of Professor Basil Metaxas* (Piraeus: University of Piraeus Press, 1997).

Chapter 3

1.   BIMCO and ISF, (1995), *The World Wide Demand for and Supply of Seafarers*, Manpower update (University of Warwick, 1995).
2.   Minghua, Zhao, *Women Seafarers in the EC* (Cardiff: SIRC, 1998).
3.   Economic Commission, 'Report on Training Facilities in China, India, Indonesia and the Philippines' (SIRC and WMU (World Maritime University), 1998, unpublished).
4.   Nicolaides, P., 'The Growing Role of the Cyprus Shipping Council', *Cyprus Mail*, 22 July 1995.
5.   Harlaftis, Gelina, *A History of Greek-owned Shipping* (London: Routledge, 1996) pp. 212–15.
6.   Hill, J.M.M., *The Seafaring Career* (London, Tavistock Institute, 1972) p. 60.
7.   SIRC, *Multi-cultural and Multi-national Crews*, Report to EC (DG VII) (Cardiff: SIRC, forthcoming).
8.   SIRC, management interviews for *MARCOM* Project, 1997.
9.   Ibid.
10. SIRC, interviews with management and crews, 1997.
11. Couper, A.D., Recordings of Anwar the Cook for BBC Radio 4 programme, *The British Seafarer*, broadcast 1978.
12. Oubre, Sinclaire, 'Apostleship of the Sea', unpublished report on ship observations, Port Arthur, Texas, 1997.
13. Borisova, Yevgeria, 'Abandoned crew starves in city port', *The St Petersburg Press*, 5–11 December 1995, p. 1. For comparisons with pre-Second World War conditions see Hope, Ronald, *A New History of British Shipping* (London: John Murray, 1990).
14. Lloyd's Register, *The World Casualty Statistics* (London: Lloyd's Register, 1996).

15. SIRC, *Proceedings of a Research Workshop on Fatigue in the Maritime Industry* (Cardiff: SIRC, 1996).

16. Roberts, Steven, *Mortality Among Seafarers* (Cardiff: SIRC, 1998).

17. Ibid.

18. Nielsen, D. and Roberts, Steven, *Fatalities among the World's Merchant Seafarers (1990–1994)* (Cardiff: SIRC, 1998).

19. Grey, Andrew, Table 'Comparison of the Types of Attack 1991–1996', *Lloyd's List*, 16 July 1996: regional attacks see IMB (1997) *Piracy and Armed Robbery against Ships*, ICC, I Linton Rd, Barking 1G11.

20. Accounts of the *Anna Sierra* hijack, International Maritime Bureau, 1995 and in *Lloyd's List*, 16 November 1995 and 1 February 1996, and (amongst others) Ellen, Eric, 'Piracy: a Myriad of Reasons, but a Simple Solution', *BIMCO Bulletin*, 1997, vol. 92, no. 1.

21. Taylor, Rex, et al., 'The Psycho-Social Consequences of Intermittent Husband Absence: an Epidemiological Study', *Social Science and Medicine*, vol. 20, no. 9, 1985, pp. 877–85.

22. Forsyth, C. 'Determinants of Family Integration among Merchant Seamen', *International Journal of Sociology of the Family*, vol. 18, 1998, pp. 33–4.

    Forsyth, C., 'Father Alienation, A further analysis of familial management startegy among merchant seamen', *International Journal of Sociology of the Family*, vol. 22, no. 2, 1992, pp. 1–9.

    Forsyth, C., 'Sea Daddy, An Exercise into an endangered social species', *Maritime Policy and Management*, vol. 11, 1984, pp. 53–60.

    Forsyth, C. and Brankston, W.B., 'The social psychological consequences of a life at sea: A Causal Model', *Maritime Policy and Management*, vol. 11, 1984, pp. 123–34.

    Forsyth, C. and Gramling, R., 'Adaptive familial strategies among merchant seafarers' lifestyles', *Family and Economic Issues*, vol. 11, no. 2, 1990, pp. 183–98.

    Morrice, J.K.W., et al., 'Oil Wives and Intermittent Husbands', *British Journal of Psychiatry*, vol. 147, 1985, pp. 479–83.

    Morrice, J.K.W., et al., 'The Intermittent Husband Syndrome', *New Society*, vol. 43, no. 796, January 1978.

Shera, M., Shipping Out: *A Sociological study of the American Merchant Seaman* (Cambridge, MD: Cornell Maritime Press Inc., 1973).

23. Lai, Karen, Recording made in March 1996 at Seamen's Central United Ministry to Port of Galveston (personal communication).

Chapter 4

1. Dury, C. and Stokes, P., *Ship Finance: the credit crisis*, (London: Lloyd's of London Press, 1983).
2. Ibid.
3. Ibid.
4. Ibid.
5. Glass, D., 'The Rise and Fall of Adriatic Tankers', *Seatrade Review*, December, 1995, pp. 6–9.
6. Ibid.
7. Brooks, M.R., *Ship Finance, the banker's perspective* (Halifax, Canada: Centre for International Business Studies, Dalhousie University, 1990).
8. Tinsley, D., 'Sanko orders anchor handlers', *Lloyd's List*, 24 February 1997, p. 1.
9. Lowry, N., 'Regency applies for Chapter XI', *Lloyd's List*, 10 November 1995.
10. Anon., 'Seizures & Arrests: Regency Cruises', *Lloyd's List*, 18 November 1995.
11. Bray, J., 'Russia bid to control Baltic Shipping', *Lloyd's List*, 12 October 1996.
12. Borisova, Y. and Donaldson, L., 'Creditors agree BSC rescue plan', *Lloyd's List*, 5 April 1997, p. 1.
13. Shuker, L., 'P&I cover withdrawn from Unimar', *Lloyd's List*, 7 December 1996, p. 1.
14. Anon., *Lloyd's List*, 14 November 1997.
15. Anon., *Lloyd's List*, 18 November 1997.
16. ITF records, unpublished data from SSD Actions Unit, 1997.
17. Ibid.
18. *Maritime News*, no. 2, 1997, p.2.
19. Garland, Geoff, 'Adriatic Tankers ship called "dirty" and "dangerous"', *TradeWinds*, 1 September 1995, p.6.
20. Morris, Jim, *Houston Chronicle*, 18 August 1996, p.1.
21. MORI, Survey for ITF, unpublished, 1997.

Chapter 5

1. Harlaftis, G., *Greek Shipowners and Greece 1945–1975*, (London: Athlone Press, 1993).
2. Ibid.
3. UNCTAD, *Review of Maritime Transport* (New York and Geneva: United Nations, 1995).
4. Lillestolen, T., 'Panagis Zissimatos: The man behind the myth', *TradeWinds*, 11 June 1993, p. 28.
5. Ibid.
6. Ibid., p. 1.
7. Lillestolen, T., 'Adriatic Tankers' fleet is large and diversified', *TradeWinds*, 11 June 1993, pp. 30–1.
8. Anon., 'Trade upturn adds momentum of recovery', *Lloyd's List*, 15 June, 1995.
9. Lillestolen, T., 'Dipping into crude, but not diving in', *TradeWinds*, 11 June 1993, p. 29.
10. Ibid.
11. Glass, D., 'The rise and fall of Adriatic Tankers', *Seatrade Review*, December 1995, pp. 6–9.
12. Stallstrom, T., 'DNV responds in Adriatic case', *TradeWinds*, 16 June 1995, p. 2.
13. Knutsen, T.S., 'Letter blew the whistle for banned "Rokko San"', *TradeWinds*, 20 March 1992, p. 28.
14. Knutsen, T.S., 'Adriatic Tankers to sue Stavanger Tank', *TradeWinds*, 3 April 1992, p. 4.
15. Letter to the ITF, London, from the crew of the *Stainless King*, January 1996.
16. Garfield, G., 'Adriatic Tankers ship called "dirty" and "dangerous"', *TradeWinds*, 1 September 1995, p. 6.
17. Anon., 'Adriatic Tankers', *ITF Seafarers' Bulletin*, no. 10, 1996, pp. 26–7.
18. Anon., 'Adriatic loses Australian case', *Fairplay*, 2 February 1996.
19. Letter to the ITF legal department, London from Paco Carreria, a Panamanian lawyer.
20. Garfield, G. and Landells, J., 'Adriatic faces new crewing claim', *TradeWinds*, 1 September 1995, p. 7; Guest, A., 'Registers delete Adriatic vessels', *Lloyd's List*, 1 September 1995.
21. Anon., 'Adriatic defends itself', *TradeWinds*, 25 August 1995, p. 3.

22.   Anon., 'Adriatic loses P&I cover', *Lloyd's List*, 16 January 1996.
23.   Anon., 'First Step', *Fairplay*, 1 June 1995, p. 3.

Chapter 6

1.   Lillestolen, T., 'Panagis Zissimatos: The man behind the myth', *TradeWinds*, 11 June 1993, p. 28.
2.   Ibid.
3.   Macalister, Terry, 'New Exec Promise to Revive Adriatic Without Ship Sales',*TradeWinds*, 18 August 1995, p. 7.
4.   Harlaftis, Gelina, *A History of Greek-owned Shipping,,* (London: Routledge, 1996) p. 173.
5.   'Newsfront', *Seatrade Week*, 17–23 November 1995, p. 1.
6.   Glass, D., 'Banking on Greek Shipping', *SeaTrade Review*, November 1996, p. 19.
7.   Grammenos, Costas, 'Financing the International Fleet', *Seaways*, July 1991, p. 9.
8.   Stokes, P., 'Assessing Shipping Investment', *Lloyd's Shipping Economist*, October 1992, p. 11.
9.   Anon., 'Adriatic Tankers Finalises $50 million Private Debt Placement', *Marine Monitor*, 14 February 1995, p. 1.
10.   Lowrey, Nigel, 'New sources of capital are shaking up shipping market', *Lloyd's List*, 29 October 1997, p. 7.
11.   Macalister, Terry, *Evening Standard*, 21 February 1995.
12.   Arntzen, M., in a paper at *Lloyd's Shipping Economist*'s 8th Shipping Finance Conference in London, 1995.
13.   Stokes, 'Assessing Shipping Investment'.
14.   Anon., 'Banking on experience is what really counts', *Lloyd's Shipping Economist*, January 1996, p. 7.
15.   Ibid.
16.   Whittiker, Gillian and Bradey, Joe., 'Greek Tragedies May Not Deter Investors', *TradeWinds*, 10 November 1995.
17.   Grammenos, Costas, 'Shipping Investments in Capital Markets within a Dynamic International Environment', paper given at the American Stock Exchange Shipping Conference, 1989.
18.   Rissik, D., 'Sentrachem is hit by Adriatic Loan Claims', *Lloyd's List*, 23 October 1995.
19.   Anon., 'DnB Explore Deal on 20 Adriatic Vessels', *Seatrade Week*, 24–30 November 1995.
20.   Wade, S., 'Money Talks', *Fairplay*, 1 April 1993, p. 20.

21. Lillestolen, T., 'Panagis Zissimatos: The Man Behind the Myth'.
22. Landells, J., 'Lavish Parties and Bounced Cheques', *TradeWinds*, 10 November 1995, p.20.
23. Landells, J. and Macalister, T. 'Management Firm Irons Out Payment Deal with Adriatic', *TradeWinds*, 4 August 1995.
24. Brooks, Mary, (1990), *Ship Finance: a Banker's Perspective*, (Halifax, Canada: 1990) (Halifax, Canada: Centre for International Business Studies, Dalhousie University) p. 57.
25. Larsen, G., 'Instructive Example', *Lloyd's Shipping Economist*, May 1992, p. 5.
26. Brooks, *Ship Finance: a Banker's Perspective*.
27. Stokes, 'Assessing Shipping Investment', p. 14.
28. Anon., 'Value of Adriatic Fleet Questioned', *Seatrade Week*, 17–23 November 1995.
29. Guy, J., 'Money Talks', *Fairplay*, 7 June 1990, p. 15.
30. Symes, Roger, 'The demise of AT', *Storing Ships News*, February 1996.
31. Symes, 'The demise of AT'.
32. Landells, John, 'Zissimatos Defends Adriatic Tankers' Record', *TradeWinds*, 9 December 1994, p. 6.
33. Anon., 'Chemical Trade Stays at Core', *TradeWinds*, 9 December 1994, p. 6.
34. Bray, J., 'CIT Affirms Support for Shipping', *Lloyd's List*, 16 April 1996.
35. Lillestolen, Trond and Landells, John, 'Adriatic Suezmay Stuck at Trieste', *TradeWinds*, 10 February 1995, p. 4.
36. Anon., 'Adriatic in Denial of ITF Charges', *Seatrade Week*, 24–30 March 1995, p. 1.
37. Anon., 'Adriatic Sails into Smoother Waters', *Seatrade Week*, 9–15 June 1995, p. 2.
38. Anon., 'Hard Hit Adriatic Made Scapegoat', *Seatrade Week*, 26 May–1 June 1995, p. 4.
39. Landells, John and Lillestolen, Trond, 'Adriatic Fights Back', *TradeWinds*, 26 May 1995, p. 4.
40. Anon., 'First Step', *Fairplay*, 1 June 1995, p. 3.
41. Guest, Andrew, 'Adriatic head may buy back vessels', *Lloyd's List*, 12 January 1996.
42. Anon., 'Adriatic bankruptcy decisions imminent', *Lloyd's List*, 8 January 1996.
43. Anon., 'Comeback attempt by Adriatic ends in anger and writs', *TradeWinds*, 14 November 1996.

44. Anon., 'Skaugens Petrotrans caught up in tangled affairs', *TradeWinds*, 8 November 1996, p. 15.
45. Anon, 'Zissimatos was key player in move to trade vessels', *TradeWinds*, 8 November 1996, p. 14.
46. Macalister, Terry, 'BNB catches flak from creditors of Adriatic Tankers', *TradeWinds*, 8 October 1996.
47. Lowrey, Nigel, 'New sources of capital are shaping up shipping market', *Lloyd's List*, 29 October 1997, p. 7.
48. Macalister, Terry, 'Brokers face firing line over Adriatic', *TradeWinds*, 2 February 1996, p. 6.
49. Anon., 'One of the wounded vows to seek justice against Zissimatos', *TradeWinds*, 8 November 1996, p. 15.

Chapter 7

1. Whittaker, Gillian, 'Piraeus court sentences head of collapsed Adriatic Tankers', *TradeWinds*, 10 October 1996, p. 3.
2. Rankin, Philip, 'Question – What shall we do with the abandoned sailor?', *Lloyd's List*, 4 November 1996, p. 1.

Chapter 8

1. ITF data files.
2. Ibid.
3. Dickey, Alan, 'Russian seafarers still trapped in Netherlands', *Lloyd's List*, 19 August 1995.
4. ITF data files.
5. Cockroft, David, 'Beyond 2000: Some thoughts on Maritime Trade Unionism', *Maritime Policy and Management*, vol. 24, no. 1, 1997, pp. 3–8. The account of the ITF is based partly on this Guest Editorial.
6. Ibid.
7. Ibid.
8. Landells, J., 'Zissimatos defends Adriatic Tankers' record', *TradeWinds*, 9 December 1994, p. 96.
9. Editorial, 'Adriatic in demand of ITF charges', *Seatrade Week Newsfront*, 24–30 March 1995, p. 1.
10. Anon., 'Adriatic Tankers in deal with ITF', *Lloyd's List*, 4 May 1995.
11. Landells, J., 'Adriatic Tankers makes peace with the ITF', *TradeWinds*, 5 May 1995.

12.   Landells, J., 'Adriatic set to escape ITF blacklist', *TradeWinds*, 9 June 1995.
13.   Landells, J. and Macalister, T., 'Top ITF official jumps ship to join Adriatic Tankers team', *TradeWinds*, 14 July 1995, p. 5.
14.   Macalister, T., 'Adriatic promises to pay up as ITF warns of "all out war"', *TradeWinds*, 21 July 1995.
15.   Anon., 'It's war ITF warns Adriatic', *Seatrade Week Newsfront*, 28 July 1995, p. 3.
16.   Statement by Adriatic, *Lloyd's List*, 26 July 1995.
17.   'The ITF and Adriatic Tankers', ITF Press release, 28 July 1995.
18.   Landells, J. and Macalister, T., 'Management firm irons out payment deal with Adriatic', *TradeWinds*, 4 August 1995.
19.   Jones, Glyn, *Lent Appeal*, the Missions to Seamen, London, 1996.
20.   Rodriguez-Martos, Ricardo, Personal correspondence with Apostolados Del Mar, Barcelona, 1997.
21.   Jones, Glyn, *Lent Appeal*.
22.   Lai, Karen, 'From the National Catholic Conference for Seafarers', *Catholic Maritime News*, Washington, DC, vol. 52, April 1996, p. 3.
23.   Jones, Glyn, *Lent Appeal*.

Chapter 9

1.   Maritime Transport Committee of the Organisation for Economic Co-operation and Development (OECD), *Competitive advantages obtained by some shipowners as a result of non-observance of applicable international rules and standard* (Paris: OECD, 1996).
2.   Conventions and other legal instruments passed by the IMO affect seafarers through, *inter alia*, improving standards of training and certification, fire safety, life-saving appliances, standards of medical care, responsibilities of flag states and quality in management rather than through direct interference in standards of pay, etc.
3.   A Convention is a legal instrument that is required to be ratified by the country concerned and will usually come into force twelve months later. Thereafter, reports must be submitted to the ILO, at appropriate intervals, on the working of the Convention. Any member of the ILO may file a complaint that another member is failing to observe a

Convention that both have ratified and the ILO is obliged to investigate any such complaint. Such a complaint may also be made by a delegate of the ILO or an industrial association of employers or workers. A Recommendation, on the other hand, puts much less onerous obligations upon a state.

4.   *Maritime Labour Conventions and Recommendations* (Geneva: International Labour Office, 1994).

5.   Ibid.

6.   This table does not include the laws of the 'new' maritime powers such as Thailand and Vietnam, who have virtually non-existent maritime codes but whose laws do allow the arrest of foreign flagged vessels by foreign crews or even crews of nationally flagged vessels for unpaid wages.

7.   Chapman, P., *Trouble on Board: The Plight of the International Seafarer* (New York: ILR Press, 1992) pp. 37–8.

8.   (1995) 134 ALR 92.

9.   This particular point evidences the lack of evolution of Panamanian law – shipowners do not hire stevedores directly any more.

10.   'Report of the International Law Commission to the General Assembly', *Yearbook of the International Law Commission 1956*, Vol. II, p. 253 at p.279, *Commentary* on draft article 30 on status of ships, quoted in Brown, E.D., *The International Law of the Sea: Volume 1 – Introductory Material* (Dartmouth: Aldershot, 1994) p. 288.

11.   McConnell, M.L., 'Darkening Confusion Mounted Upon Darkening Confusion: The Search for the Elusive Genuine Link', *Journal of Maritime Law and Commerce*, vol. 16, 1985, p. 382.

12.   Hodges, S., *Law of Marine Insurance* (London: Cavendish Publishing Limited, 1996) p. 37.

13.   His clause is the same both in the old 1983 version and the new 1995 version of the Institute Time Clauses (Hulls), as well as the ITC(H) Restricted Perils policy and clause 14 of the Institute Voyage Clauses (Hulls).

14.   (1836) 4 Ad & E 420.

15.   Perhaps the most concise definition of what a P&I club is can be found in the Marine Insurance Act of 1906. Section 85 of this Act states that: 'Where two or more persons mutually agree to insure each other against marine losses there is said to be a mutual insurance.' Today's P&I clubs are corporations rather than groups or individuals and hence liability in modern times will fall upon the club rather than the indi-

vidual member, but the basic premise upon which the P&I clubs are founded remains essentially the same: each member responds to a 'call' for payment by contributing to a central fund from which the claims of the members are met. There may be few claims in a financial year, enabling members to have some part of their contribution returned, though in a year of heavy claims supplementary calls may have to be made. Hence upon joining a club, an owner or other interested party takes on the benefit of insurance cover of the scope set out in the club rules and the burden of contributing to the losses of fellow members. Entry into a P&I club is often effected by means of an application form, although many clubs will merely ask for those details required for underwriting purposes such as the extent of P&I cover required, the nature of the management of the vessel, the geographical area over which the vessel trades and the nationality of the crew.

16.   Hill, C., Robertson, B. and Hazelwood, S., *Introduction to P&I*, 2nd edn (London: Lloyd's of London Press Limited, 1994) p. 34.

17.   Mulrenan, J., 'Adriatic Loses P&I Cover', *Lloyd's List*, 16 January 1996.

18.   [1969] A.M.C. 1669.

19.   The club member's trustee in bankruptcy had paid the claim against the member and the court decided that it was not essential that judgment debts should be paid by a member's own funds and that member had not offended such a rule if he paid the judgment debt by using a loan or a gift.

20.   *Johnson* v. *The Salvage Association* (1887) 19 Q.B.D. 458 at p. 460 *per* Lindley L.J.; *The 'Padre Island' (No.2)* [1987] 2 Lloyd's Rep. 529, at p. 540.

21.   [1990] 2 Lloyd's Rep. 191, especially at p. 197 *per* Lord Brandon, and pp. 200–202 *per* Lord Goff and pp. 204–206 *per* Lord Jauncey.

22.   The relevant parts of section 1(3) of the Third Parties (Rights Against Insurers) Act 1930 state: 'In so far as any contract of insurance … in respect of any liability of the insured to third parties purports, whether directly or indirectly, to avoid the contract or to alter the rights of the parties … the contract shall be of no effect.'

23.   [1990] 2 Lloyd's Rep. 191 (HL) at p. 204.

Chapter 10

1. Whittaker, Gillian, 'Piraeus court sentences head of collapsed Adriatic Tankers', *TradeWinds*, 10 October 1996.
2. Bruyn, Severyn T., 'The civil world of business', in Boyle, E.J. (ed.), *Social Economics* (London and New York: Routledge, 1996) p. 146.
3. Grey, Michael, 'When crew pay is a low priority', *Lloyd's List*, 8 February 1995, p. 5.
4. ICS/ISF, *Code of good management practice in safe ship operation*, issued by the International Chamber of Shipping and the International Shipping Federation (London: ICS/ISF, 1981).
5. Lane, A.D., 'Global Seafarers, Citizens or Displaced Persons', *Seaways*, June 1998, pp. 9–11.
6. Castells, Manuel, *End of Millenium* (London: Blackwell, 1998) p. 355.
7. Hirst, Paul and Thomson, Graham, *Globalization in Question* (London: Blackwell, 1996) p. 184.
8. Ibid.
9. Ibid.
10. Everard, E.M., 'Rogue Ships – A Shipowner's View', in *Maritime Policy and Management* (London: Taylor and Francis, 1995) p. 199.

Appendix 1
Flags of Convenience and Second Registries, June 1997

Flag of Convenience Registries

Antigua & Barbuda
Aruba
Bahamas
Barbados
Belize
Bermuda
Burma
Cambodia
Canary Islands
Cayman Islands
Cook Islands
Cyprus
Germany (GIS)
Gibraltar

Honduras
Lebanon
Liberia
Luxembourg
Malta
Marshall Islands
Mauritius
Netherlands Antilles
Panama
St Vincent
Sri Lanka
Tuvalu
Vanuatu

Second Registers

(Status depends on ownership being from the flag country and agreements acceptable to that country's unions)
Denmark   (DIS)
Isle of Man   (UK)
Kerguelen   (France)
Madeira(Portugal)
Norway (NIS)

Source: ITF, London.

Appendix 2
Ship losses by Flag (1996)

This table does not represent the total losses for the year but shows the top 14 by flag.

	No.	DWT Lost	Total DWT	% Loss
Panama	27	185,964	82,871,307	0.224
USA	14	2,781	17,095,496	0.016
Japan	10	5,303	19,235,690	0.027
Russia	10	29,145	13,825,898	0.211
Belize	10	7,719	1,015,838	0.759
Honduras	9	6,109	1,200,981	0.508
China	7	45,209	17,004,116	0.266
Cyprus	7	137,673	23,804,046	0.578
St Vincent	6	30,493	7,134,362	0.427
Spain	6	3,904	1,686,619	0.231
Turkey	6	35,639	6,433,465	0.554
Malta	5	77,803	19,490,707	0.399
Greece	5	25,872	27,527,903	0.094
France	3	519	4,385,450	0.012

Source: World Casualty Statistics, 1996, Lloyd's Register.

Appendix 3

Examples of Flag of Convenience and Second Registry Enactment of National Laws giving effect to ILO recommendations and conventions on repatriation and wages[1]

Country	Enacting Legislation	Main Features of National Legislation	
		Repatriation	Wages
Panama	Labour Code of the Republic of Panama	Article 255: The employer shall always be under an obligation to return the employee to the place or port of employment before terminating their work relationship, regardless of the type of contract. However, when the employee has been employed in Panama, regardless of the port of enlistment, the employer shall be under an obligation to return him to the place where he was employed. The expenses in connection with his return must include those related to transportation, lodging, wages and support during the trip, as well as the expenses agreed upon for his departure.	Article 31: The maximum regular shift is eight hours a day up to 48 hours in a week, after which overtime must be paid.
			Article 261: There is a 25% minimum increase of wages for all overtime work on a commercial vessel.
			Article 145: If the wages the seafarer receives are remarkably unfair in comparison with the average wage for his or her job in the maritime industry, then the seafarer has the right, through judicial proceedings, to claim the establishment of the corresponding wage.
		Article 256: If a Panamanian vessel should change nationality, all shipping articles relating to her shall be deemed to be terminated from the moment the obligation referred to in Article 255 has been complied with.	Article 148: Wages must be paid in full in each period of payment.
			Article 166: In case of bankruptcy or insolvency of the employer, the wages, benefits and indemnities owed to the workmen shall enjoy priority over any other

Country	Enacting Legislation	Main Features of National Legislation	
		Repatriation	Wages
			credits, except those guaranteed with liens, and is effective on all of the employer's property.
			Article 169: In case of any delay in payment of your wages, you will receive interest at 10% per year when payment is settled.
			Article 159: It is illegal to reduce the agreed wage during the contract period.
			Article 264: Allotments may be made to relatives: spouse, children, grand-children, parents, grandparents, brothers and sisters, or to a private bank account approved by an official of the Republic of Panama. These allotments are to be noted in the articles at the beginning of the voyage.
Liberia	Liberian Maritime Law & Regulations, 1993 Series.	Section 342(1): When the seafarer's contract ends he or she has the right to be repatriated (at no expense to the seafarer) to either the port where they joined the vessel or to another port that the seafarer and the master agree upon.	Section 327(1): The seafarer's wages start on the date given in the contract, or at the start of their work aboard the ship.
		Section 342(2): If the seafarer is put ashore in a port other than where he or she signed Articles, for reasons for which the seafarer is not responsible, they must be repatriated (at no expense to them) to the port where they signed on,	Section 341: The normal hours of work at sea or in port are eight hours per day. Any work the seafarer does after the normal eight hours must be paid at overtime rates, except in emergency situations as agreed in Paragraph 11 of the Articles.

Section 327(3): The Master must pay the seafarer one |

Country	Enacting Legislation	Main Features of National Legislation	
		Repatriation	Wages

the port where the voyage began, a port in their own country or another port agreed between the seafarer and the shipowner or master. If the seafarer's contract has not ended the shipowner may transfer them to another ship until the end of their contract.

Section 342(3): The seafarer will lose the right to repatriation if he fails to request it within one week of the time he is eligible for repatriation.

Section 342(3): The seafarer cannot be required to purchase in advance his or her own repatriation transportation as a condition of their employment. The seafarer loses his or her right to repatriation if they:

(a) Desert their duties, or

(b) Enter into a new agreement with another owner within one week of discharge, or

(c) Break their own contract through their own fault, or

(d) Are guilty of a criminal offence under Section 346 (Intoxication, alcohol or drug related), Section 348 (Incitement of Seamen to Revolt or Mutiny) or Section 349 (Revolt or Mutiny of Seamen) of the Liberian Maritime Law.

half of their earned wages when they ask him ("on demand") at any port in which the ship loads or unloads cargo before the end of the voyage. The seafarer may ask for ("demand") this payment only once every ten days. If the Master does not pay on demand, and he is wrong, the seafarer has the right to be paid their full earned wages.

Section 327(2): The seafarer is to be paid at the times specified in his or her contract (for example, every month). If no time period is specified, then he or she is to be paid within two days after the termination of their contract, or at the time when they are discharged, whichever is first.

Section 327(1): The seafarers wages stop on the date given in their contract or when they are discharged.

Section 323(3): If the voyage for which the seafarer signed Articles is extended (made longer), then they will continue to be paid until the actual end of the voyage. If the voyage is cut short, then they will be paid up until the new end of the voyage.

Country	Enacting Legislation	Main Features of National Legislation	
		Repatriation	Wages
		Section 351: If the seafarer is abandoned by the master through no fault of their own in any foreign place, he or she keeps their right to repatriation.	Section 324: If the seafarer's contract ends because of:-
			(a) Change of flag; or
			(b) Change of ownership; or
			(c) Abandonment of vessel; or
			(d) Loss of the vessel
			... then he or she has the right to fifteen days' base wages, or base wages until the end of their contract, whichever is less. They will not be paid if they work as a seafarer on another vessel during this period or if they refuse similar work at sea.
			Section 328: If the seafarer is discharged through no fault of their own before the voyage begins or before they have earned one month's wages, they have the right to receive wages for their service on the vessel plus one month's wages.
			Section 335: The seafarer's right to wages is not dependent on the earning of freight by the vessel. Section 331: All advances of wages are illegal.
			Section 331: It is illegal for money to be deducted from a seafarer's wages to pay an agent to find them

Country	Enacting Legislation	Main Features of National Legislation	
		Repatriation	Wages
			employment aboard a Liberian vessel.
			Section 331: The seafarer may allot some of their wages to be paid directly to their husband or wife, children, parents, grandchildren, grandparents, brothers or sisters, or to a bank account in their name.
			Section 327: The seafarer has the right to a full account of their wages and all deductions before they sign off.
			Section 331: The following are legal deductions:
			(a) Deductions according to the laws of the country or the place where the seafarer signed on.
			(b) Dues or other obligations paid directly to a labour organisation of which the seafarer is a member.
			(c) Deductions paid into a fund for the benefit of seafarers and their families (with their written consent) to supply hospital care, pensions on the retirement or death of a seafarer, life insurance, unemployment benefits and compensation for illness and injury.
			Section 332: The seafarer's wages and clothing are

Country	Enacting Legislation	Main Features of National Legislation	
		Repatriation	Wages
			exempt from attachment by all courts of law.
			Section 334: The seafarer cannot lose their right to place a lien on the ship for recovery of wages nor can they be made to give up any salvage rights.
Cyprus	Merchant Shipping (Masters & Seamen) Law, as revised 31 December 1977.	Part X, 65: If the seafarer's employment is terminated at the end of their contract, or without their consent before the contract ends they have a right to be repatriated at the owner's expense to the port where they signed onto the ship, or to their home country, or to a port mutually agreed by them and the Master.	Part IV, 25: The seafarer has the right to be paid the wages promised in the Agreement, and all wages due must be paid before their agreement is terminated.
		Part X, 65: Travel costs and the cost of food and lodging while the seafarer travels shall by paid by the shipowner.	Part VI, 25(2): The seafarer's right to wages starts when the voyage begins or at another time specified in the Agreement, whichever comes first.
		Part X, 67: If the seafarer is shipwrecked or abandoned or left behind and the owner fails to repatriate them, the Republic of Cyprus will take ultimate responsibility for their maintenance and repatriation.	Part VI, 36(1): The seafarer's right to wages does not depend upon the ship's earnings.
			Part VI, 35: The seafarer cannot be required to give up the right to place a lien on the ship for his or her unpaid wages.
			Part VI, 37: If the ship is wrecked or lost, or sold at public auction, before a Contract of Employment ends, and the seafarer remains unemployed, he or she is entitled to receive wages for up to two additional months.

Country	Enacting Legislation	Main Features of National Legislation	
		Repatriation	Wages
			Part VI, 44: Any seafarer on board a ship flying the Cypriot flag (including the Master) who has not been paid the wages owed to them has the right to sue the shipowner in a Cypriot court for the payment of the wages owed.
Bahamas	Merchant Shipping Act	Section 162: When the seafarer is discharged he or she has the right to be repatriated at the owner's expense to a "return port" which is the port from which they began, a port in their home country or some other port which they agree on; except that if they began in the Bahamas they will be returned to the Bahamas unless they agree to be sent elsewhere. Section 153(3): If the seafarer decides to cease working on the ship before the end of their contract the owner will not be responsible for paying their repatriation expenses. Section 163: If, at the time of discharge, the seafarer is fit for duty he may be required to work on a ship going to his "return port" and, in this case, he or she must be paid for the work they do on the voyage to their "return port". They may also be repatriated by public transportation. Also, the owner must provide for all of the seafarer's	Section 99: A seafarer has the right to be paid the wages promised in the agreement. He or she begins to earn wages when they start working, or on a date shown in the agreement, whichever comes first. Section 101(1): The seafarer has the right to receive all wages which they have earnt according to their contract. Under no condition can a shipowner reduce a seafarer's wages because the shipowners have not earnt enough money. Section 95: If the agreement that the seafarer has signed provides for it, the seafarer may receive up to 2 weeks' wages in advance of joining the ship, except in a United States port where he or she may not receive any wages before they have actually earnt them (46 USC 599). Section 96: The agreement may include an arrangement between the seafarer and the shipowner for the

Country	Enacting Legislation	Main Features of National Legislation	
		Repatriation	*Wages*
		expenses during the trip to their "return port".	former to have a portion of his or her wages forwarded to a near relative or a bank.
			Section 102(1): If the seafarer stops working because they miss the ship, or because they are sick, or for any other reason, they will receive no more wages than they have earned. If, however, the seafarer has stopped working because the ship founders or is lost then they are entitled to two (2) months' additional pay, unless they begin work on another ship.
Norwegian International Registry (NIS)	Seamen's Act of 30 May 1975 (Chapter II) and Seamen's Regulations of 31 January 1986.	Unless the seafarer has agreed upon a port of departure, he or she is entitled to free passage home with maintenance if he or she is dismissed by their employer. This applies if the seafarer is hired for a specific period of time, or for a specific voyage. Free passage and maintenance includes food and lodging en route as well as during waiting periods prior to and during the journey. If the seafarer is a Norwegian national or has a residence in Norway he or she is entitled to free passage home with maintenance after six months' service on the same ship with the same employer.	The seafarer's articles will state the day on which wages begin. The latest date will be the day that they begin work on board. If they must travel to the ship from the place where they entered into the contract their wages shall begin the day that they start their journey to the ship. Wages run up to and include the final day of employment unless otherwise agreed upon in a collective wage agreement. Each month the seafarer is entitled to receive a written statement of the wages they have earnt. The statement will include the amount of wages earned, the method of calculation and any possible deductions. At the end of their employment the seafarer will receive a

Country	Enacting Legislation	Main Features of National Legislation	
		Repatriation	Wages

settlement of wages form from his employer which will be signed by both him and the employer.

If wages are calculated per day based on monthly wages, one day's wage will equal 1/30 of the monthly wage. If wages are calculated per day, based on the entire voyage, the entire wage for the voyage will be divided by the total number of days to reach a daily amount. If the actual voyage is shorter than expected the seafarer is entitled to the entire wage stated in their articles. If the actual voyage is longer, they are entitled to additional wages based on the daily fraction of the expected period. The seafarer is not entitled to wages for any period during which they unlawfully refuse to work.

The seafarer is entitled to payment of their wages whenever the ship is in port but not more than once every seven days in each country. Wages will be paid in cash in the local currency of the port their ship is in at the current rate of exchange unless they ask for a draft on the shipping company. The seafarer may have part of their wages paid monthly to a specified beneficiary in Norway or deposited in a Norwegian bank. If other

Country	Enacting Legislation	Main Features of National Legislation	
		Repatriation	Wages

payment arrangements are required then they must be agreed upon prior to signing the contract.

The employer may not deduct any amount from a seafarer's wages without their written consent unless the deduction is authorised by law, or the collective wages agreement, to compensate for damages caused by the seafarer's gross negligence which they have admitted to in writing or which has been established in court.

Under no circumstances shall deductions be made from the seafarer's wages which are needed to sustain the seafarer and his family.

If the seafarer unlawfully leaves the service of the ship and is still owed wages then those remaining wages will be held by a designated authority. This amount may be used to pay the expenses of the government or of the seafarer's employer that result from his or her unlawful action.

If the seafarer is still owed wages after settlement of any expenses but the seafarer does not claim those wages within three years after the termination of their employment, the money will be forfeited for use by the Norwegian gov-

Country	Enacting Legislation	Main Features of National Legislation	
		Repatriation	Wages
			ernment for the benefit of seamen or their relatives. If the number of crew used is smaller than that originally expected by the shipowner, or if the number of fit members of the crew falls during the course of a voyage, the seafarer is entitled to a portion of the wages saved by the shipowner because of the smaller crew.
Malta	Maltese Merchant Shipping Act 1973	MSA 130: If the seafarer is dismissed at the end of their contract of employment or if they are discharged from their contract against their will before it has expired and the seafarer is outside of Malta, he or she has the right to be repatriated at the shipowner's expense to Malta or to a "proper return port". Repatriation includes travel costs and expenses. MSA 130: If the seafarer is shipwrecked, abandoned or left behind and the shipowner fails to repatriate him or her, the Government of Malta will take ultimate responsibility for their maintenance and repatriation.	MSA 131: The seafarer has the right to be paid the wages specified in the Agreement, and all the wages due to them must be paid before or at the time their employment is terminated. MSA 138: The seafarer's right to wages begins when he or she begins working on the ship or at the time specified in the Agreement, whichever happens first. MSA 40: The seafarer's right to wages does not depend on the ship's earnings. MSA 145: If the seafarer is discharged through no fault of their own before the voyage begins or before they have earned one month's wages, they have the right to receive wages for their services on the vessel plus one month's wages.

[1] *Source*: The Centre For Seafarers' Rights, Seamen's Church Institute of New York and New Jersey, 241 Water Street, New York, NY 10038, USA.

Glossary

Allotments – Monthly payments sent to a seafarer's family by his or her employer while the seafarer is away at sea.

Beneficial ownership – National ownership of ships registered under flags of convenience.

Bilge – Drainage area contained between the side and bottom plating of a ship.

Bo'sun – Petty officer supervising deck crew.

Bulk carrier – Vessel carrying large consignments of loose cargo usually carried in full shiploads.

Bulkhead – Vertical subdivision within the ship's hull.

Chain locker – Stowage area for the ship's hull.

Charter party – The written agreement setting forth the terms and conditions under which the owner makes a ship available to a shipper.

Classification society – A society classifying ships which are built to its specifications. The society surveys vessels during building and during their lifetime to ensure that they remain in compliance with its rules and regulations.

Coastal state – The extension of national jurisdiction seawards from the coast.

Conferences – Any type of formal or informal agreement between shipowners which restricts competition.

Container ship – One designed to take large standardised metal boxes containing different types of cargo.

Deadweight tonnage (DWT) – The difference between light and load displacements. It is a measure of the carrying capacity of a vessel and is the weight of cargo, fuel, fresh water and stores that it is able to carry at a specified draught. It is the normal unit for bulk carriers and tankers.

Flag of convenience (FOC) – 'A flag of a state whose government sees registration not as a procedure necessary to impose sovereignty and hence control over its shipping but as a sevice which can be sold to foreign shipowners wishing to escape the fiscal or other consequences of registration under their own flags' (Marlow, P.B. and Bergantino, A., *An Analysis of the Decision to Flag Out* (Cardiff: SIRC/Neptune Report, 1998).

Flag state – Nation under whose flag a vessel sails.

Gross registered tonnage (GRT) – The registered tonnage (100 cu. ft.) plus the measured tonnage 'over deck', such as the spaces for the bridge, accommodation, etc. GRT is a normal unit for passenger ships and cargo liners and is used as a basis for safety requirements and manning.

Inmarsat – International Maritime Satellite Organisation. An IMO-sponsored global communication system used by shipping.

Innocent passage – Foreign shipping has a right of innocent passage through the terrritorial sea. Such passage must not prejudice the peace, good order or security of the coastal state.

Laid up – A ship which is out of commission and has no cargo to carry.

Manning agency – An agency which recruits and supplies crews to shipowners.

MARCOM – The Impact of Multicultural and Multilingual Crews on MARitime COMmunication. A project funded by the European Commission under the Transport RTD programme of the 4th Framework Programme.

MARPOL – International Convention for Prevention of Pollution of the Sea from Ships. An IMO Convention 1973, received sufficient signatures in October 1982 to partially enter into force in October 1983.

Net registered tonnage (NRT) – A measure of the earning capacity of a vessel, expressed in units of 100 cu. ft. It is the GRT less the volumes of spaces not used for the carriage of cargo (engine room, certain water tanks, etc.). NRT is frequently the basis on which harbour dues and pilotage fees are levied. It is a normal unit for passenger ships and cargo liners.

P&I club – Shipowners' mutual insurance club covering claims other than those protected by hull and cargo insurance.

Pay off – When a seafarer leaves a vessel he is said to pay off.

Panamax ships – Ships so constructed that the dimensions of the Panama Canal are taken into account in their width and draught.

Port-state control – A state-run body which inspects the condition of a visiting vessel and its safety and insurance documents. A state has a right to carry out inspections to protect its coastline against pollution and against substandard shipping.

Reefer ships – Ships designed for carrying refrigerated cargo.

Ro-ro (roll on/roll off) ships – Ships designed to carry cargo-loaded road vehicles and trailers which drive on and off when embarking and disembarking.

Second registry (GIS, DIS, NIS) – A registry under a national flag that allows shipowners some reduction in taxation and freedom to choose the nationalities of their crews.

Ship's agent – A shipowner's or charter's representative in a port. The agent will arrange for the handling of the cargo, stores, fuel and any other requirements that the ship may have.

Sign on – When a seafarer joins a vessel, they sign the ship's articles or a contract.

SOLAS – The International Convention on Safety of Life at Sea. The 1974 SOLAS Convention entered into force on 25 May 1980. The Convention covers all aspects of safety of life at sea and has undergone regular amendments since it came into force.

Suezmax – Ships so constructed that the dimensions of the Suez Canal are taken into account in their width and draught.

Supercargo – A supernumerary member of the ship's company who is not one of the crew. A supercargo may be a company representative on a vessel that is on charter.

Tanker – A vessel subdivided into a number of tanks designed to carry oil in bulk.

ULCC – Ultra-large crude carrier: the largest crude oil tankers afloat, above 330,000 DWT.

VLCC – Very large crude carrier: a very large crude oil carrier which is subdivided into a number of tanks. Above 200,000 DWT.

Index